Emergence

Dimensions of a New World Order

edited by Charles Lerche

© Bahá'í Publishing Trust 1991
27 Rutland Gate
London SW7 1PD

All rights reserved

British Library Cataloguing-in-Publication Data

A catalogue record for this book is
available from the British Library

ISBN 1 870989 22 8

The world's equilibrium hath been upset through the vibrating influence of this most great, this new World Order. Mankind's ordered life hath been revolutionized through the agency of this unique, this wondrous System – the like of which mortal eyes have never witnessed.

Bahá'u'lláh

CONTENTS

Introduction	vii
An Analysis of the Bahá'í World Order Model *Loni Bramson-Lerche*	1
From League of Nations to World Commonwealth *Brian Lepard*	71
Human Nature and the Problem of Peace *Charles Lerche*	101
A Universal Political Thesis *Peter Mühlschlegel*	131
Bahá'í Development Strategy; A Meeting of Social Ideologies *Holly Hanson*	145
The World Order of Nature *Arthur Lyon Dahl*	161
Index	175

INTRODUCTION

THE last decade of the twentieth century is already shaping up to be one of tumult and change, challenge and opportunity. In all areas of life startling events have become commonplace. At times euphoric, at times insecure, we find it difficult to assimilate so many new developments. Most would agree, however, that our experiences of the past do not provide sufficient guidance for the present, let alone the future. But just how do we begin to change our world — to cast it in a new form, more suited to the needs of our time?

It is becoming increasingly clear that the various 'crises' in our world are not discrete events, but are highly inter-related. Considered in this light, they suggest that many fundamental patterns of social organization, and the values represented by these patterns, require urgent re-examination. Throughout the ages social problems have stimulated such re-appraisal, but unique to our era is the fact that these issues must be addressed in a global context. No single state, society, or economy can regulate its affairs in isolation, and all, willingly or not, are compelled to address the common 'macro' problem of planetary management. The challenge of our time is the creation of a new world order.

The study of world order entails the elaboration of models of civilization, including both value structures and institutions which are responsive to the current needs of humanity. Though there are many dimensions to this field, contemporary debate has focused mainly on political and economic issues. A survey of the available literature would reveal three basic approaches to the subject:

1. A fundamentally conservative outlook which argues that the contemporary global political and economic systems, based on national sovereignty and the market mechanism, are sufficient in themselves to guarantee the global future;

2. A reformist attitude that promotes certain modifications in world political and economic institutions and practices to remove or reduce some of our most acute problems — for instance, certain innovative approaches to the global debt crisis,

or some of the suggested approaches to arrest global environmental decay;

3. A commitment to the need for global transformation — to the foundation of a new world order, planetary in scope, based on new social values and institutions such as those proposed by movements such as World Federalists, Planetary Citizens, and the World Order Models Project.

It would be generally correct to say that the Bahá'í approach falls into the last of the three listed above, since such principles as the need for more comprehensive and authoritative global political institutions and a more equitable world economic structure figure prominently in the Bahá'í plan for world order.

The Bahá'í view entails much more than this, however, and brings a unique perspective to bear on the problem of world order. The far-reaching change in world civilization which Bahá'ís advocate is as much spiritual — involving a profound re-orientation in the inner life and the outlook of the individual — as it is economic, political or social. To Bahá'ís the emergence of a new world order represents the 'coming of age' of the human race as well as the fulfilment of past and present eschatological hopes.

The guiding principles of the world-wide Bahá'í community are contained in the writings of its founder, Bahá'u'lláh (1817-1892), who announced over one hundred years ago the advent of a new era of world civilization which would be animated by a consciousness of planetary citizenship and the recognition of a common origin and destiny for the human race. This theme is one of the fundamental elements of Bahá'í belief. It has been further elaborated by Bahá'u'lláh's eldest son, 'Abdu'l-Bahá (1844-1921), appointed sole interpreter of his father's writings; by Shoghi Effendi (1897-1957), grandson of 'Abdu'l-Bahá and designated World Head and Guardian of the Bahá'í Faith after 'Abdu'l-Bahá's passing; and by the Universal House of Justice, the internationally elected council which has guided the progress of the world-wide Bahá'í community since 1963.

Though dealing with an apparently secular topic, the essays contained in this book are written from a religious perspective. The authors take as given the existence of a benevolent God, whose purpose for the human race is being worked out through history. The broad outlines of this purpose, and the means by which to fulfil it are revealed in the teachings and example of the Manifestations of God — inspirational figures in whose name great civilizations have been raised — among whom are Abraham, Moses, the Buddha, Christ and Muḥammad. The authors also accept the authority of the revealed scriptures of the world's religious traditions, and particularly the writings of Bahá'u'lláh, being the bearer of the latest revelation of God's purpose for the human race. These essays accept the authority of the 'Bahá'í writings'* in both descriptive and prescriptive terms: they explain the root cause of humanity's current predicament, and recommend effective solutions.

Many principles and values not always linked by contemporary thinkers with the subject of world order are central to the Bahá'í agenda for global reform. Among these are a belief in the common foundation of the major world religions, the equality of men and women, the elimination of all forms of prejudice, and the need for a universal auxiliary language as a tool for the promotion of international communication. All of these precepts contribute directly to forging that true human unity which Bahá'u'lláh advocated as the essential prerequisite and foundation for future peace and prosperity on this planet.

Bahá'ís have been in the forefront of those promoting the further development of international law and organization as a necessary antidote to the anarchy of contemporary international politics. To this end they have actively supported the United Nations, which they view (as they did the League of Nations before it) as an important preliminary step towards the planetary institutions necessary to regulate and guide world affairs.

The Bahá'í community itself is increasingly being recognized as a model for the re-organization of global society. Its world-wide membership reflects a remarkable social diversity and its system of administration has demonstrated a competence for mobilizing human potential and creating dynamic consensus at the local, national, and international levels. In addition, Bahá'í institutions

---

* The collective term by which the books and letters of Bahá'u'lláh, and their interpretation and elucidation by 'Abdu'l-Bahá, Shoghi Effendi and the Universal House of Justice are described throughout this volume.

the world over have begun to apply their resources more directly to practical problems of socio-economic development, both in their own communities and within the societies around them.

One prominent authoritative Bahá'í statement on world order, *The Promise of World Peace*, is a message from the Universal House of Justice to the peoples of the world, widely distributed to government officials and leaders of thought since 1986, the United Nations International Year of Peace. The articles in this book may be viewed as commentaries on that document: most cite it, and all deal with subjects found among its many themes.

In 'An Analysis of the Bahá'í World Order Model' Loni Bramson-Lerche provides an overview of our subject. She compares the Bahá'í model with others, explains some of its most prominent features and analyses the significant changes in world civilization foreseen in the Bahá'í writings.

Brian Lepard's 'From League of Nations to World Commonwealth' reflects the particular perspective of the Bahá'í community on the modern development of international organization. He shows clearly how the current situation contributes to, and demonstrates the need for, even more extensive international integration.

'Human Nature and the Problem of Peace', by Charles Lerche, focuses on a passage from *The Promise of World Peace* which highlights a 'fundamental' and 'paralysing' contradiction in world affairs. The roots of this contradiction are explored, and alternatives, drawn from the Bahá'í teachings, are suggested.

The subject of sovereignty is the main theme of Peter Mühlschlegel's 'The Universal Political Thesis'. In this essay he shows how our understanding of this key political concept must evolve to meet contemporary social and spiritual needs.

Holly Hanson's 'Bahá'í Development Strategy: A Meeting of Social Ideologies' is a path-breaking effort to demonstrate how the Bahá'í teachings as applied to problems of socio-economic development can help to reconcile the goals and methods of the two most prominent schools of thought in this field.

Arthur Dahl's 'The World Order of Nature' both considers the effect of world order on the management of the environment, and takes nature itself as a model for certain principles of human organization. Dr Dahl argues that a new approach to ecological issues requires new spiritual values, and shows how the Bahá'í teachings contribute directly to the evolution of such a new ethic.

INTRODUCTION

As wide-ranging as this selection of topics is, it represents only an initial gleaning of the insights into contemporary world order issues which the Bahá'í teachings provide. Among the more notable subjects not treated here are: Bahá'í principles pertinent to reform of the global economy; the impact of a universal auxiliary language on global social evolution; and the influence of advanced communication technology on our understanding of human unity. Some discussion of these topics can be found in other Bahá'í publications, but much remains to be written. We hope this volume will encourage others to carry the study further.

The Contributors

Loni Bramson-Lerche is a historian of religion and has published several articles on various aspects of Bahá'í history. She has also taught comparative religion at two universities in Nigeria.

Brian Lepard is a lawyer practising in Philadelphia, USA. He has worked as Special Assistant in Human Rights at the United Nations Office of the Bahá'í International Community, and has a special interest in international affairs and organization.

Charles Lerche is a professor of International Relations with the Boston University Overseas Programme in Europe. He lived and taught in Nigeria for several years. His primary interests and publications are in the fields of African and international politics.

Peter Mühlschlegel, an economist and banker, has written and lectured widely on Bahá'í teachings pertinent to economics. He has published (in German) *The World Central Bank President: Essays on the Expansion of our Economic Consciousness* (Rosenheim: Horizonte Verlag, 1989), and plans a book on voluntary sharing.

Holly Hanson served in the Office of Social and Economic Development at the Bahá'í World Centre, and is the author of *Social and Economic Development: A Bahá'í Approach* (Oxford: George Ronald, 1989).

Arthur Dahl has held a number of influential posts in the environmental sciences, and is presently Deputy to the Director of the Oceans and Coastal Areas Programme Activity Centre of the United Nations Environmental Programme in Nairobi, Kenya. He has published widely in the fields of coral reef ecology and island environment management, and is the author of *Unless and Until; A Bahá'í Focus on the Environment* (London: Bahá'í Publishing Trust, 1990).

AN ANALYSIS OF THE BAHÁ'Í WORLD ORDER MODEL
Loni Bramson-Lerche

HEDLEY Bull, in *The Anarchical Society*, states that, prior to the mid-nineteenth century, no political system could be said to have corresponded to various allusions to a 'great society of all mankind.'[1] According to Bull, it was only from the late nineteenth to the early twentieth century that a global political system began to develop. He states that previous to this time the world order system 'was simply the sum of the various political systems that brought order to particular parts of the world.'[2] Bull defines this newly developing world order as being 'those patterns or dispositions of human activity that sustain the elementary or primary goals of social life among mankind as a whole.'[3]

Bull's definition of world order is one of the most highly regarded, but in the field of international relations there is no agreement on the nature of these patterns, dispositions or goals, and consequently no generally accepted or comprehensive view of what a system of world order might be. It is therefore of interest to examine the Bahá'í world order model as it is one of the earliest, and still one of the most comprehensive, to be proposed. The main characteristic distinguishing the Bahá'í model from all others is that while they remain at the level of informed speculation, the Bahá'í world order model is the only one actually being implemented. Those concerned with the broad questions of world order will thus be interested in undertaking detailed studies of the Bahá'í model, at the levels of both theory and practice. This essay is a preliminary attempt at such a study. It will primarily examine the concept of world order as expressed in the Bahá'í writings,[4] what the members of this highly diverse community understand by the term 'world order', why they feel that the current political and societal system needs to be changed, what transition process is envisaged, and what the outlines of their world order model are.

A detailed analysis of the writings of Bahá'u'lláh[5] reveals the blueprint for a new system of world order:

> O ye men of wisdom among nations! Shut your eyes to estrangement, then fix your gaze upon unity. Cleave tenaciously unto that which will lead to the well-being and tranquillity of all mankind. This span of earth is but one homeland and one habitation.[6]
>
> Address yourselves to the promotion of the well-being and tranquillity of the children of men. Bend your minds and wills to the education of the peoples and kindreds of the earth, that haply the dissensions that divide it may, through the power of the Most Great Name [i.e., Bahá'u'lláh], be blotted out from its face, and all mankind become the upholders of one Order, and the inhabitants of one City.[7]

Bahá'u'lláh designated his eldest son, 'Abdu'l-Bahá,[8] his successor and sole authorized interpreter of his writings. Although 'Abdu'l-Bahá developed various world order themes present in his father's writings, it was his eldest grandson, Shoghi Effendi,[9] appointed Guardian of the Bahá'í Faith in 'Abdu'l-Bahá's *Will and Testament*, who was the first to synthesize and analyse the world order themes in the Bahá'í sacred writings, and to develop them further.

The Bahá'í Concept of World Order

In *The Promise of World Peace*, the Universal House of Justice explains the goal of world order in the light of Bahá'í teachings on moral and spiritual values:

> We join with all who are the victims of aggression, all who yearn for an end to conflict and contention, all whose *devotion to principles of peace and world order promotes the ennobling purposes for which humanity was called into being by an all-loving Creator.*[10]

The world order model pursued by Bahá'ís is mainly concerned with what they believe to be God's purposes in creating humanity, and how these purposes ennoble the human race. Humanity is seen as having been created to know and to love God, and to promote the evolution of society.[11] Human beings, thus, have two aspects to their nature, material and spiritual. The main purpose of human existence, for Bahá'ís, is to learn to control the material side and develop the spiritual side as much as possible through emulating divine virtues and qualities, and through orienting oneself towards the service of humanity.[12]

AN ANALYSIS OF THE BAHÁ'Í WORLD ORDER MODEL

In order to study the Bahá'í world order model it is necessary to understand the concept of human nature which shapes this religion's perspective toward social and political issues. This concept is essential to the Bahá'í perspective on how best to promote transition towards a new world order. The Universal House of Justice explains that the intense suffering caused by the extensive social ills and conflict found in all societies has led people to believe that since aggressive behaviour is so commonplace it 'is intrinsic to human nature and therefore ineradicable.'[13] The Universal House of Justice states that this belief has led to a paralysis of will, with the consequence that, although world leaders recognize the global nature of contemporary problems, they are unable to meet the challenge, and cannot seriously consider the possibility of subordinating their national self-interests in order to establish a world order which would include a 'united world authority'. This paralysis is also due to the fact that the uneducated and oppressed masses are not able to express their desires for a new world order based on 'peace, harmony and prosperity' for all humanity.[14]

'Abdu'l-Bahá emphatically states that humankind is quite capable of establishing a preferred world order:

> A few, unaware of the power latent in human endeavor, consider this matter as highly impracticable, nay even beyond the scope of man's utmost efforts. Such is not the case, however. On the contrary, thanks to the unfailing grace of God, the loving-kindness of His favored ones, the unrivaled endeavors of wise and capable souls, and the thoughts and ideas of the peerless leaders of this age, nothing whatsoever can be regarded as unattainable. Endeavor, ceaseless endeavor, is required. Nothing short of an indomitable determination can possibly achieve it. Many a cause which past ages have regarded as purely visionary, yet in this day has become most easy and practicable. Why should this most great and lofty Cause — the day-star of the firmament of true civilization and the cause of the glory, the advancement, the well-being and the success of all humanity — be regarded as impossible of achievement?[15]

Bahá'í theology explains that God has created human beings with spiritual and physical needs and capabilities. Individuals have free will and thus choose how to fulfil their needs and develop their capacities. These choices are not preordained or predetermined. In addition to this, Bahá'ís believe that the capacity to perfect oneself and acquire qualities and virtues is unlimited. Bahá'u'lláh describes man as 'the supreme Talisman', and 'a mine rich in gems of inestimable value'.[16] To be able to develop this potential, each person needs to be educated so that he or she is capable of properly exercising free will. 'Abdu'l-Bahá explains that physical capacities and needs are not subject to personal regulation, that is, one can neither control the need to eat and sleep, nor getting sick, growing old or dying. But people have virtually total control over whether they do good or bad; for instance one can be just or unjust, aggressive or non-aggressive.[17] With regard to the capacity for aggression, the Bahá'í teachings differ sharply from the opinions of the 'realist' school of political science.

The Universal House of Justice wrote that God's purpose in creating humankind is

> as far removed from current concepts of human well-being and happiness as is possible. We should constantly be on our guard lest the glitter and tinsel of an affluent society should lead us to think that such superficial adjustments to the modern world as are envisioned by humanitarian movements or are publicly proclaimed as the policy of enlightened statesmanship — such as an extension to all members of the human race of the benefits of a high standard of living, of education, medical care, technical knowledge — will of themselves fulfill the glorious mission of Bahá'u'lláh. Far otherwise. These are the things which shall be added unto us once we seek the Kingdom of God, and are not themselves the objectives for which the Báb gave His life, Bahá'u'lláh endured such sufferings as none before Him had ever endured, the Master ['Abdu'l-Bahá] and after Him the Guardian [Shoghi Effendi] bore their trials and afflictions with such superhuman fortitude. Far deeper and more fundamental was their vision, penetrating to the very purpose of human life.[18]

The Bahá'í teachings strongly suggest, then, that an analysis of humanity's needs must go beyond the usual scope of academic writings on world order to examine the very values implicit in the subject. One summary of the key elements of the Bahá'í new world order system is: peace, unity in diversity, the equality of men and women,[19] conflict resolution and the complete transformation of society. Hossain Danesh, a Bahá'í psychiatrist, summarizes the Bahá'í world order model as being

> characterized by unity in diversity, the harmony of science and religion, the equality of men and women, and by the eradication of

prejudices of all kinds, the preservation of human rights, and the promotion of justice and freedom — in short, by the assertion of the fundamental nobility of every human being and the ultimate victory of the human spirit.[20]

Gregory Dahl, a Bahá'í economist, defines world order as being the organization of 'the laws and institutions of the world to promote global prosperity and security'.[21]

It is very clear in Bahá'u'lláh's writings that he believes contemporary problems are due to irreparable defects in the social system:

> The winds of despair are, alas, blowing from every direction, and the strife that divideth and afflicteth the human race is daily increasing. The signs of impending convulsions and chaos can now be discerned, inasmuch as the prevailing order appeareth to be lamentably defective.[22]

The Bahá'í world order model proposes the creation of a new social system in order to correct the inadequacies of the current system.

Critiques of the State System

Many scholars have written on the development of a rapidly evolving universal awareness that society is in a state of crisis. There is first the crisis of direct violence and the threat of direct violence (for instance war, terrorism, the fact that violence is increasingly destructive) which has been analysed as being endemic and pervasive in the world's social organization.[23] Related to violence is the problem of disarmament, as well as the problem of the amount of money involved in arms spending.

There is also the crisis of poverty, including malnutrition, lack of proper educational opportunities, unemployment and underemployment, insufficient and inadequate housing and lack of proper medical care. Over the last forty years or so, conscious efforts have been made by various governments and organizations to help resolve the problems of poverty, specifically in countries outside of the First World. Third World scholars have analysed these efforts and have ascertained that economic benefits invariably go to the elite, especially those in the city, and the problems of poor people and poor regions become worse as ethnic and class cleavages widen. The economic gap between the world's poor and rich is widening, and there seems to be no way to stop its progression if current policies continue.[24]

Alienation is another serious problem. People of both the First and Third Worlds are becoming desperate as they see that business and governmental organizations with large vested interests in the status quo are not willing to alter their patterns of behaviour or restrain their disruptive and destructive technologies and activities.[25]

The problem of structural violence — violence that is integral to the social structure — is also of great concern. This can occur on a person-to-person basis, such as the exploitation of people because of their sex, race or ethnic origin, or it can take the form of colonialism, neo-colonialism or imperialism within cultural, economic, political, scientific or technological relationships. It characterizes the domination-dependence syndrome within and between societies. Structural violence develops when any person is denied the possibility of participating in social processes which are considered necessary for that person's full development. It results in the rich becoming richer and the poor poorer, shorter life spans for certain groups of people, and interesting work being reserved for the elite while mind-numbing work is reserved for the lower classes.[26]

There is also a crisis concerning human rights and repression. At times governments feel that they have the right to violate human rights, as can be seen, for instance, in the official use of torture.[27] There are also the problems of population growth, political unrest, the deterioration of the environment, resource shortages, the lack of control of new technologies and personal and collective insecurity.[28]

Central to the consideration of these universal crises is the identification of a root cause and the possibility of implementing a solution which would go to that root. The most widely held position among political scientists is that the various problems currently endemic to society require, at most, a reform of the state system. A growing number of political analysts, however, believe that these problems are global in nature, and that trying to resolve them within the structure of a nation-state system will not only fail to solve the problems, but may well serve only to aggravate them. These scholars feel that if an attempt is to be made to confront

AN ANALYSIS OF THE BAHÁ'Í WORLD ORDER MODEL

these issues, then new normative standards and a substantial change in the world's social structure are needed.[29] What these new values should be and what and how extensive the changes should be are still very much open questions.

Bahá'í Views

The Bahá'ís believe that the cause of these problems is basically two-fold: the failure to adapt social structures to a rapidly changing world, and the widespread turning away from religion to man-made ideologies. Specifically, Bahá'ís believe that the nation-state system is outmoded and that new values are needed to evolve a social and political system appropriate for the unification of the human race, which is the principal Bahá'í doctrine.

In the 1930s Shoghi Effendi explained how the crises of contemporary society are not merely the result of a temporary disruption in the world's various political and social organizations. He described the problems causing these crises and stated that, if a change was not brought about in the social system, the consequences would be severe:

> The recrudescence of religious intolerance, of racial animosity, and of patriotic arrogance; the increasing evidences of selfishness, of suspicion, of fear and of fraud; the spread of terrorism, of lawlessness, of drunkenness and of crime; the unquenchable thirst for, and the feverish pursuit after, earthly vanities, riches and pleasures; the weakening of family solidarity; the laxity in parental control; the lapse into luxurious indulgence; the irresponsible attitude towards marriage and the consequent rising tide of divorce; the degeneracy of art and music, the infection of literature, and the corruption of the press; the extension of the influence and activities of those 'prophets of decadence' who advocate companionate marriage, who preach the philosophy of nudism, who call modesty an intellectual fiction, who refuse to regard the procreation of children as the sacred and primary purpose of marriage, who denounce religion as an opiate of the people, who would, if given free rein, lead back the human race to barbarism, chaos, and ultimate extinction — these appear as the outstanding characteristics of a decadent society, a society that must either be reborn or perish.[30]

In *The Promised Day is Come*, written in 1941, Shoghi Effendi analysed how traditional religious values were being undermined by 'an unbridled and obsolete nationalism.'[31] In the same book he defines nationalism, racialism and communism as the three false gods of society,

> at whose altars governments and peoples, whether democratic or totalitarian, at peace or at war, of the East or of the West, Christian or Islamic, are, in various forms and in different degrees, now worshipping. Their high priests are the politicians and the worldly-wise, the so-called sages of the age; their sacrifice, the flesh and blood of the slaughtered multitudes; their incantations outworn shibboleths and insidious and irreverent formulas; their incense, the smoke of anguish that ascends from the lacerated hearts of the bereaved, the maimed, and the homeless.
>
> The theories and policies, so unsound, so pernicious, which deify the state and exalt the nation above mankind, which seek to subordinate the sister races of the world to one single race, which discriminate between the black and the white, and which tolerate the dominance of one privileged class over all others — these are the dark, the false, and crooked doctrines . . .[32]

The Universal House of Justice, in *The Promise of World Peace*, contends that the dramatic resurgence of religious fanaticism only disguises the increasing number of people turning away from religion because they believe it to be irrelevant to modern life. They have turned instead to materialistic indulgence and to various man-made ideologies which they believe will solve the world crises. The Universal House of Justice claims that these materialistic ideologies are doomed to failure because they do not have as their fundamental basis the concept of the unity of the human race:

> All too many of these ideologies, alas, instead of embracing the concept of the oneness of mankind and promoting the increase of concord among different peoples, have tended to deify the state, to subordinate the rest of mankind to one nation, race or class, to attempt to suppress all discussion and interchange of ideas, or to callously abandon starving millions to the operations of a market system that all too clearly is aggravating the plight of the majority of mankind, while enabling small sections to live in a condition of affluence scarcely dreamed of by our forbears.[33]

The Universal House of Justice condemns these ideologies for contributing substantially to the contemporary social and economic malaise as well as being responsible for 'the apathy that has gripped the mass of the peoples of all nations and . . . the extinction of hope in the hearts of deprived and anguished millions.'[34]

The Contemporary Debate over World Order

The question of how we should get from the 'old world order' — that is, a society based on a nation-state structure — to a 'new world order' — one with a global identity and international form of government — is an essential one, for as some scholars have pointed out, there is no evident reason to believe that a world government would not be tyrannical, inhumane, or authoritarian, or that having a global government will necessarily solve the problems of extreme poverty, violence, unjust social stratification or ecological irresponsibility.[35]

When examining the transition issue and other questions dealing with models of world order, it can be seen that there is little agreement as to what is necessary to get from the current situation to something else. The following is a synopsis of what can be found in the writings of those scholars who believe that a form of world order is necessary.

One change suggested as necessary during the transition process concerns attitudes; that is, humankind must understand the necessity of accepting the concept of global interdependence in order to ensure human survival.[36]

Another proposal is to develop a new theory of social change, in order to study and understand the currently existing social forces oriented towards actively changing the world and overcoming perceived injustices. The purpose of understanding the forces involved in social change is to be able to use them to evolve to a form of world order. Among the analysts who advocate social change there are those who call first for reforming national societies before attempting a global social change, and there are those who feel that global reform should come first because it will not be possible to make reforms within a national society without first controlling transnational actors.[37]

Richard Falk proposes the re-orientation of political consciousness. He believes that the elements of a new world order are already latent in the present political structure and that the transition period should serve to hasten the restructuring of society and the redistribution of structural functions, while shaping these processes away from possible repressive features. In other words, according to Falk, a new political consciousness is needed before deciding on any new institutional forms.[38]

Many of those involved in world order studies believe that new values must be established that will aid in the development of a global consciousness and the reform of our social structure. The world order models developed are based on these values.

William Coffin suggests five core values for the promotion of a global perspective and enhancement of individual autonomy and dignity: peace, economic welfare, social justice, 'ecophilia' and sharing in decision-making processes.[39]

The World Order Models Project (WOMP) established four core values: peace, economic well-being, social justice and environmental stability.[40]

Rajni Kothari, although a member of WOMP, has established a somewhat different set of values: autonomy for nations in the political realm, and for individuals so that they can realize their potential and creativity; minimum and maximum standards of living and consumption; non-violence, implying the right of survival and the right to be protected from uniformity in social structures and behaviour models; justice, implying the equality of all people and the establishment of economic and social justice; and participatory democracy.[41] Kothari points out that a great deal is said about the First World's concern for the condition of the Third World, but there is little respect for the dignity and freedom of the people who are the targets for development projects, or for the great diversity in social systems which give people their identity.[42]

Robert Johansen proposes the following set of values: peace; universal economic well-being and social justice; human rights; co-operation and solidarity; ecological concern and preservation; people-orientation as a priority when making economic and political decisions; the consideration of the human race as a whole rather than just people within a particular national boundary when deciding upon policy; and the establishment of community bonds vertically between classes and horizontally between all nations.[43] He emphasizes that what people believe about how the world functions, and about how it will function in the future, contributes to making the world function in exactly that way.[44] Thus, the values implicit in a society are integral to its development and transformation.

Saul Mendlovitz points out that when discussing the establishment of global values, it is necessary to expand the present limits of the theory of social knowledge. That is, currently, the field of social knowledge is culturally and geographically limited to the scholar's background, which determines what problems the scholar chooses to study and what remedies he or she will propose for them. Thus, even if a problem is felt to be global in nature it will be interpreted by different people according to their particular cultural, social and economic backgrounds. Mendlovitz suggests establishing transnational and cross-cultural perspectives when studying world order problems through international and intercultural collaborative research.[45]

Again, questions must be asked: what must be done to get people to adopt a new set of values, and, more specifically, how is it possible to create new values on a world-wide scale? Falk has, perhaps more than others, tried to answer these questions. He advocates the development of a new political energy, animated by a set of new global values and a coherent vision of what one is trying to do, taking into consideration that all four WOMP norms are important and must be developed at the same time. The transition will come about through widespread education; the growth of a world order reform movement (a social movement or populist mobilization) manifesting widespread attitudinal changes, which will make reforms through organizational activism; self-interest and the development of a sense of urgency to solve the world's problems which will spur people into non-violent action; and last, with a new global consciousness, institutions themselves will implement innovation in their structures.[46]

Another aspect of the transition process, as noted by some scholars, is that the perception of human nature must change. As mentioned earlier, it is widely felt that violence is inherent to human nature and that we have only limited ability to control it. Falk explains that if there is to be a reduction of large-scale violence, it is necessary that there be a change in the conviction that violence is an acceptable means of social control and change. As a corollary, there must be an increase in the belief that non-violent means can be used instead. In addition to this, progress towards social, political and economic dignity for all people is necessary; the four WOMP values must be adopted and pursued around the world to develop convergent lines of consciousness; reliable institutions are to be developed to settle disputes; and respect for these institutions is to be cultivated.[47]

These transition scenarios are widely criticized. 'Political realists', such as Raymond Aron, state that norms are not a valid basis for the study of world order. Others, such as Hedley Bull and Stanley Hoffmann propose other norms, but based on the retention of the nation-state system. Hoffmann criticizes WOMP and those sympathetic to its goals for several basic reasons: that they are never able to adequately describe how society will move from its current lethal games to a world-oriented government; that their proposals are too extreme in that the present structures are considered to be completely bad; and that they require their proposals — based on their values — to be considered the preferred solutions.[48]

Hoffmann states that the efforts discussed above to develop world order models are based on 'pure arbitrariness'. He states that Robert Johansen, for instance, 'does not explain how the values of global humanism, which he espouses, would overcome national hatreds and prejudices, or the obstacles erected by so many regimes that show no fondness for citizens' movements at all.'[49] Johan Galtung, Hoffmann asserts, 'envisages a global community of small societies, but . . . leaves us in the dark about how to transform today's world of 'structural violence' into tomorrow's ideal, perhaps because in his obsession with center-periphery relations he takes practically no account of the resilience of nations.'[50] Rajni Kothari, Hoffmann explains, never states how the world will reform itself to be comprised of only about twenty-five States.[51]

Bahá'í Views on the Transition Process

It is at this point that we can begin to see the major differences between the Bahá'í world order model and those produced by academics in the field of international relations. The Bahá'í model calls for a complete change in all systems around the world based on new universal values, and offers institutions through which this radical change can be effected.

AN ANALYSIS OF THE BAHÁ'Í WORLD ORDER MODEL

The Universal House of Justice calls for the wiping away of past ideologies and the search for new solutions:

> That materialistic ideals have, in the light of experience, failed to satisfy the needs of mankind calls for an honest acknowledgement that a fresh effort must now be made to find the solutions to the agonizing problems of the planet. The intolerable conditions pervading society bespeak a common failure of all, a circumstance which tends to incite rather than relieve the entrenchment on every side. Clearly, a common remedial effort is urgently required. It is primarily a matter of attitude. Will humanity continue in its waywardness, holding to outworn concepts and unworkable assumptions? Or will its leaders, regardless of ideology, step forth and, with a resolute will, consult together in a united search for appropriate solutions?[52]

The Universal House of Justice then quotes Shoghi Effendi:

> If long-cherished ideals and time-honoured institutions, if certain social assumptions and religious formulae have ceased to promote the welfare of the generality of mankind, if they no longer minister to the needs of a continually evolving humanity, let them be swept away and relegated to the limbo of obsolescent and forgotten doctrines. Why should these, in a world subject to the immutable law of change and decay, be exempt from the deterioration that must needs overtake every human institution? For legal standards, political and economic theories are solely designed to safeguard the interests of humanity as a whole, and not humanity to be crucified for the preservation of the integrity of any particular law or doctrine.[53]

From the Bahá'í point of view, efforts to solve the world's problems cannot be solely pragmatic in orientation. Specifically addressing the problems related to establishing a durable peace, the Universal House of Justice states that

> the primary challenge in dealing with issues of peace is to raise the context to the level of principle, as distinct from pure pragmatism. For, in essence, peace stems from an inner state supported by a spiritual or moral attitude, and it is chiefly in evoking this attitude that the possibility of enduring solutions can be found.[54]

The main feature of the Bahá'í world order model, then, is the belief that there needs to be a new system of values and a new form of government to implement them. The most important of these values is a profound sense of the oneness of humanity. The Universal House of Justice states that a new world order can only be founded once the human race has chosen to abandon all of its prejudices. The consciousness of the oneness of humankind, it contends, is a prerequisite for the reorganization of society and the administration of the world.[55]

Bahá'ís believe that in order to establish a new set of values it is necessary for all people to have a renewed sense of spirituality. Shoghi Effendi's secretary stated on his behalf that new social laws and institutions could not be implemented without accepting spiritual principles (or what some call human values) and putting them into practice in one's daily individual and community life.[56] Bahá'ís are pursuing these aims of establishing a new set of values and a renewed sense of spirituality both within their own communities and in society at large.

In regards to their efforts in the world at large, the Bahá'í Faith has enjoyed the status of an international Non-Governmental Organization since 1948, under the title 'Bahá'í International Community'. It has consultative status with UNESCO and UNICEF and a working association with UNEP and WHO. The Bahá'í International Community also has a working association with the South Pacific Commission. In 1987 the Bahá'í International Community became a member of the World Wide Fund for Nature's Network on Conservation and Religion. Through these associations Bahá'ís participate officially in international conferences on a wide variety of subjects and present statements and reports giving the Bahá'í teachings and points of view on these topics.[57] On a national and local level, Bahá'í communities around the world have working relations with a variety of governmental and non-governmental organizations with which they share goals.

The greatest effort of Bahá'ís, however, is directed towards their own individual and community lives.[58] Bahá'u'lláh enjoined his followers to pray daily and to meditate on a portion of his writings every morning and evening.[59] The prayers and writings of Bahá'u'lláh, the Báb and 'Abdu'l-Bahá are oriented towards fostering a complete transformation of the individual and society towards their preferred goals:

> ... is not the object of every Revelation to effect a transformation in the whole character of mankind, a transformation that shall manifest itself

both outwardly and inwardly, that shall affect both its inner life and external conditions? For if the character of mankind be not changed, the futility of God's universal Manifestations would be apparent.[60]

This daily, personal effort to consciously change their mode of behaviour to that prescribed in their religion's teachings is supported by the efforts of the various Bahá'í administrative institutions. The efforts of the Bahá'ís to implement transformation towards a preferred goal has been analysed by Dr Janet Khan, a Bahá'í psychologist. She states that the Bahá'í world community,

> far from seeing itself as already complete and self-sufficient, is embarked on an infinite series of experiments at the local, national, and international levels in its efforts to realize the vision of mankind's oneness which it finds in the writings of its founder.[61]

She explains that the process begins with the spiritual principles found in the Bahá'í writings which 'promote change by inducing an attitude, an aspiration, which facilitates the discovery of practical solutions to social problems.'[62] 'Change', she continues,

> is promoted through such means as the exercise of individual will and effort, through education, the transformation of individual and group behavior to accord with spiritual principle, cooperative activity, the practice of consultation as a means of group decision-making, and the fostering of diversity within the framework of unity and reciprocity.[63]

She gives as an example the putting into practice of the Bahá'í principle of the equality of men and women:

> Individuals strive to put the principle of equality into practice in their daily lives. The community supports such efforts by arranging activities to focus attention on the importance of the principle and by harnessing the newly developed skills of both women and men for the service of the community.[64]

The Two-fold Process: Disintegration and Integration

Bahá'ís believe that the transition process towards their model of world order began in the nineteenth century with the onset of

Bahá'u'lláh's ministry, if not even earlier, during the time of the Báb. In his most important book, the Kitáb-i-Aqdas, Bahá'u'lláh wrote:

> The world's equilibrium hath been upset through the vibrating influence of this most great, this new World Order. Mankind's ordered life hath been revolutionized through the agency of this unique, this wondrous System — the like of which mortal eyes have never witnessed.[65]

Shoghi Effendi divided this transition period into phases, of which humanity is still in the first. He refers to this phase as the beginnings of a two-fold process: of disruption and disintegration (the death of the old world order) and integration (the birth of the new world order).[66]

In several letters Shoghi Effendi described at length his interpretation of political and social events and trends and how these were part of the process of disintegration.[67] He analysed, among other aspects of the world situation, the breakdown of the world's political and economic structures; the moral decadence and the degradation of society due to the decline of religion as a social force; the necessity of the disintegration of religious institutions; the reason for the proliferation of sects and cults; and the cause of the fall of the European, Christian and Islamic empires and monarchies.[68]

The process of disintegration is part of what Bahá'ís call 'the major plan of God'. They believe that when Bahá'u'lláh proclaimed his message it became 'the spirit of the age', that is, in order for humanity to progress it became necessary to implement Bahá'u'lláh's social and economic teachings, such as the oneness of humankind, the equality of men and women, the establishment of a just economy, universal education, the elimination of prejudices and the establishment of a world government.[69] By disregarding or denying these principles and instead trying to reform 'national processes, suited to the ancient days of self-contained nations',[70] the leaders of the world are steering humanity along the path of destruction. The Universal House of Justice explains that the major plan of God 'proceeds mysteriously in ways directed by Him alone.' It is 'tumultuous in its progress, working through mankind as a whole, tearing down barriers to world unity and forging humankind into a unified body in the fires of suffering and experience.'[71] Bahá'u'lláh, referring to this dual process of tearing down and rebuilding, wrote: 'Soon will the present-day order be rolled up, and a new one spread out in its stead';[72] and 'The day is approaching when We will have rolled up the world and all that is therein, and spread out a new order in its stead.'[73]

The second, integrative, process is the replacing of old world values by those found in Bahá'u'lláh's teachings. Shoghi Effendi refers to it as: 'the gradual diffusion of the spirit of world solidarity which is spontaneously arising out of the welter of a disorganized society.'[74] It is also the growth and development of the Bahá'í Faith as seen in the accomplishment of the various plans created by the Bahá'í institutions and given to the Bahá'ís to carry out.[75] The role of the Bahá'ís in the process of integration is to spread — to the best of their ability — awareness of Bahá'u'lláh's teachings and encourage their practical application. This enterprise is usually referred to by Bahá'ís as 'teaching'.

The Universal House of Justice has stated that 'the paramount purpose of all Bahá'í activity is teaching.'[76] Every individual Bahá'í is encouraged, by the Bahá'í writings as well as by Bahá'í institutions, to practise the personal virtues endorsed in the Bahá'í teachings, and to inform those with whom they come in contact of the existence, nature and purpose of Bahá'u'lláh's revelation. Pursuit of these goals is tempered by moderation — proselytism is forbidden in their religion.

The pursuit of teaching is of immense significance to Bahá'ís in their endeavour to raise the new world order envisaged in the Bahá'í writings. It is an activity which serves to redirect the goal orientation of not only the Bahá'ís involved, but also the generality of humanity with whom they come in contact, towards a radical and comprehensive transformation of society from the grass roots. The source of their motivation for teaching comes, in part, from an acute awareness of

> the pitiful plight of masses of humanity, suffering and in turmoil, hungering after righteousness, but 'bereft of discernment to see God with their own eyes, or hear His Melody with their own ears'. They must be fed. Vision must be restored where hope is lost, confidence built where doubt and confusion are rife. . . .
> Teaching is the food of the spirit; it brings life to unawakened souls

and raises the new heaven and the new earth; it uplifts the banner of a unified world . . .'[77]

The Universal House of Justice explains that even when the world will finally be able to unite politically, it will be like a body 'without life.'[78] The Bahá'ís, by implementing these plans for growth and development are accomplishing 'the task of breathing life into this unified body.' The House of Justice calls this programme of overt Bahá'í activity the 'minor plan of God'.[79]

The transition period, according to Shoghi Effendi's interpretation of world history, is the current stage in the very long development of human civilization. He explained that civilization passes through stages of development similar to that in the life of an individual. Humankind has passed through the stages of infancy and childhood. This evolution has been slow and, accordingly, 'the measure of Divine Revelation, in every age, has been adapted to, and commensurate with, the degree of social progress achieved in that age by a constantly evolving humanity.'[80] Currently humanity is in the final throes of its 'painful, adolescent' stage, which will lead eventually to the stage of maturity: 'The tumult of this age of transition is characteristic of the impetuosity and irrational instincts of youth, its follies, its prodigality, its pride, its self-assurance, its rebelliousness, and contempt of discipline.'[81]

In Shoghi Effendi's analysis the process of integration began thousands of years ago, starting with the development of the family, followed by that of the tribe, the city-state, and the nation. The final stage is 'the unification of the whole world, the final object and the crowning glory of human evolution on this planet. It is this stage which humanity, willingly or unwillingly, is resistlessly approaching.'[82]

The Lesser Peace

Bahá'ís call the second phase of the transition period the 'Lesser Peace'. The processes of disintegration and integration previously described are to continue in this next phase and throughout the entire transition period.

In 1863 (in Edirne) and again from 1868 to 1872 (the early Acre period), Bahá'u'lláh proclaimed his station as a manifestation of God to the kings and rulers of the world in a series of powerful letters. In these letters he exhorted the rulers, both secular and ecclesiastical, to recognize his divine authority and follow his teachings. He also advised them how to be just in their dealings with their peoples.[83] When both his claims and advice were rejected Bahá'u'lláh made the following declaration to these rulers:

> Now that ye have refused the Most Great Peace,[84] hold ye fast unto this, the Lesser Peace, that haply ye may in some degree better your own condition and that of your dependents.[85]

The Bahá'í writings do not state how long the Lesser Peace will last, but they do make clear that it will pass through several stages, and that its evolution is an organic process.[86] Shoghi Effendi wrote that it involves 'the reconstruction of mankind, as the result of the universal recognition of its oneness and wholeness.'[87] Initially it will be marked by the world becoming politically unified.[88]

In a letter known to Bahá'ís as the 'Seven Candles of Unity', 'Abdu'l-Bahá explains how the world will evolve towards the 'Most Great Peace':

> . . . this century — the century of light — hath been endowed with unique and unprecedented glory, power and illumination. Hence the miraculous unfolding of a fresh marvel every day. Eventually it will be seen how bright its candles will burn in the assemblage of man.
>
> Behold how its light is now dawning upon the world's darkened horizon. The first candle is unity in the political realm, the early glimmerings of which can now be discerned. The second candle is unity of thought in world undertakings, the consummation of which will ere long be witnessed. The third candle is unity in freedom which will surely come to pass. The fourth candle is unity in religion which is the corner-stone of the foundation itself, and which, by the power of God, will be revealed in all its splendour. The fifth candle is the unity of nations — a unity which in this century will be securely established, causing all the peoples of the world to regard themselves as citizens of one common fatherland. The sixth candle is unity of races, making of all that dwell on earth peoples and kindreds of one race. The seventh candle is unity of language, i.e., the choice of a universal tongue in which all peoples will be instructed and converse.[89]

The Bahá'í writings state that these seven steps will not necessarily be taken in the order given by 'Abdu'l-Bahá,[90] and do not state how many of them will be taken during the Lesser Peace. Nor do they go into detail as to the nature of the Lesser Peace. An outline is given, as well as a description of its purpose and characteristics, and these have given rise to a variety of speculative definitions by Bahá'í authors. John Huddleston, a Bahá'í economist, interprets the Lesser Peace as the gradual adoption by all nations of a global collective security system in order 'to avoid total disaster.'[91] Philip Hainsworth also describes the establishment of the Lesser Peace as a gradual process. During the Lesser Peace, according to Hainsworth, the nations of the world will first unite in a confederation to establish world peace. This will evolve into a federation. He believes that once peace is established, the solving of structural problems could take centuries.[92]

The Bahá'í writings do not give an exact date for the initial establishment of the Lesser Peace.[93] In several instances 'Abdu'l-Bahá indicates that it is to be by the end of the twentieth century. These statements have been confirmed by Shoghi Effendi and the Universal House of Justice.[94] Although the Bahá'í writings indicate that the era of the Lesser Peace should be inaugurated by the year 2000, they also indicate that the process of its establishment is gradual and will most likely extend beyond the turn of the century.[95]

Bahá'u'lláh states that the Lesser Peace will be established by all humankind, and by the united actions of the rulers of the world:

> ... may God aid [the kings of the earth] through His strengthening grace — to establish the Lesser Peace. This, indeed, is the greatest means for insuring the tranquillity of the nations. It is incumbent upon the Sovereigns of the world — may God assist them — unitedly to hold fast unto this Peace, which is the chief instrument for the protection of all mankind. It is Our hope that they will arise to achieve what will be conducive to the well-being of man.[96]

> We have enjoined upon all mankind to establish the Lesser Peace — the surest of all means for the protection of humanity. The sovereigns of the world should, with one accord, hold fast thereunto, for this is the supreme instrument that can ensure the security and welfare of all peoples and nations.[97]

The initial phase of the Lesser Peace, then, is to be the result of a political effort by the governments of the world, independent of the Bahá'í community, and, Bahá'ís acknowledge, without any conscious realization on the part of the generality of humankind of the impact of Bahá'u'lláh's revelation.[98] Although the Bahá'í writings clearly state that the Bahá'ís will not have a direct hand in the establishment of the Lesser Peace, this does not mean that Bahá'ís are dissuaded from playing any part at all. For instance, Bahá'u'lláh states that one of the duties of the Universal House of Justice is to promote the Lesser Peace, so that 'the people of the earth may be relieved from the burden of exorbitant expenditures.'[99] A letter from the Secretariat of the Universal House of Justice explains that as the Lesser Peace evolves through its various stages, direct Bahá'í influence will grow:

> ... later on, in God's good time, the Faith will have a direct influence on it in ways indicated by Shoghi Effendi in his *The Goal of a New World Order*. In connection with the steps that will lead to this latter stage, the Universal House of Justice will certainly determine what has to be done, in accordance with the guidance in the Writings . . . In the meantime, the Bahá'ís will undoubtedly continue to do all in their power to promote the establishment of peace.[100]

During the transition process the Bahá'í community itself will undergo transformation, and will follow its own course of evolution. The more it develops, the more impact it is likely to have on the course of the Lesser Peace. This process of growth that the Bahá'í community is currently undergoing

> will carry the steadily evolving Faith of Bahá'u'lláh through its present stages of obscurity, of repression, of emancipation and of recognition — stages one or another of which Bahá'í national communities in various parts of the world now find themselves in — to the stage of establishment, the stage at which the Faith of Bahá'u'lláh will be recognized by the civil authorities as the state religion, similar to that which Christianity entered in the years following the death of the Emperor Constantine, a stage which must later be followed by the emergence of the Bahá'í state itself, functioning, in all religious and civil matters, in strict accordance with the laws and ordinances of the Kitáb-i-Aqdas, the Most Holy, the Mother-Book of the Bahá'í Revelation, a stage which, in the fullness of time, will culminate in the establishment of the World Bahá'í Commonwealth.[101]

It is possible to find in the Bahá'í writings descriptions of certain processes and political institutions which are stated to be necessary for the establishment of a political peace. For instance, Bahá'u'lláh states that the Lesser Peace is to be established by the rulers of the world convening a general assembly to be attended by the rulers themselves or their ministers (although he emphasizes that it would be better for the rulers to attend). Those attending this assembly must decide on and 'enforce whatever measures are required to establish unity and concord amongst men.'[102] There are no indications in the Bahá'í writings whether the Lesser Peace will be established at one gathering, or whether a series of such congresses will need to be held. Nor, if there are to be a series of assemblies, is there any indication whether these will be completely independent from each other or connected in some way. Also, there is no indication whether the actual drafting of an agreement will be done by the rulers, their ministers, or others. There are some indications which seem to point to the possibility of having a series of universal assemblies on different subjects attended by delegates or specialists in the field being discussed, for instance, in establishing an international auxiliary language.[103]

The Bahá'í Principle of Disarmament

One important topic which Bahá'u'lláh stipulated to be discussed at such an assembly is disarmament, which is an essential element of his plan for collective security. However, this disarmament is to be comprehensive and universal, not limited only to certain States. In addition, the disarmament process is to occur simultaneously in all countries. Bahá'u'lláh calls upon the rulers of the world to come to a reconciliation so that they will need only a minimum number of arms to protect their territories and maintain internal security. If one country attacks another, then all the world should unite to stop the aggressor. This, it is stated, will promote peace and greatly reduce the financial burdens on the people.[104]

A survey of the writings of Bahá'u'lláh and 'Abdu'l-Bahá on disarmament shows that they feel economic factors will be the prime motivation for the governments of the world to finally come to agreement on this issue: 'The awful burdens of taxation for war purposes will get beyond human endurance. . . .'[105] Such

AN ANALYSIS OF THE BAHÁ'Í WORLD ORDER MODEL

a drastic cut in expenditures on armaments is in itself not considered to be sufficient. The money saved should be reallocated to socially constructive ends; especially to finding solutions to the many urgent social and economic problems. Bahá'u'lláh states:

> We cherish the hope that through the earnest endeavours of such as are the exponents of the power of God — exalted be His glory — the weapons of war throughout the world may be converted into instruments of reconstruction and that strife and conflict may be removed from the midst of men.[106]

'Abdu'l-Bahá also discussed how money no longer used for military purposes should be allocated and how this change in economic priorities would eliminate poverty, improve education, increase social and economic development and promote culture. Once the world is disarmed 'these huge sums will be diverted to other more useful channels, pauperism will disappear . . .'.[107]

'Abdu'l-Bahá explained the moral and social benefits of disarmament:

> . . . the entire population would, first of all, be relieved of the crushing burden of expenditure currently imposed for military purposes, and secondly, great numbers of people would cease to devote their time to the continual devising of new weapons of destruction — those testimonials of greed and bloodthirstiness, so inconsistent with the gift of life — and would instead bend their efforts to the production of whatever will foster human existence and peace and well-being, and would become the cause of universal development and prosperity.[108]

In addition to economic and social considerations, 'Abdu'l-Bahá states that disarmament is also necessary to ensure security, for as long as any country increases military expenditures, other countries will feel the need to participate in 'this crazed competition through her natural and supposed interests.'[109] Through disarmament humanity would be delivered from 'international confusion'.[110] Every government's stock of arms must be strictly limited, because increase of military forces and other preparations for war will cause nations to be suspicious of others' motives. A binding pact must be made so that no country will feel the need to stockpile weapons or produce new ones. Each country's military will only need to be large enough to ensure internal security, control criminal and disorderly manifestations and prevent local disturbances. An international police force will maintain security on an international level.[111]

Besides explaining why disarmament is necessary, 'Abdu'l-Bahá suggested several means by which a lasting disarmament could be achieved. The first is through education. Each person's intellectual capacity must be developed so that everyone can understand the compelling reasons for disarmament, and all institutions should be inculcated with 'peaceful ideals'.[112]

Another means is through refusal to participate in unjust wars. Thus, bankers must refuse to loan governments money to wage unjust wars; presidents and managers of transportation companies must refuse to transport war material across international borders; and soldiers must require from their government clear explanations as to first, how and why conditions had degenerated to such a state that war has become necessary, and second, that the war to be waged is just.[113]

'Abdu'l-Bahá also calls for the establishment of an impartial, international commission to firmly establish international borders. This will allow countries to maintain their national integrity and protect their independence and vital interests.[114]

One of Bahá'u'lláh's apparent goals is for society to evolve to such a point that the thought of war will be abhorrent. There are indications in the Bahá'í writings that this evolution is to occur within the period of the Lesser Peace, but there are no clear indications that all violent international conflicts will be forever eliminated at any particular point during the Lesser Peace. For instance, 'Abdu'l-Bahá states that

> The sovereigns of the world . . . must conclude a binding treaty, and establish a covenant. the provisions of which shall be sound, inviolable and definite. They must proclaim it to all the world, and obtain for it the sanction of all the human race . . . All the forces of humanity must be mobilized to insure the stability and permanence of this Most Great Covenant . . . The fundamental principle underlying this solemn Pact should be so fixed that if any government later violate any one of its provisions, all the governments on earth should arise to reduce it to utter submission, nay the human race as a whole should resolve, with every power at its disposal, to destroy that government.[115]

'Abdu'l-Bahá indicates that the decision to disarm will be made, and the process of disarmament begun before the end of the twentieth century,[116] though he gives no clear statements of a date by which the process will be completed, or by which peace will be established.[117]

Institutions to be Developed during the Lesser Peace

An institution mentioned in the Bahá'í writings which is to evolve during the Lesser Peace is that of the 'Supreme Tribunal'.[118] This body is to be a final court of appeal, with the authority to settle disputes, define exact national boundaries and determine, proportional to each population, the size of each national military force. Through arbitration it is to settle all issues which could become a cause of war. Its main purpose, therefore, is to prevent war and establish peace.[119] There are to be similar institutions on a local and national level.[120]

The Supreme Tribunal is to be established by the governments and peoples of the world (perhaps as a result of one of the general assemblies mentioned above). Its members are to come from each country. If any country refuses to abide by a decision made by the Supreme Tribunal, this body should have the authority, power and support to order the other countries to unite and execute its decision.[121]

During the period of the Lesser Peace, a form of world super-state is to be established which will evolve into a commonwealth based on a federal system of government (though such a body politic will not necessarily come into existence during the Lesser Peace). This super-state is to have, besides a supreme tribunal, an international executive and a world parliament. Shoghi Effendi gives an outline of this government:

> Some form of a world Super-State must needs be evolved, in whose favor all the nations of the world will have willingly ceded every claim to make war, certain rights to impose taxation and all rights to maintain armaments, except for purposes of maintaining internal order within their respective dominions. Such a state will have to include within its orbit an International Executive adequate to enforce supreme and unchallengeable authority on every recalcitrant member of the commonwealth; a World Parliament whose members shall be elected by the people in their respective countries and whose election shall be confirmed by their respective governments; and a Supreme

Tribunal whose judgment will have a binding effect even in such cases where the parties concerned did not voluntarily agree to submit their case to its consideration. A world community in which all economic barriers will have been permanently demolished and the interdependence of Capital and Labor definitely recognized; in which the clamor of religious fanaticism and strife will have been forever stilled; in which the flame of racial animosity will have been finally extinguished; in which a single code of international law — the product of the considered judgment of the world's federated representatives — shall have as its sanction the instant and coercive intervention of the combined forces of the federated units; and finally a world community in which the fury of a capricious and militant nationalism will have been transmuted into an abiding consciousness of world citizenship — such indeed, appears, in its broadest outline, the Order anticipated by Bahá'u'lláh, an Order that shall come to be regarded as the fairest fruit of a slowly maturing age.[122]

In the Bahá'í writings, there is no indication that the three basic institutions of the proposed world super-state will necessarily come into being at the same time: for instance, the Supreme Tribunal might evolve first. This is suggested by some of its responsibilities mentioned above, such as defining national boundaries and determining the size of military forces, which are usually the responsibility of a legislature.

The Catastrophic Nature of the Disintegration Process

In *The Promise of World Peace*, the Universal House of Justice wrote that not only is peace possible, it is the inevitable next stage in the evolution of the human race. This peace can be attained, it continues, either through 'consultative will' or through 'unimaginable horrors' due to our 'stubborn clinging to old patterns of behaviour.'[123] The Universal House of Justice describes the process of disintegration, which is to include a confused period of a calamitous nature, as being organic in character. It is to lead the peoples of the world to unite in a single, planetary social order.[124]

Bahá'u'lláh related this catastrophic process of disintegration to the fulfilment of ancient scriptural prophecies:

> The allusions made in the Scriptures have been unfolded, and the signs recorded therein have been revealed, and the prophetic cry is continually being raised. . . .

AN ANALYSIS OF THE BAHÁ'Í WORLD ORDER MODEL

> Witness how the world is being afflicted with a fresh calamity every day. Its tribulation is continually deepening. . . . At one time it hath been agitated by contentions and disputes, at another it hath been convulsed by wars, and fallen a victim to inveterate diseases. Its sickness is approaching the stage of utter hopelessness, inasmuch as the true Physician [Bahá'u'lláh] is debarred from administering the remedy, whilst unskilled practitioners are regarded with favor, and are accorded full freedom to act.[125]

Some western Bahá'ís have reduced this complex concept of a process of disintegration to that of 'the catastrophe' or 'calamity', a sudden event which will occur in a brief period of time. Among some of these Bahá'ís there is also a belief that 'the catastrophe' will take the form of a nuclear World War III. Such an interpretation is partially based on the following quote from Bahá'u'lláh:

> The world is in travail, and its agitation waxeth day by day. Its face is turned towards waywardness and unbelief. Such shall be its plight, that to disclose it now would not be meet and seemly. Its perversity will long continue. And when the appointed hour is come, there shall suddenly appear that which shall cause the limbs of mankind to quake. Then, and only then, will the Divine Standard be unfurled, and the Nightingale of Paradise warble its melody.[126]

Although the source of the idea that the human race will have to suffer through catastrophic events in order to prepare it for a new world order clearly comes from the writings of Bahá'u'lláh, the western Bahá'ís' understanding of these writings comes primarily from their interpretation of Shoghi Effendi's letters elucidating these writings and analysing the social, political and economic events of his day.

In one of Shoghi Effendi's earliest major letters to the Bahá'ís of the West, 'The Goal of a New World Order' (1933), he introduced the Bahá'ís to the dual implications of the principle of the 'oneness of mankind'. This principle 'implies at once a warning and a promise — a warning that in it lies the sole means for the salvation of a greatly suffering world, a promise that its realization is at hand.'[127]

Shoghi Effendi's analysis of the process of disintegration includes predictions, based on deduction, of chaotic and catastrophic events which, he declares, must go to the very core of society. Writing in 1932, he compared this process to the development of the federation of the United States of which the Civil War was a necessary part:

> Who knows that for so exalted a conception to take shape a suffering more intense than any it has yet experienced will have to be inflicted upon humanity? Could anything less than the fire of a civil war with all its violence and vicissitudes — a war that nearly rent the great American Republic — have welded the states, not only into a Union of independent units, but into a Nation, in spite of all the ethnic differences that characterized its component parts? That so fundamental a revolution, involving such far-reaching changes in the structure of society, can be achieved through the ordinary processes of diplomacy and education seems highly improbable. We have but to turn our gaze to humanity's blood-stained history to realize that nothing short of intense mental as well as physical agony has been able to precipitate those epoch-making changes that constitute the greatest landmarks in the history of human civilization.[128]

Continuing, Shoghi Effendi explained that only through such suffering can humankind be chastened and prepared to undertake its new responsibilities:

> Great and far-reaching as have been those changes in the past, they cannot appear, when viewed in their proper perspective, except as subsidiary adjustments preluding that transformation of unparalleled majesty and scope which humanity is in this age bound to undergo. That forces of a world catastrophe can alone precipitate such a new phase of human thought is, alas, becoming increasingly apparent. That nothing short of the fire of a severe ordeal, unparalleled in its intensity, can fuse and weld the discordant entities that constitute the elements of present-day civilization, into the integral components of the world commonwealth of the future, is a truth which future events will increasingly demonstrate.[129]

In 1934 Shoghi Effendi wrote:

> Might not this process of steady deterioration which is insidiously invading so many departments of human activity and thought be regarded as a necessary accompaniment to the rise of this almighty Arm of Bahá'u'lláh? Might we not look upon the momentous happenings which, in the course of the past twenty years, have so deeply agitated every continent of the earth, as ominous signs

AN ANALYSIS OF THE BAHÁ'Í WORLD ORDER MODEL

simultaneously proclaiming the agonies of a disintegrating civilization and the birthpangs of that World Order — that Ark of human salvation — that must needs arise upon its ruins?[130]

Shoghi Effendi explains that such suffering is necessary because humankind, by rejecting the message of Bahá'u'lláh, has shown it must be made ready for the new Bahá'í world order:

> For the revelation of so great a favor a period of intense turmoil and wide-spread suffering would seem to be indispensable. Resplendent as has been the Age that has witnessed the inception of the Mission with which Bahá'u'lláh has been entrusted, the interval which must elapse ere that Age yields its choicest fruit must, it is becoming increasingly apparent, be overshadowed by such moral and social gloom as can alone prepare an unrepentant humanity for the prize she is destined to inherit.[131]

This suffering — which elsewhere Shoghi Effendi refers to as being a retributory judgement of God[132] — is more than a divine punishment in the theological sense, since it involves the destruction of old social, political and economic institutions to make room for the new order which humankind has refused voluntarily to construct. This process of disintegration is fuelled by the destructive forces found in 'a civilization that has refused to answer to the expectation of a new age, and is consequently falling into chaos and decline.'[133] Therefore the retribution spoken of in the Bahá'í writings is the consequence of the human race having refused the 'word of God' and thus having to suffer the very painful demolition of its social, political and economic order.[134] Since this retribution will necessarily involve intense suffering, it could be viewed as a punishment, but at the same time it directs the peoples of the world toward the 'Most Great Peace': 'My calamity is My providence, outwardly it is fire and vengeance, but inwardly it is light and mercy.'[135]

In 1979 the Universal House of Justice made reference to a 'universal anarchy' which would necessarily affect all the people of the world, from which the Bahá'ís would not be exempt:

> The decline of religious and moral restraints has unleashed a fury of chaos and confusion that already bears the signs of universal anarchy. Engulfed in this maelstrom, the Bahá'í world community, pursuing with indefeasible unity and spiritual force its redemptive mission,

inevitably suffers the disruption of economic, social and civil life which afflicts its fellowmen throughout the planet.[136]

These and other statements have led an appreciable number of western Bahá'ís to speculate on the nature and timing of the 'catastrophe' or 'calamity'. For most of those who speculate on this subject, this event, or series of events, is yet to occur. For instance, Philip Hainsworth, in 1986, wrote that it is not known 'at what point in time major upheavals will occur', implying that the major upheavals these Bahá'ís associate with their concept of the 'catastrophe' had not yet occurred or were not currently in process.[137] Jay Tyson, also in 1986, wrote that 'the catastrophe' has not yet begun.[138] Tyson's personal interpretation of 'the catastrophe' comes down on the side of a nuclear war, but specifies that, as the calamity is to be unparalleled in nature, it could also take another form, such as 'environmental collapse, chemical or biological warfare, falling asteroids from outer space, or some other calamity that is totally unforeseen'.[139]

While the suggestion of such dramatic events can be found in the Bahá'í writings, it is possible to find records of attempts to place these prophecies in perspective. In 1928 Shoghi Effendi's secretary wrote on his behalf:

> What Shoghi Effendi says is that in certain Tablets ['Abdu'l-Bahá] speaks of another war.... Exactly when it will be and what form it will take, and what will be the extent of its field of operation, no one can foretell. Shoghi Effendi does not feel it advisable to harbour such dark thoughts, for that may affect our activities and rob us of that optimism and hopefulness which every person needs in striving for the realization of his ideals.[140]

In 1946 his secretary wrote again on his behalf:

> ... as regards the possibility of a future war; we cannot state dogmatically it will or will not take place – all we know is that mankind must suffer and be punished sufficiently to make it turn to God.[141]

And in 1949:

> We have no indication of exactly what nature the apocalyptic upheaval will be: it might be another war ... but as students of our Bahá'í writings it is clear that the longer the 'Divine Physician' (i.e.,

AN ANALYSIS OF THE BAHÁ'Í WORLD ORDER MODEL

Bahá'u'lláh) is withheld from healing the ills of the world, the more severe will be the crises, and the more terrible the sufferings of the patient.[142]

Peter Khan has for a number of years promoted the concept that the 'catastrophe' or 'calamity' has, in fact, already begun, with World Wars I and II being the first two stages.[143] While a member of the International Teaching Centre (the international executive body of the Bahá'í administrative order based at the Bahá'í World Centre in Haifa), Dr Khan visited North America and became concerned by the preoccupation of some Bahá'ís with the thought of an impending catastrophe.[144] The report he made upon his return prompted the International Teaching Centre to write an extensive letter concerning this subject.

This letter first explains that much of the speculation regarding Bahá'u'lláh's prophecies derives from reports made by Bahá'ís who had gone to Haifa to visit Shoghi Effendi. It reminds the Bahá'ís that these hearsay reports of statements Shoghi Effendi had made during conversation have no authority: indeed, Shoghi Effendi had himself corrected many of these interpretations.[145] The letter also emphasizes that there are many statements in the Bahá'í writings explaining that the form, intensity and duration of the suffering to be experienced by humanity are unknown. For instance:

> . . . although there is every reason to expect that the world will experience travails and testing as never before, we do not know what form these upheavals will take, when exactly they will come, how severe they will be, nor how long they will last.[146]

This letter also cites a communication from the Universal House of Justice, in response to a question from the Board of Counsellors in Europe, stating that Bahá'ís

> should understand that a catastrophic breakdown of human society as a result of mankind's ignoring His Message has been clearly foretold by Bahá'u'lláh, and that we are, indeed, in the midst of such a breakdown.[147]

Further, the Secretariat of the Universal House of Justice wrote on its behalf that the calamities prophesied in the Bahá'í writings have already begun:

The House of Justice points out that calamities have been and are occurring and will continue to happen until mankind has been chastened sufficiently to accept the Manifestation for this day.[148]

An important point made in the letter from the International Teaching Centre is that calamities are to continue until the human race has accepted Bahá'u'lláh's message. The Bahá'í writings imply, then, that catastrophes are not to end with the advent of the Lesser Peace, as they are generated by the breakdown of society which is to continue well into the period of the Lesser Peace itself.[149]

A recent widespread statement by the Universal House of Justice interprets current global developments as 'indications that the Lesser Peace cannot be too far distant . . .', sketches the obstacles which stand in the way of its achievement, and stresses the tumult of the transition period:

> The winds of God rage on, upsetting old systems, adding impetus to the deep yearning for a new order in human affairs . . . The rapidity of the changes being wrought stirs up the expectations which inspire our dreams in the closing decade of the twentieth century. The situation is equally a bright portent and a weighty challenge.
>
> It is portentous of the profound change in the structure of present-day society which attainment to the Lesser Peace implies. Hopeful as are the signs, we cannot forget that the dark passage of the Age of Transition[150] has not been fully traversed; it is as yet long, slippery and tortuous. For godlessness is rife, materialism rampant. Nationalism and racism still work their treachery in men's hearts, and humanity remains blind to the spiritual foundations of the solution to its economic woes.[151]

The Universal House of Justice cites the Gulf crisis as illustrating the contrast between the integrative and disintegrative characteristics which make up the transition period:

> The overwhelming danger which, as a result of the turmoil in the Middle East . . . was a poignant reminder of the contrast between the unobtrusive, steadily developing, distinctly integrative System of Bahá'u'lláh and the turbulent character of the Age of Transition, 'whose tribulations', Shoghi Effendi avers, 'are the precursors of that Era of blissful felicity which is to incarnate God's ultimate purpose for all mankind.' It was another of the 'ominous signs simultaneously proclaiming the agonies of a disintegrating civilization and the birth

pangs of that World Order — that Ark of human salvation — that must needs arise upon its ruins.'[152]

The Most Great Peace

In the Bahá'í teachings, the transition process is to lead to Bahá'u'lláh's prescribed world order, 'the Most Great Peace'. This will be civilization's 'golden age'. In 1981 the Universal House of Justice wrote:

> Without minimizing the serious situation facing a world heedless of Bahá'u'lláh's admonitions, it must be remembered that He also refers to the Golden Age of civilization to come.[153]

For Bahá'ís, this Most Great Peace represents the spiritual, social and political transformation of the world into a unified body. It is the goal towards which all Bahá'ís are to work.[154] Shoghi Effendi linked it with the prophecies of Isaiah and the Christian hope for the establishment of the Kingdom of God on Earth.[155] In *The Promised Day is Come*, he described the glory of this future period:

> God's purpose is none other than to usher in, in ways He alone can bring about, and the full significance of which He alone can fathom, the Great, the Golden Age of a long-divided, a long-afflicted humanity. Its present state, indeed even its immediate future, is dark, distressingly dark. Its distant future, however, is radiant, gloriously radiant — so radiant that no eye can visualize it.[156]

The Bahá'í world order model can be categorized as system-transforming, but, as will be seen, it distinguishes itself from other world order models in several important aspects.[157]

World Unity

The unification of the world is the keystone of Bahá'u'lláh's religion. All of his spiritual and social principles revolve around and derive from this one central theme. Shoghi Effendi wrote in 1931:

> Are not these intermittent crises that convulse present-day society due primarily to the lamentable inability of the world's recognized leaders to read aright the signs of the times, to rid themselves once for all of

their preconceived ideas and fettering creeds, and to reshape the machinery of their respective governments according to those standards that are implicit in Bahá'u'lláh's supreme declaration of the Oneness of Mankind — the chief and distinguishing feature of the Faith He proclaimed? For the principle of the Oneness of Mankind, the cornerstone of Bahá'u'lláh's world-embracing dominion, implies nothing more or less than the enforcement of His scheme for the unification of the world — the scheme to which we have already referred. 'In every Dispensation,' writes 'Abdu'l-Bahá, 'the light of Divine Guidance has been focussed upon one central theme.... In this wondrous Revelation, this glorious century, the foundation of the Faith of God and the distinguishing feature of His Law is the consciousness of the Oneness of Mankind.'[158]

Expounding further on the importance of this theme for the Bahá'í religion, Shoghi Effendi explained that unification does not imply uniformity. The Bahá'í Faith

> does not ignore, nor does it attempt to suppress, the diversity of ethnical origins, of climate, of history, of language and tradition, of thought and habit, that differentiate the peoples and nations of the world. It calls for a wider loyalty, for a larger aspiration than any that has animated the human race. It insists upon the subordination of national impulses and interests to the imperative claims of a unified world. It repudiates excessive centralization on one hand, and disclaims all attempts at uniformity on the other. Its watchword is unity in diversity...
>
> The call of Bahá'u'lláh is primarily directed against all forms of provincialism, all insularities and prejudices....
>
> Let there be no mistake. The principle of the Oneness of Mankind — the pivot round which all the teachings of Bahá'u'lláh revolve — is no mere outburst of ignorant emotionalism or an expression of vague and pious hope. Its appeal is not to be merely identified with a reawakening of the spirit of brotherhood and good-will among men, nor does it aim solely at the fostering of harmonious co-operation among individual peoples and nations. Its implications are deeper, its claims greater than any which the Prophets of old were allowed to advance. Its message is applicable not only to the individual, but concerns itself primarily with the nature of those essential relationships that must bind all the states and nations as members of one human family. It does not constitute merely the enunciation of an ideal, but stands inseparably associated with an institution adequate to embody its truth, demonstrate its validity, and perpetuate its influence.[159] It implies an organic change in the structure of present-day

AN ANALYSIS OF THE BAHÁ'Í WORLD ORDER MODEL

society, a change such as the world has not yet experienced. It constitutes a challenge, at once bold and universal, to outworn shibboleths of national creeds — creeds that have had their day and which must, in the ordinary course of events as shaped and controlled by Providence, give way to a new gospel, fundamentally different from, and infinitely superior to, what the world has already conceived.

It calls for no less than the reconstruction and the demilitarization of the whole civilized world — a world organically unified in all the essential aspects of its life, its political machinery, its spiritual aspiration, its trade and finance, its script and language, and yet infinite in the diversity of the national characteristics of its federated units.

It represents the consummation of human evolution . . .[160]

It is clear that Shoghi Effendi perceived the establishment of a true world commonwealth and world civilization during the Most Great Peace to be a gradual and continuing process, both organic and flexible in nature, as would be the case with the evolution of social, economic and political institutions during the Lesser Peace.

Whereas the establishment of the Lesser Peace will primarily be the result of efforts made outside the Bahá'í community, the Bahá'ís are responsible for the establishment of the Most Great Peace through the building up of their administrative order and the spiritualization of humanity, which the Universal House of Justice calls 'the task of breathing life into this unified body'.[161] In many letters Shoghi Effendi emphasized that the spirit and manner in which the Bahá'ís perform their work would determine at least the speed with which the Most Great Peace would be established.[162]

In 1936 Shoghi Effendi gave a description of his vision of a future Bahá'í world commonwealth, at least in its early stages:

The unity of the human race, as envisaged by Bahá'u'lláh, implies the establishment of a world commonwealth in which all nations, races, creeds and classes are closely and permanently united, and in which the autonomy of its state members and the personal freedom and initiative of the individuals that compose them are definitely and completely safeguarded. This commonwealth must, as far as we can visualize it, consist of a world legislature, whose members will, as the trustees of the whole of mankind, ultimately control the entire resources of all the component nations, and will enact such laws as shall be required to regulate the life, satisfy the needs and adjust the relationships of all races and peoples. A world executive, backed by an international Force, will carry out the decisions arrived at, and apply the laws enacted by, this world legislature, and will safeguard the organic unity of the whole commonwealth. A world tribunal will adjudicate and deliver its compulsory and final verdict in all and any disputes that may arise between the various elements constituting this universal system. A mechanism of world inter-communication will be devised, embracing the whole planet, freed from national hindrances and restrictions, and functioning with marvellous swiftness and perfect regularity. A world metropolis will act as the nerve center of a world civilization, the focus towards which the unifying forces of life will converge and from which its energizing influences will radiate. A world language will either be invented or chosen from among the existing languages and will be taught in the schools of all the federated nations as an auxiliary to their mother tongue. A world script, a world literature, a uniform and universal system of currency, of weights and measures, will simplify and facilitate intercourse and understanding among the nations and races of mankind. In such a world society, science and religion, the two most potent forces in human life, will be reconciled, will cooperate, and will harmoniously develop. The press will, under such a system, while giving full scope to the expression of the diversified views and convictions of mankind, cease to be mischievously manipulated by vested interests, whether private or public, and will be liberated from the influence of contending governments and peoples. The economic resources of the world will be organized, its sources of raw materials will be tapped and fully utilized, its markets will be coordinated and developed, and the distribution of its products will be equitably regulated.

National rivalries, hatreds, and intrigues will cease, and racial animosity and prejudice will be replaced by racial amity, understanding and cooperation. The causes of religious strife will be permanently removed, economic barriers and restrictions will be completely abolished, and the inordinate distinction between classes will be obliterated. Destitution on the one hand, and gross accumulation of ownership on the other, will disappear. The enormous energy dissipated and wasted on war, whether economic or political, will be consecrated to such ends as will extend the range of human inventions and technical development, to the increase of the productivity of mankind, to the extermination of disease, to the extension of scientific research, to the raising of the standard of physical health, to the sharpening and refinement of the human brain, to the exploitation of the unused and unsuspected resources of the planet, to the prolongation of human life, and to the furtherance of any other agency that can

AN ANALYSIS OF THE BAHÁ'Í WORLD ORDER MODEL

stimulate the intellectual, the moral, and spiritual life of the entire human race.

A world federal system, ruling the whole earth and exercising unchallengeable authority over its unimaginably vast resources, blending and embodying the ideals of both the East and the West, liberated from the curse of war and its miseries, and bent on the exploitation of all the available sources of energy on the surface of the planet, a system in which Force is made the servant of Justice, whose life is sustained by its universal recognition of one God and by its allegiance to one common Revelation — such is the goal towards which humanity, impelled by the unifying forces of life, is moving.[163]

The Most Great Peace is the period in which the world government, which will have developed during the Lesser Peace, will begin to function as a Bahá'í government, that is, a world commonwealth functioning strictly according to Bahá'í law and principles.[164] From this world commonwealth, a world civilization will evolve. Shoghi Effendi, concluding his description of the future world commonwealth, emphasizes his belief in the future glory of human civilization:

Who can doubt that such a consummation — the coming of age of the human race — must signalize, in its turn, the inauguration of a world civilization such as no mortal eye hath ever beheld or human mind conceived? Who is it that can imagine the lofty standard which such a civilization, as it unfolds itself, is destined to attain? Who can measure the heights to which human intelligence, liberated from its shackles, will soar? Who can visualize the realms which the human spirit, vitalized by the outpouring light of Bahá'u'lláh, shining in the plenitude of its glory, will discover?[165]

The Bahá'í Administrative Order: Pattern for the Bahá'í World Commonwealth

The Bahá'í administrative order has been called the nucleus, pattern, framework, instrument, guardian and forerunner of the future Bahá'í world commonwealth.[166] Shoghi Effendi described this administrative order as being unique in conception and different from democratic, autocratic, dictatorial, monarchical, republican and aristocratic forms of government, as well as from the Hebrew Commonwealth, the Imamate, the Caliphate and the various Christian ecclesiastical organizations.[167]

The Bahá'í administrative order has also been called Bahá'u'lláh's 'social order'.[168] The dual foundation of this social order is the family and the individual. In the Bahá'í Faith the family takes on a special function as it is there, through interrelation and implementation of the Bahá'í principles, that individuals can change their perspective of basic social roles, then, implementing these transformed perspectives in social relations on a larger scale, will be able to alter basic patterns and functions in society as a whole.[169] The Bahá'í teachings guarantee and protect the rights and privileges of the individual within the family unit. It is in the context of family life that individuals can most commonly learn, and practise, their responsibilities towards others.[170] This enhances awareness of wider social responsibilities, which the individual holds towards the community. The Bahá'í Faith has no clergy, and every Bahá'í is encouraged to participate in the Bahá'í administrative order, and to help it function properly. This can be done by voting for and serving on a variety of institutions, consulting with these bodies and implementing decisions made by them. Access to, and participation in the Bahá'í administrative order is seen as a basic right of every Bahá'í, no matter their culture, economic standing or educational background.

The basic administrative institution in the Bahá'í Faith is that of the Nineteen Day Feast, a gathering held once every Bahá'í month.[171] This institution, unique to the Bahá'í community, is highly significant in their world order model:

> The World Order of Bahá'u'lláh encompasses all units of human society; integrates the spiritual, administrative and social processes of life; and canalizes human expression in its varied forms towards the construction of a new civilization. The Nineteen Day Feast embraces all these aspects at the very base of society. Functioning in the village, the town, the city, it is an institution of which all [Bahá'ís] are members. It is intended to promote unity, ensure progress, and foster joy.[172]

That Bahá'ís consider the Nineteen Day Feast 'the foundation' of their new world order emphasizes the importance of the grass roots in their model. The Bahá'í preferred world order model is primarily to be a matter of everyday living, a process in which all people can fully participate:

> . . . the [Nineteen Day] Feast is rooted in hospitality, with all its implications of friendliness, courtesy, service, generosity and conviviality. The very idea of hospitality as the sustaining spirit of so

significant an institution introduces a revolutionary new attitude to the conduct of human affairs at all levels, an attitude which is so critical to that world unity which the Central Figures of our Faith laboured so long and suffered so much cruelty to bring into being. It is in this divine festival that the foundation is laid for the realization of so unprecedented a reality.[173]

At the Nineteen Day Feast, members of the local spiritual assembly and individuals within its jurisdiction consult on a variety of issues concerning the well-being of their community. During the Feast individuals may make suggestions to the local spiritual assembly. Whereas the Nineteen Day Feast is the basic administrative institution, the local spiritual assembly is the basic administrative unit. A local spiritual assembly is currently elected once a year in every municipality, village or unincorporated local area where there are at least nine adult Bahá'ís. It operates on the first level of society, that is with individuals and families. Its duties are to encourage the Bahá'ís 'to unite in a distinctive Bahá'í society, vitalized and guarded by the laws, ordinances and principles of Bahá'u'lláh's revelation.'[174] Local spiritual assemblies are also, among other duties, to do what is necessary to help the poor, sick, disabled, orphans and widows; ensure the spiritual and intellectual education of children; communicate with other Bahá'í communities and institutions; arrange the regular meetings of the community, (the Nineteen Day Feast and the commemoration of Bahá'í holy days and anniversaries); arrange meetings to promote the 'social, intellectual and spiritual interests' of the general community (including those people in their area of jurisdiction who are not Bahá'ís); and supervise the translation and publication of Bahá'í literature intended for local use.[175]

That there are also national spiritual assemblies in the Bahá'í administrative order acknowledges the role of the nation-State in the development of the Bahá'í world commonwealth.[176] The members of the national spiritual assembly are currently nine in number, and are elected at an annual national convention, by delegates who are themselves elected by much smaller-scale local or regional conventions. The national spiritual assembly performs many functions similar to those of the local assembly, but at a national level. It initiates any measure which it considers will be beneficial to the welfare of its community, and has legislative and judicial authority within its geographical area of jurisdiction. It is solely responsible for directing the general affairs of the Bahá'í community on a national scale. Among its duties it is to 'stimulate, unify and coordinate' the activities of the local spiritual assemblies and Bahá'ís through frequent consultation. It is also to keep in close contact with the international level of the Bahá'í administrative order, that is, the Universal House of Justice.[177] The members of all national spiritual assemblies also have the collective duty of electing, currently once every five years, the members of the Universal House of Justice.

The Universal House of Justice is the supreme legislative and judicial body both in the Bahá'í administrative order and the Bahá'í world order model. 'Abdu'l-Bahá calls the Universal House of Justice 'the consummate union and blending of church and state' as it has both political and religious functions.[178] Thus, this body exemplifies the Bahá'í conviction that there is no distinction between the sacred and the profane. Religion is to be an integral part of everyday life.

In his *Will and Testament*, 'Abdu'l-Bahá ensured the organic flexibility of the Bahá'í community by specifying that the Universal House of Justice could change any laws it may enact, or any clarifications of the Bahá'í writings it may make, according to the needs of the times.[179] The Universal House of Justice is considered by Bahá'ís to be infallibly guided in the making of its decisions.[180] Bahá'u'lláh gives the members of the Universal House of Justice the responsibility of ensuring 'the protection and safeguarding of men, women and children. It is incumbent upon them to have the utmost regard for the interests of the people at all times and under all conditions.'[181] Elsewhere, Bahá'u'lláh gives the Universal House of Justice — along with 'just kings and presidents' — responsibility for the affairs of the human race.[182] He also gives them the task of 'the training of peoples, the upbuilding of nations, the protection of man and the safeguarding of his honour.'[183] In addition the Universal House of Justice has the right of taxation.

The Universal House of Justice, the national spiritual assembly and the local spiritual assembly form what Bahá'ís call the arm of the 'rulers'. There is a complementary arm of the 'learned', currently comprised of the International Teaching Centre, the continental boards of counsellors, the members of the auxiliary board and the assistants to the auxiliary board.[184] This arm has some executive capacities, whereas most of this power belongs to the Universal House of Justice and the spiritual assemblies. It is not yet clear how executive authority in the future will be distributed within the Bahá'í administrative order.[185] Currently the primary duty of the members of these institutions is to encourage and advise the institutions of the 'rulers' and the generality of the Bahá'í community.[186]

Bahá'í Consultation

At the heart of the Bahá'í administrative order is the practice of consultation, the method used by Bahá'ís to make decisions, and their primary tool for conflict resolution. Consultation is so fundamental to the Bahá'í pattern of relations, both between individuals and between institutions, that a brief consideration of its theoretical basis and practical use is worthwhile here.

Consultation is to be used by the various Bahá'í administrative institutions, but also by businesses, and by individuals in any kind of group activity. It is to be used whenever a decision needs to be made, either personal or commercial, for a crisis or in an ordinary situation, within a family or for a commercial or governmental institution, or to resolve a personal difficulty with the aid of friends, family, professionals or a spiritual assembly.[187] In the Bahá'í writings consultation has been called a principle and a law; Shoghi Effendi called it the bedrock of the Bahá'í administrative order.[188]

'Abdu'l-Bahá, during his travels in the West, often spoke about consultation. While in Paris he attended a parliamentary session which resulted in a fist fight. He used this example to explain what consultation should be, that is, the attainment of truth for the questions presented, at the same time stressing that it is not an opportunity for self-opinion or for the opposition, in a parliamentary situation, to create a battleground. Consultation should not be the voicing of personal views, antagonism, or contradiction. When putting forth an opinion, it should be given as a contribution towards a consensus and not as something that is considered correct and right. Consultation should take place in a state of serenity, calm and composure. Before advancing one's own opinion, views previously expressed must be considered, and if another idea is better, then it should be immediately accepted and one's own relinquished. This, 'Abdu'l-Bahá claimed, is how unity and truth can be achieved. 'Abdu'l-Bahá described consultation as being a spiritual conference in attitude, held in an atmosphere of love. One should never insist on one's own opinion. Consultation is to be the investigation of reality with love and fellowship.[189]

'Abdu'l-Bahá explained in detail the basic qualities required for participating in consultation and the fundamental procedural steps to be followed. The first step is the continual effort of the individual to develop qualities such as purity of motive, radiance of spirit, detachment from all but God, humility, lowliness, patience, long-suffering in difficulties, servitude, lack of ill-feeling or discord, and the ability to freely express one's opinions.[190]

Another step, to be practised throughout the consultation, is the use of prayer to receive divine aid in order to arrive at a unified decision, and to develop, among the people consulting, a spirit of mutual love, harmony, sincerity and freedom from estrangement.

A third step is to 'search out the truth',[191] a process which is composed of two sub-steps. The first of these is agreement on the issue under consultation and the gathering of relevant information required for the consultation, including material from the Bahá'í writings for the establishment of the spiritual principles involved. The second sub-step is for those consulting to

> proceed with the utmost devotion, courtesy, dignity, care and moderation to express their views. They must . . . not insist upon their own opinion, for stubbornness and persistence in one's views will lead ultimately to discord and wrangling and the truth will remain hidden. The honored members must with all freedom express their own thoughts, and it is in no wise permissible for one to belittle the thought of another . . .[192]

For this aspect of the consultation process, emphasis is placed on the 'right of the individual to self-expression' and the freedom of the individual 'to declare his conscience and set forth his views.'[193] This is because, as 'Abdu'l-Bahá states: 'The shining spark of truth cometh forth only after the clash of differing opinions.'[194]

The last step is the arrival at a decision. The Bahá'í writings express a preference for decision-making by consensus, but if this is not possible then the issue should be put to a vote and the majority opinion is to be put into effect. Once a decision is made the Bahá'í writings make clear that there are to be no objections or censuring of the decision, either inside or outside of the meeting, as it would then be impossible to properly implement the decision, and thus it would never be known if it were right or wrong.[195] There is a right of appeal if an individual or institution does not agree with the decision, but while the appeal is under consideration the principle is that it should be implemented.[196]

An Embryonic World Community

The Bahá'í administrative order has been described as only the first shaping of what in the future will evolve into the social life and laws of the world community.[197] The Bahá'í teachings imply, then, that whereas the Bahá'í electoral process and the institutions of the Universal House of Justice, 'the learned', the national spiritual assembly, the local spiritual assembly and the Nineteen Day Feast will endure, this will not necessarily be in a form that would be recognizable to the Bahá'ís of today. It is also possible that other institutions will be created or that some of those currently operating will evolve into, or be replaced by, others more suited to the changing needs of an evolving society.[198]

The Bahá'í Community as Model

There are many reasons why the concept of world order is not easily accepted. Among the arguments often encountered are that there would be too many possibilities for oppression, especially of the poor and weak; that it is too utopian, naive and idealistic; that it is irrelevant to practical leaders of action; that States and rulers do not want to give up their power; and, in the end, that it is mere rhetoric.

Bahá'ís are convinced that their community life has already evolved to such a point that a thorough study of its workings would show how these objections can be overcome; for they believe they are already living at the dawn of a new world civilization. The Universal House of Justice has offered the Bahá'í community as a model for study:

It is a community of some three to four million people* drawn from many nations, cultures, classes and creeds, engaged in a wide range of activities serving the spiritual, social and economic needs of the peoples of many lands. It is a single social organism, representative of the diversity of the human family, conducting its affairs through a system of commonly accepted consultative principles, and cherishing equally all the great outpourings of divine guidance in human history. Its existence is yet another convincing proof of the practicality of its Founder's vision of a united world, another evidence that humanity can live as one global society, equal to whatever challenges its coming of age may entail. If the Bahá'í experience can contribute in whatever measure to reinforcing hope in the unity of the human race, we are happy to offer it as a model for study.[199]

Several specific features of Bahá'í community life merit further study in the light of questions raised by efforts in the field of international relations to develop new and viable world order models.

One concerns the acceptance of a world order system in the Third World, as, to date, the development of a new global system has primarily been a western intellectual exercise. Third World concerns are largely oriented towards survival under harsh and difficult conditions, many of which have been created by the rich nations. There is little trust of First World efforts to help, especially if changes to social, political and economic structures are proposed. The Third World looks for a just distribution of the world's goods and resources and equitable participation in decision-making at all levels, but has no reason to believe that the First World will voluntarily give up its current economic and political advantages.

The writings of Shoghi Effendi, and the Universal House of Justice's *The Promise of World Peace* insist that the Bahá'í vision of world government is something new and is not based on current western ways of organizing society and accomplishing goals. For instance, Shoghi Effendi's secretary wrote on his behalf:

> Though it is premature to try and endeavour to foresee on what basis various nations would be represented on any international Council, or

---

* In October 1985. The most recent figure (August 1990) is close to six million (editor's note).

AN ANALYSIS OF THE BAHÁ'Í WORLD ORDER MODEL

in any international form of Government, it is clear that from the Bahá'í standpoint it could only be carried out on a basis of true justice; and justice does not imply one race having a preponderating vote over some other race's representatives, and thus being in a position to dominate them.[200]

The Bahá'í world order model is to have a role in the daily lives of individuals. This might seem particularly challenging in the Third World where such broad and abstract concepts are not usually seen as pertinent to most peoples' daily lives. However, the Bahá'í model provides, at the grass roots, a right of self-determination through its electoral procedures and consultative institutions. This helps the poor to define their own needs and act to meet them.[201] A systematic and thorough study of how the Bahá'í model is being developed in the Third World is needed to reveal the full significance of its influence there.

Also worth noting are the differences between proposed new world order models and the current Bahá'í form of administration. The Bahá'í administrative order is hierarchical, with, currently, international, national and local levels. Each level has a large amount of authority and freedom to make decisions based on the needs and conditions of the area within its jurisdiction. The system fosters both vertical and horizontal (and in some cases diagonal) interaction between all the levels, with the individual being able to have indirect input via the national convention and direct input via the Nineteen Day Feast, and through letters to and personal consultation with institutions on all levels.[202] Aspects of the Bahá'í administrative order can be found in other governmental types, such as democratic, monarchical and aristocratic forms of government, but there are also many features which distinguish it from all of these.[203] A further analysis of these differences would be of interest.

This concludes an outline of the Bahá'í world order model as defined primarily in the Bahá'í writings. The Bahá'í model is the only one actually being implemented, therefore hopefully it has been demonstrated that it merits more in-depth study, both at the theoretical and practical levels, by those interested in the broad questions of world order.

NOTES

1. From at least as long ago as the time of Dante (1265-1321) there have been philosophers and savants who have written about the desirability of establishing a 'great society of all mankind'. These societies, though, were not universalistic in nature. They excluded groups of people such as 'the barbarians', 'the savages' and 'the infidels'.
2. Hedley Bull, *The Anarchical Society: A Study of Order in World Politics* (New York: Columbia University Press, 1977), p. 20.
3. Ibid. Bull differentiates between 'world order' and 'international order', the latter being 'order among states'.
4. In this essay, 'Bahá'í writings' includes those of Bahá'u'lláh, the Báb (1819-50), 'Abdu'l-Bahá, Shoghi Effendi and Universal House of Justice. In some sections it will be of interest to also examine the writings of certain other Bahá'ís or communications from other Bahá'í institutions, which for Bahá'ís do not have the binding authority of the 'Bahá'í writings', but nevertheless throw interesting light on the subjects under discussion. Bahá'ís consider the Báb to be a manifestation of God (see note 60), and Bahá'u'lláh's precursor. For more information on his life, see H. M. Balyuzi, *The Báb: The Herald of the Day of Days* (Oxford: George Ronald, 1973).
5. For a biography of Bahá'u'lláh see H. M. Balyuzi, *Bahá'u'lláh: The King of Glory* (Oxford: George Ronald, 1980).
6. Bahá'u'lláh, *Tablets of Bahá'u'lláh revealed after the Kitáb-i-Aqdas* comp. Research Department of the Universal House of Justice, trans. Habib Taherzadeh and others, rev. ed. (Haifa: Bahá'í World Centre, 1982), p. 67. Except where the context makes it obvious, the conventional use of the words 'man' and 'men' in quotations from the Bahá'í writings translates the concept of 'humanity'.
7. Bahá'u'lláh, *Gleanings from the Writings of Bahá'u'lláh* trans. Shoghi Effendi, 2nd rev. ed. (Wilmette, IL: Bahá'í Publishing Trust, 1976), pp. 333-4.
8. For a biography of 'Abdu'l-Bahá see H. M. Balyuzi, *'Abdu'l-Bahá: The Centre of the Covenant of Bahá'u'lláh* (Oxford: George Ronald, 1971).
9. For a biography of Shoghi Effendi see Rúḥíyyih Rabbaní, *The Priceless Pearl* (London: Bahá'í Publishing Trust, 1969).
10. The Universal House of Justice, *The Promise of World Peace: A Statement by the Universal House of Justice* (London: Bahá'í Publishing Trust, 1985), p. 25 (emphasis added).
11. See for instance, Bahá'u'lláh, *Gleanings*, pp. 65, 70 and 215.
12. For more information on this aspect of Bahá'í theology see in this book, Charles Lerche, 'Human Nature and the Problem of Peace', pp. 101-30. The reader may also refer to 'Abdu'l-Bahá, *Some Answered Questions* comp. and trans. Laura Clifford Barney, 5th ed., (Wilmette, IL: Bahá'í Publishing Trust, 1981), part 4: 'On the Origin, Powers, and Conditions of Man', pp. 177-259.
13. The Universal House of Justice, *The Promise of World Peace*, p. 2.
14. Ibid., p. 11.
15. 'Abdu'l-Bahá, *The Secret of Divine Civilization* trans. Marzieh Gail, 2nd ed. (Wilmette, IL: Bahá'í Publishing Trust, 1970), p. 66.

16. Bahá'u'lláh, *Tablets*, pp. 161 and 162.
17. 'Abdu'l-Bahá, *Some Answered Questions*, p. 248.
18. The Universal House of Justice, *Wellspring of Guidance: Messages 1963-1968* rev. ed. (Wilmette, IL: Bahá'í Publishing Trust, 1976), pp. 113-14.
19. Two essays on the Bahá'í concept of the equality of men and women are in preparation by this author. One will be published in the 'Bahá'í Focus' series of the Bahá'í Publishing Trust of the United Kingdom.
20. H.B. Danesh, *Unity: The Creative Foundation of Peace* rev. ed. (Ottawa: Bahá'í Studies Publications, 1986; Toronto: Fitzhenry-Whiteside, 1986), p. 118.
21. Gregory C. Dahl, 'Evolving toward a Bahá'í Economic System', Association for Bahá'í Studies, ed., *Bahá'í Studies Notebook: Towards an Ever-Advancing Civilization*, vol. III, nos. 3 & 4 (February 1984), (Ottawa: Association for Bahá'í Studies, 1984), p. 46.

For the purpose of comparison, it would be of interest to mention here just a few additional definitions of world order made by non-Bahá'í academics:

John Radano defines the world order movement as being 'the quest for a responsible world society, one capable of keeping the peace, based on social justice for all persons, with respect for the centrality and sovereignty of the human person.' (John Radano, 'Ecumenism and World Order', in Patricia M. Mische, ed., *Christian Voices on World Order*, The Whole Earth Papers, vol. 1, no. 10, (East Orange, NJ: Global Education Associates, 1978), p. 30).

Stanley Hoffmann states that 'order is what provides the states and their subjects with security of life and possessions.' (Stanley Hoffmann, *Primacy or World Order: American Foreign Policy Since the Cold War* (New York: McGraw-Hill Book Company, 1980), p. 149).

Antony Dolman's definition of world order is 'a pattern of power relations among international actors capable of ensuring the functioning of various activities according to a set of rules, written and unwritten.' (Antony J. Dolman, *Resources, Regimes, World Order*, Pergamon Policy Studies on International Development, (New York: Pergamon Press, 1981), p. 9). An international actor is any entity which has influence on world affairs). Dolman goes on to explain that 'the study of world order is concerned with the structures of power, authority and influence, types of conflict and methods of settlement used by international actors in the pursuit of their goals.' (Ibid.).

22. Bahá'u'lláh, *Tablets*, p. 171.
23. See, for instance, Johan Galtung, *The True Worlds: A Transnational Perspective* (New York: The Free Press, 1980), pp. 1 and 18-19; Richard A. Falk, 'Toward a New World Order: Modest Methods and Drastic Visions', in Saul H. Mendlovitz, ed., *On the Creation of a Just World Order: Preferred Worlds for the 1990s* (New York: The Free Press, 1975), p. 218; and Robert C. Johansen, *The National Interest and the Human Interest: An Analysis of U.S. Foreign Policy* (Princeton, NJ: Princeton University Press, 1980), p. 5.

24. See, for instance, Galtung, *The True Worlds*, pp. 1, 18-19; and Rajni Kothari, 'World Politics and World Order: The Issue of Autonomy', pp. 40-5, and Falk, 'Toward a New World Order: Modest Methods and Drastic Visions', p. 215, in Mendlovitz, ed., *On the Creation of a Just World Order*.
25. See, for instance, Falk, 'Toward a New World Order: Modest Methods and Drastic Visions', p. 218, and Kothari, 'World Politics and World Order: The Issue of Autonomy', pp. 47-8, in Mendlovitz, ed., *On the Creation of a Just World Order*.
26. See, for instance, Gustavo Lagos, 'The Revolution of Being', p. 83, and Galtung, 'Nonterritorial Actors and the Problem of Peace', pp. 151-52, in Mendlovitz, ed., *On the Creation of a Just World Order*, and Johan Galtung, *The True Worlds*, pp. 107-78.
27. See, for instance, Galtung, *The True Worlds*, p. 1, and Falk, 'Toward a New World Order: Modest Methods and Drastic Visions', in Mendlovitz, ed., *On the Creation of a Just World Order*, p. 218.
28. See, for instance, Galtung, *The True Worlds*, p. 1; Johansen, *The National Interest and the Human Interest*, p. 5; and Falk, 'Toward a New World Order: Modest Methods and Drastic Visions', in Mendlovitz, ed., *On the Creation of a Just World Order*, p. 218.

The following is a list of concerns in regards to the current state of society gleaned from Barbara J. Wien, ed., *Peace and World Order Studies: A Curriculum Guide* 4th ed. (New York: World Policy Institute, 1984); Falk, 'What New System of World Order?' in Richard Falk, Samuel S. Kim and Saul H. Mendlovitz, eds., *Toward a Just World Order*, Studies on a Just World Order, vol. 1 (Boulder, Co: Westview Press, 1982) pp. 537-8; Brian Lepard in this book, pp. 71-99; Johansen, *The National Interest and the Human Interest;* and Miriam Therese Macgillis, 'Theology and World Order: Remember the Garden' in Mische, ed., *Christian Voices on World Order*, pp. 4-7: excessive efforts to achieve national security; arms spending; hunger; unemployment; lack of decent housing; lack of decent health care; education; aggression; excessive competition; feelings of alienation, powerlessness, and frustration; violence; terrorism; economic justice; social justice; human rights; ecological justice; the threat of nuclear war; civil wars; regional wars; the arms race in the First and Third Worlds; overpopulation; poverty; oppression of certain peoples; depletion and waste of human and material resources; inadequately managed technology; peace; conflict mediation; social and economic development; constructive negotiations; the unity of the human race; changing the framework and normative basis of international relations; transformation of societal organization; the elimination of prejudice; activating the grass roots level; the power structure; the armed forces; energy; the equality of women; the international legal structure; decolonization; freedom of the press and other forms of communication; land reform; personal security; and better intercultural understanding and acceptance.
29. See, for instance, Johansen, *The National Interest and the Human Interest*, pp. 4-5; and Carl-Friedrich von Weizsäcker, 'A Sceptical

Contribution', p. 118, and Falk, 'Toward a New World Order: Modest Methods and Drastic Visions', p. 211, in Mendlovitz, ed., *On the Creation of a Just World Order*.
30. Shoghi Effendi, *The World Order of Bahá'u'lláh: Selected Letters* 2nd rev. ed. (Wilmette, IL: Bahá'í Publishing Trust, 1974), pp. 187-8.
31. Shoghi Effendi, *The Promised Day is Come* rev. ed. (Wilmette, IL: Bahá'í Publishing Trust, 1980), p. 105.
32. Ibid., pp. 113-14.
33. The Universal House of Justice, *The Promise of World Peace*, p. 7.
34. Ibid., p. 8.
35. See, for instance, Johansen *The National Interest and the Human Interest*, p. 19; Saul H. Mendlovitz, introduction to Rajni Kothari, *Footsteps into the Future: Diagnosis of the Present World and a Design for an Alternative*, with an introduction by Saul H. Mendlovitz (New York: The Free Press, 1974), p. xviii; and Richard A. Falk, *A Study of Future Worlds* (New York: The Free Press, 1975), p. 180.
36. Radano, 'Ecumenism and World Order', in Mische, ed., *Christian Voices on World Order*, p. 31.
37. See, for instance, Mendlovitz, introduction to Kothari, *Footsteps into the Future*, pp. xi and xvii.
38. Falk, *A Study of Future Worlds*, pp. 152 and 158.
39. William Sloane Coffin, 'A World for All of Us: A Proposal', in Mische, ed., *Christian Voices on World Order*, pp. 42-3.
40. See, for instance, Mendlovitz, introduction to Kothari, *Footsteps into the Future*, p. xiv. The WOMP values are sometimes stated as peace, social and economic well-being, human dignity and environmental quality (Falk, 'Toward a New World Order: Modest Methods and Drastic Visions', in Mendlovitz, ed., *On the Creation of a Just World Order*, p. 212).
41. Kothari, *Footsteps into the Future*, pp. 10-11 and 39-42.
42. Ibid., p. 32.
43. Johansen, *The National Interest and the Human Interest*, pp. 20-2.
44. Ibid., 36-7.
45. Mendlovitz, introduction to Kothari, *Footsteps into the Future*, pp. ix-xii.
46. Falk, 'Toward a New World Order: Modest Methods and Drastic Visions', in Mendlovitz, ed., *On the Creation of a Just World Order*, pp. 213-14; Falk, *A Study of Future Worlds*, pp. 152 and 220; and Johansen, *The National Interest and the Human Interest*, pp. 31-2.
47. Falk, *A Study of Future Worlds*, pp. 154-6.
48. Stanley Hoffmann, *Duties Beyond Borders: On the Limits and Possibilities of Ethical International Politics* (Syracuse, NY: Syracuse University Press, 1981), pp. 192-3.
49. Ibid., p. 192.
50. Ibid.
51. Ibid.
52. The Universal House of Justice, *The Promise of World Peace*, p. 8.
53. Ibid., p. 9. See also Shoghi Effendi, *The World Order of Bahá'u'lláh*, p. 42.

54. The Universal House of Justice, *The Promise of World Peace*, p. 15.
55. See ibid., p. 17. See also Lepard, in this book, pp. 71-99. Compilations of the Bahá'í writings which highlight some of the more important values in the Bahá'í teachings have been issued by the Universal House of Justice and its Research Department. See, for instance, *Consultation* comp. Research Department of the Universal House of Justice rev. ed. (London: Bahá'í Publishing Trust, 1990); *The Importance of Prayer, Meditation and the Devotional Attitude* comp. Research Department of the Universal House of Justice (London: Bahá'í Publishing Trust, 1981); *The Power of Divine Assistance* comp. Research Department of the Universal House of Justice (London: Bahá'í Publishing Trust, 1981); *Excellence in All Things* comp. Research Department of the Universal House of Justice rev. ed. (London: Bahá'í Publishing Trust, 1989); *Family Life* comp. Research Department of the Universal House of Justice (London: Bahá'í Publishing Trust, 1982). *Bahá'í Education* comp. Research Department of the Universal House of Justice rev. ed. (London: Bahá'í Publishing Trust, 1987); *Peace* comp. Research Department of the Universal House of Justice (London: Bahá'í Publishing Trust, 1985). *Preserving Bahá'í Marriages* comp. Research Department of the Universal House of Justice (London: Bahá'í Publishing Trust, 1991); *Ḥuqúqu'lláh: The Right of God* comp. Research Department of the Universal House of Justice rev. ed. (London: Bahá'í Publishing Trust, 1989); *Women* comp. Research Department of the Universal House of Justice rev. ed. (London: Bahá'í Publishing Trust, 1990); *Trustworthiness* comp. Research Department of the Universal House of Justice (London: Bahá'í Publishing Trust, 1987); and *A Chaste and Holy Life* comp. Research Department of the Universal House of Justice (London: Bahá'í Publishing Trust, 1988).
56. 'Concerning the idea of the Bahá'í World Order and the proper emphasis which should be laid on the social aspect of the Faith; the Guardian feels the necessity for all teachers [of the Bahá'í Faith] to stress the fact that the World Order of Bahá'u'lláh can, under no circumstances, be divorced from the spiritual principles and teachings of the Cause; that the social laws and institutions of the Faith are inseparably bound up and closely interwoven with the moral and spiritual principles enunciated by Bahá'u'lláh, Who, Himself, indeed, has time and again emphasized the underlying oneness and the identity of purpose of all His spiritual, doctrinal, and social teachings. The Friends, while emphasizing both of these aspects, should, in particular, point out that they constitute parts of one and the same plan, and elements of a single, divine and world-embracing system.' (Extract from a letter written on behalf of Shoghi Effendi to Leroy Ioas, dated 14 April 1939, in *Bahá'í News*, no. 134 (March 1940), p. 2.)
57. For a sample listing of conferences attended by the Bahá'í International Community and the statements and reports presented at these conferences, see *The Bahá'í World*, vol. XVIII (1979-1983) (Haifa: Bahá'í World Centre, 1986), pp. 410-12.
58. The transformation of personal and community lives has recently become a focal point for Bahá'í activity. See, for instance, the 'Riḍván'

message from the Universal House of Justice to the Bahá'ís of the World, in *Bahá'í Journal*, vol. 6, no. 2 (May 1989), pp. 1-2.
59. The Bahá'ís may also choose a passage from the writings of the Báb or 'Abdu'l-Bahá.
60. Bahá'u'lláh, *Kitáb-i-Íqán: The Book of Certitude* trans. Shoghi Effendi, 2nd ed. (Wilmette, IL: Bahá'í Publishing Trust, 1970), pp. 240-1. A 'manifestation of God' is Bahá'í terminology for the great prophets, such as Moses, Buddha, Jesus, Muḥammad, the Báb and Bahá'u'lláh. The manifestation is chosen by God to perfectly reflect his attributes and qualities; the manifestation is sent by God to reveal his teachings to the human race.
61. *Bahá'í News*, no. 682 (January 1988), p. 2. This article was originally a paper presented at the 1987 annual meeting of the International Society for General Systems Research held in Budapest.
62. Ibid., p. 3.
63. Ibid.
64. Ibid., pp. 3-4.
65. The Universal House of Justice, *A Synopsis and Codification of the Laws and Ordinances of the Kitáb-i-Aqdas: The Most Holy Book of Bahá'u'lláh* (Haifa: Bahá'í World Centre, 1973), p. 27.
66. Shoghi Effendi, *The Promised Day is Come*, p. 17, and Shoghi Effendi, *The World Order of Bahá'u'lláh*, p. 170.
67. See, for instance, the following works by Shoghi Effendi, *The World Order of Bahá'u'lláh*; *The Promised Day is Come*; and *The Advent of Divine Justice* (Wilmette, IL: Bahá'í Publishing Trust, 1984).
68. See, for instance, Shoghi Effendi, *The Promised Day is Come*, pp. 114-15 and Shoghi Effendi, *The World Order of Bahá'u'lláh*, pp. 170-90.
69. See, for instance, 'Abdu'l-Bahá, *Selections from the Writings of 'Abdu'l-Bahá* comp. Research Department of the Universal House of Justice, trans. Marzieh Gail and others, rev. ed. (Haifa: Bahá'í World Centre, 1982), p. 109.
70. Shoghi Effendi, *The World Order of Bahá'u'lláh*, p. 36.
71. The Universal House of Justice, *Wellspring of Guidance*, pp. 133 and 134.
72. Bahá'u'lláh, *Gleanings*, p. 7.
73. Ibid., p. 313.
74. Shoghi Effendi, *The World Order of Bahá'u'lláh*, p. 44.
75. Ibid., pp. 43-4. Based on 'Abdu'l-Bahá's *Tablets of the Divine Plan* rev. ed. (Wilmette, IL: Bahá'í Publishing Trust, 1977), Shoghi Effendi implemented a series of national and international plans to help the Bahá'ís organize the growth and development of their communities and administrative institutions. Later these plans were given by the Universal House of Justice. Currently each national spiritual assembly develops its own based on guidelines given by the Universal House of Justice.
76. *Bahá'í News*, no. 687 (June 1988), p. 2.
77. Ibid.
78. The Universal House of Justice, *Wellspring of Guidance*, pp. 133-4.
79. Ibid., p. 134.

80. Shoghi Effendi, *The Promised Day is Come*, p. 118.
81. Ibid., p. 117.
82. Ibid., p. 118.
83. Shoghi Effendi, *God Passes By* (Wilmette, IL: Bahá'í Publishing Trust, 1970), pp. 158-9, 171-6 and 206-13. For some of the letters see Bahá'u'lláh, *The Proclamation of Bahá'u'lláh to the Kings and Leaders of the World* (Haifa: Bahá'í World Centre, 1972).
84. Bahá'í terminology for Bahá'u'lláh's prescribed system of world order.
85. Bahá'u'lláh, *Gleanings*, p. 254.

It should be pointed out that for Bahá'ís the establishment of peace is more than just the ending of war, which 'Abdu'l-Bahá defines as being political, commercial, patriotic or racial. (Bahá'u'lláh, 'Abdu'l-Bahá and Shoghi Effendi, *Waging Peace: Selections from the Bahá'í Writings on Universal Peace*, Los Angeles: Kalimát Press, 1984, p. 19). 'Abdu'l-Bahá calls peace the 'panacea' of every societal disease (ibid., p. 43). For Bahá'ís it includes the subordination of national self-interest to the requirements of a world order, educating the masses, liberating the subjugated, eliminating all forms of racism, eliminating the extremes of wealth and poverty, establishing the full equality of women, eliminating nationalism and religious strife, establishing an international auxiliary language, eliminating excessive and unjust taxes and ending the wasting of resources on militarization. (See ibid.; the Universal House of Justice, *The Promise of World Peace*, pp. 11-16; and *World Order*, vol. 5, no. 2 (Winter 1970-71), p. 1).
86. *Peace*, p. 45; Shoghi Effendi, *Citadel of Faith: Messages to America, 1947-1957* (Wilmette, IL: Bahá'í Publishing Trust, 1970), pp. 6-7; and Shoghi Effendi, *The Promised Day is Come*, p. 124.
87. Shoghi Effendi, *The Promised Day is Come*, p. 123.
88. *Peace*, p. 45, and The Universal House of Justice, *Wellspring of Guidance*, p. 133.
89. 'Abdu'l-Bahá, *Selections from the Writings of 'Abdu'l-Bahá*, p. 32. The historical background to this letter, and its implications for world peace and unity from a Bahá'í point of view can be found in Anjam Khursheed, *The Seven Candles of Unity; The Story of 'Abdu'l-Bahá in Edinburgh* (London: Bahá'í Publishing Trust, 1991), pp. 45-54 and 159-78.
90. *Peace*, p. 41 (this letter was written to Dr Glenn L. Shook; see *Bahá'í News*, no. 210, August 1948, p. 3). An earlier letter, written on behalf of Shoghi Effendi contained the following clarification: 'With reference to your question concerning 'Abdu'l-Bahá's reference to 'unity in the political realm'; this unity should be clearly distinguished from the 'unity of nations'. The first is a unity which [politically] independent and sovereign *states* achieve among themselves; while the second is one which is brought about between *nations*, the difference between a state and a nation being that the former, as you know, is a political entity without necessarily being homogeneous in race, whereas the second implies national as well as political homogeneity.' (*Peace*, p. 39).
91. John Huddleston, 'Marxism: A Bahá'í Perspective', in Anthony A. Lee, ed., *Circle of Unity: Bahá'í Approaches to Current Social Issues* (Los Angeles: Kalimát Press, 1984), p. 217.

92. Philip Hainsworth, *Bahá'í Focus on Peace* (London: Bahá'í Publishing Trust, 1986), pp. 82-3, 90.

Other Bahá'ís give definitions which appear, at least in part, to differ from explanations found in the Bahá'í writings, if these definitions are applied to a description of the establishment and development periods of the Lesser Peace. For instance Anthony Lee defines the Lesser Peace as being 'a cessation of war and a unity among nations to be established by world leaders on the basis of political necessity, motivated by fear and practical advantage.' (Anthony A. Lee, ed., *Circle of Peace: Reflections on the Bahá'í Teachings*, Los Angeles: Kalimát Press, 1985, p. xi). Jay Tyson defines the Lesser Peace as being 'the ending of war among nations' (J. Tyson, *World Peace and World Government: From Vision to Reality*, Oxford: George Ronald, 1986, p. 2).

93. 'All we know is that the Lesser Peace and the Most Great Peace *will* come — their exact dates we do not know.' (From a letter written on behalf of Shoghi Effendi, quoted by the Universal House of Justice, in *Peace*, p. 43).

94. See ibid., p. 42 and Shoghi Effendi, *The Promised Day Is Come*, p. 121. The Universal House of Justice wrote to a Bahá'í on 23 January 1980: 'The words ascribed to the Master ['Abdu'l-Bahá], which appeared in "The Montreal Daily Star", stating that permanent and universal peace will be established in the twentieth century, agree with His statement, made in writing and recorded in one of His Tablets and confirmed by Shoghi Effendi on [page 121] of "The Promised Day is Come."' ('The Lesser Peace and the Year 2000', comp. Research Department of the Universal House of Justice unpublished compilation, n.p.). The secretariat of the Universal House of Justice wrote on 31 January 1985 to a Bahá'í: 'First, there will come the Lesser Peace, when the unity of nations will be achieved . . .' ('Mass Conversion and the Golden Age', unpublished compilation, p. 9). It also wrote on 23 April 1987 to a Bahá'í: 'it is clear that 'Abdu'l-Bahá anticipates that "permanent peace" will "be universal in the twentieth century".' (Ibid., p. 13).

95. For instance, the Universal House of Justice's Secretariat wrote: "Abdu'l-Bahá anticipated that the Lesser Peace *could* be established before the end of the twentieth century.' (Secretariat of the Universal House of Justice to a Bahá'í in a letter dated 15 April 1976, quoted in International Teaching Centre, letter to the Continental Board of Counsellors in the Americas, 1 July 1984, p. 6). The emphasis is added. For more on the question of the process of the establishment of the Lesser Peace and the year 2000 see Research Department of the Universal House of Justice, 'Questions About the Lesser Peace and Executive Authority', memorandum to the Universal House of Justice, 27 June 1990, and Research Department of the Universal House of Justice, 'New Translation' memorandum to the Universal House of Justice, 16 October 1990. The author wishes to thank the Research Department of the Universal House of Justice for the material sent regarding the establishment of the Lesser Peace and the end of the Formative Age.

96. Bahá'u'lláh, *Epistle to the Son of the Wolf* trans. Shoghi Effendi (Wilmette, IL: Bahá'í Publishing Trust, 1969), p. 30.
97. Bahá'u'lláh, *Tablets*, p. 126.
98. *Peace*, pp. 40 and 45.
99. Bahá'u'lláh, *Tablets*, p. 89.
100. *Peace*, p. 45. For 'The Goal of a New World Order', see Shoghi Effendi, *The World Order of Bahá'u'lláh*, pp. 29-48.
101. Shoghi Effendi, *Messages to the Bahá'í World: 1950-1957* (Wilmette, IL: Bahá'í Publishing Trust, 1971), p. 155. In its 1986 'Riḍván' message to the Bahá'ís of the world, the Universal House of Justice announced that the Bahá'í community had now accomplished its emergence from obscurity. (*Bahá'í News*, no. 662 (May 1986), p. 1).
102. Bahá'u'lláh, *Epistle to the Son of the Wolf*, p. 31. See also Bahá'u'lláh, *Tablets*, p. 165.
103. 'Abdu'l-Bahá, *Paris Talks: Addresses Given By 'Abdu'l-Bahá in Paris in 1911-1912*, 11th ed. (London: Bahá'í Publishing Trust, 1971), p. 156, and Bahá'u'lláh, *Tablets*, pp. 165-6. One of the Bahá'í principles is that of establishing or designating an international auxiliary language as a means of creating better understanding among the peoples of the world. It is considered by Bahá'ís to be an essential element in the creating of a permanent peace (See for instance, 'Abdu'l-Bahá, *Paris Talks*, p. 156). This is the first step towards the establishment or designation by the Universal House of Justice, at some future time, of only one language to be used by the world's population (Bahá'u'lláh, *Tablets*, p. 68. See also a letter written by Shoghi Effendi's secretary to a Bahá'í dated 30 August 1928, in 'The Principle of an International Auxiliary Language', comp. Research Department of the Universal House of Justice, unpublished compilation, p. 1).
104. Bahá'u'lláh, *Epistle to the Son of the Wolf*, pp. 30-1; Bahá'u'lláh, *Tablets*, p. 165; and Bahá'u'lláh, *The Proclamation of Bahá'u'lláh*, p. 13.

'Abdu'l-Bahá states that the governments of the world must come to a consensus and make a joint agreement to end the possibility of war, and disarm. In a newspaper interview while in Canada in 1912, 'Abdu'l-Bahá declared that this decision would come in the twentieth century and that governments will be forced to come to such an agreement (See *Peace*, pp. 19-20 and 21, and Bahá'u'lláh, 'Abdu'l-Bahá and Shoghi Effendi, *Waging Peace*, pp. 68-9).

Bahá'u'lláh is quoted as having written the following to Mr. Varqa: 'Les nations du monde feront une course aux armements à tel point que la situation deviendra dangereuse. Il y aura des guerres et beaucoup de sang sera versé. Les savants du monde se réuniront pour trouver la cause et ils constateront que les causes de tous ces carnages sont les préjugés et que le plus cruel de ces préjugés est le préjugé religieux. Ils essaieront d'éliminer la religion pour qu'ils puissent éliminer les préjugés qui en sont les causes. Ils constateront que l'homme ne peut pas vivre sans religion; alors, ils vont étudier tous les principes de toutes les religions existantes pour qu'ils puissent voir laquelle de ces religions est conforme aux exigences de notre temps et c'est à ce moment-là que la Foi baha'ie

sera mondialement reconnue.' (Association Européenne Francophone pour les Etudes Bahá'íes, ed., *Approche Pluridisciplinaire des Processus de Paix: Recueil des Conférences*. n.p. Association Européenne Francophone pour les Etudes Bahá'íes, 1986), p. 90.
105. 'Abdu'l-Bahá, in *Peace*, p. 20. For an analysis of the consequences of the arms race see Marek Thee, ed., *Armaments, Arms Control and Disarmament: A UNESCO Reader for Disarmament Education* (Paris: UNESCO, 1982), pp. 44-54.
106. Bahá'u'lláh, *Tablets*, p. 23.
107. 'Abdu'l-Bahá, in *Star of the West*, vol. 5, no. 8 (1 August 1914), p. 115.
108. 'Abdu'l-Bahá, *The Secret of Divine Civilization*, pp. 65-6.
109. *Peace*, p. 21.
110. 'Abdu'l-Bahá, in Bahá'u'lláh, 'Abdu'l-Bahá and Shoghi Effendi, *Waging Peace*, p. 44.
111. 'Abdu'l-Bahá, *The Secret of Divine Civilization*, p. 65; and *Peace*, p. 20.
112. Bahá'u'lláh, 'Abdu'l-Bahá and Shoghi Effendi, *Waging Peace*, p. 44.
113. *Peace*, p. 21.
114. Ibid. 'Abdu'l-Bahá, *The Secret of Divine Civilization*, pp. 64-5.
115. Quoted in Shoghi Effendi, *The World Order of Bahá'u'lláh*, p. 192.
116. See note 104.
117. There are no indications in the Bahá'í writings that the process of disarmament will be completed or that peace will be established by the year 2000.
118. Elsewhere in the Bahá'í writings it is called the 'Great Council'; 'Court'; 'World Tribunal'; 'universal tribunal'; 'arbitral court of justice'; 'highest court of appeal'; 'parliament of man'; 'international court'; 'Great Board of Arbitration'; 'international tribunal'; 'inter-parliamentary gathering', and 'Universal Court of Arbitration'. 'Abdu'l-Bahá, *Paris Talks*, p. 155; Shoghi Effendi, *God Passes By*, p. 305; 'Abdu'l-Bahá, *The Promulgation of Universal Peace: Talks Delivered by 'Abdu'l-Bahá during His Visit to the United States and Canada in 1912* comp. H. MacNutt, 2nd ed. (Wilmette, IL: Bahá'í Publishing Trust, 1982), pp. 301, 317 and 389; 'Abdu'l-Bahá, *'Abdu'l-Bahá in London: Addresses and Notes of Conversations* (London: Bahá'í Publishing Trust, 1982), p. 29; Bahá'u'lláh, 'Abdu'l-Bahá and Shoghi Effendi, *Waging Peace*, p. 55; and Shoghi Effendi, *Bahá'í Administration*, 5th rev. ed. (Wilmette, IL: Bahá'í Publishing Trust, 1968), p. 47.
'Abdu'l-Bahá also speaks of a 'World Council', probably a reference to the Supreme Tribunal. ('Abdu'l-Bahá, *Selections*, p. 280).
In a letter written to Dr Glenn L. Shook on his behalf, the secretary of Shoghi Effendi stated that 'Supreme Tribunal' is the correct translation. (*Lights of Guidance: A Bahá'í Reference File* comp. Helen Hornby (New Delhi: Bahá'í Publishing Trust, 1983), p. 236, and *Bahá'í News*, no. 210, August 1948, p. 3).
119. *Peace: More Than an End to War* comp. Terrill G. Hayes, Richard A. Hill, Anne Marie Scheffer, Anne G. Atkinson and Betty J. Fisher (Wilmette, IL; Bahá'í Publishing Trust, 1986), p. 201; Bahá'u'lláh, 'Abdu'l-Bahá and Shoghi Effendi, *Waging Peace*, p. 55; 'Abdu'l-Bahá,

Paris Talks, p. 155; 'Abdu'l-Bahá, *The Promulgation of Universal Peace*, pp. 301, 317 and 389; and 'Abdu'l-Bahá, *'Abdu'l-Bahá in London*, p. 70.
120. 'Abdu'l-Bahá, *The Secret of Divine Civilization*, p. 38 and 'Abdu'l-Bahá, *The Promulgation of Universal Peace*, p. 301.
121. Bahá'u'lláh, 'Abdu'l-Bahá and Shoghi Effendi, *Waging Peace*, p. 55; 'Abdu'l-Bahá, *Paris Talks*, p. 155; 'Abdu'l-Bahá, *The Promulgation of Universal Peace*, pp. 301, 317 and 389; and 'Abdu'l-Bahá, *'Abdu'l-Bahá in London*, p. 70.
'Bahá'u'lláh says that the Supreme Tribunal must be established: although the League of Nations has been brought into existence, yet it is incapable of establishing universal peace. But the Supreme Tribunal which Bahá'u'lláh has described will fulfil this sacred task with the utmost might and power. And His plan is this: that the national assemblies of each country and nation — that is to say parliaments — should elect two or three persons who are the choicest of that nation, and are well informed concerning international laws and the relations between governments and aware of the essential needs of the world of humanity in this day. The number of these representatives should be in proportion to the number of inhabitants of that country. The election of these souls who are chosen by the national assembly, that is, the parliament, must be confirmed by the upper house, the congress and the cabinet and also by the president or monarch so these persons may be the elected ones of all the nation and the government. The Supreme Tribunal will be composed of these people, and all mankind will thus have a share therein, for every one of these delegates is fully representative of his nation. When the Supreme Tribunal gives a ruling on any international question, either unanimously or by majority rule, there will no longer be any pretext for the plaintiff or ground of objection for the defendant. In case any of the governments or nations, in the execution of the irrefutable decision of the Supreme Tribunal, be negligent or dilatory, the rest of the nations will rise up against it, because all the governments and nations of the world are the supporters of this Supreme Tribunal. Consider what a firm foundation this is! But by a limited and restricted League the purpose will not be realized as it ought and should.' ('Abdu'l-Bahá, quoted in *Peace: More Than an End to War*, pp. 201-2. This is extracted from a letter known to Bahá'ís as the 'Tablet to the Hague').
122. Shoghi Effendi, *The World Order of Bahá'u'lláh*, pp. 40-1.
'As regards the International Executive referred to by the Guardian in his *Goal of a New World Order* it should be noted that this statement refers by no means to the Bahá'í Commonwealth of the future, but simply to that world government which will herald the advent and lead to the final establishment of the World Order of Bahá'u'lláh. The formation of this International Executive, which corresponds to the executive head or board in present-day national governments, is but a step leading to the Bahá'í world government of the future, and hence should not be identified with either the institution of the Guardianship or that of the International House of Justice.' (From a letter written on behalf of Shoghi Effendi, *Peace*, p. 39).

123. The Universal House of Justice, *The Promise of World Peace*, p. 1.
124. See ibid., p. 3, and *Lights of Guidance*, p. 97.
125. Bahá'u'lláh, *Gleanings*, pp. 39-40.
126. Ibid., pp. 118-19.
    Shoghi Effendi, in *The Advent of Divine Justice* (first published in 1939), quotes many of Bahá'u'lláh's passages warning of catastrophic events which would come upon the peoples of the world if they did not accept his teachings:
    "'The days are approaching their end, and yet the peoples of the earth are seen sunk in grievous heedlessness, and lost in manifest error.' "Great, great is the Cause! The hour is approaching when the most great convulsion will have appeared. I swear by Him Who is the Truth! It shall cause separation to afflict everyone, even those who circle around Me." "Say: O concourse of the heedless! I swear by God! The promised day is come, the day when tormenting trials will have surged above your heads, and beneath your feet, saying: 'Taste ye what your hands have wrought!'" "The time for the destruction of the world and its people hath arrived. He Who is the Pre-Existent is come, that He may bestow everlasting life, and grant eternal preservation, and confer that which is conducive to true living." "The day is approaching when its [civilization's] flame will devour the cities, when the Tongue of Grandeur will proclaim: 'The Kingdom is God's, the Almighty, the All-Praised!'" "O ye that are bereft of understanding! A severe trial pursueth you, and will suddenly overtake you. Bestir yourselves, that haply it may pass and inflict no harm upon you." . . . "Grieve thou not over those that have busied themselves with the things of this world, and have forgotten the remembrance of God, the Most Great. By Him Who is the Eternal Truth! The day is approaching when the wrathful anger of the Almighty will have taken hold of them. He, verily, is the Omnipotent, the All-Subduing, the Most Powerful. He shall cleanse the earth from the defilement of their corruption, and shall give it for an heritage unto such of His servants as are nigh unto Him.'" (Shoghi Effendi, *The Advent of Divine Justice*, p. 81)
    Two years later, in his 1941 letter published as *The Promised Day is Come*, Shoghi Effendi again quoted many of Bahá'u'lláh's passages referring to a catastrophe or calamity, relating them to World War II:
    "'Such shall be [humanity's] plight . . . that to disclose it now would not be meet and seemly." . . . "After a time . . . all the governments on earth will change. Oppression will envelop the world. And following a universal convulsion, the sun of justice will rise from the horizon of the unseen realm.'" (Shoghi Effendi, *The Promised Day is Come*, pp. 116-17) "'The time for the destruction of the world and its people . . . hath arrived." . . . "Soon shall the blasts of His chastisement beat upon you, and the dust of hell enshroud you." "The day will soon come . . . whereon [the foolish ones of the earth] will cry out for help and receive no answer.'" (Ibid., p. 3)
127. Shoghi Effendi, *The World Order of Bahá'u'lláh*, p. 47.
128. Ibid., p. 45.

129. Ibid., p. 46.
130. Ibid., p. 155.
131. Ibid., p. 168.
132. See, for instance, Shoghi Effendi, *The Promised Day is Come*, pp. 4-5.
133. Shoghi Effendi, *The World Order of Bahá'u'lláh*, p. 170.
134. 'O ye peoples of the world! Know verily that an unforeseen calamity is following you and that grievous retribution awaiteth you. Think not the deeds ye have committed have been blotted from My sight.' (Bahá'u'lláh, *The Hidden Words* trans. Shoghi Effendi with the assistance of some English friends, rev. ed. (Wilmette, IL: Bahá'í Publishing Trust, 1970), p. 44).
'We have fixed a time for you, O people! If ye fail, at the appointed hour, to turn towards God, He, verily, will lay violent hold on you, and will cause grievous afflictions to assail you from every direction. How severe indeed is the chastisement with which your Lord will then chastise you!' (Bahá'u'lláh, quoted in Shoghi Effendi, *The Promised Day is Come*, p. 5).
'O heedless ones! Though the wonders of My mercy have encompassed all created things, both visible and invisible, and though the revelations of My grace and bounty have permeated every atom of the universe, yet the rod with which I can chastise the wicked is grievous, and the fierceness of Mine anger against them terrible.' (Bahá'u'lláh, quoted in Shoghi Effendi, *The Advent of Divine Justice*, p. 81)
135. Bahá'u'lláh, *The Hidden Words*, p. 15. 'Abdu'l-Bahá described tests, difficulties and suffering as being of two kinds, those due to the consequences of one's own actions and those given by God. For Bahá'ís suffering serves several purposes: it leads to greater perfection, it proves one's sincerity and faith, and it helps the individual remember God, as when one is happy it is possible to forget about God. See, for instance, 'Abdu'l-Bahá, *Paris Talks*, pp. 49-51.
136. Quoted in *The Power of Unity: Beyond Prejudice and Racism* comp. Bonnie J. Taylor, National Race Unity Committee and Bahá'í Publishing Trust (Wilmette, IL: Bahá'í Publishing Trust, 1986), p. 121.
137. Hainsworth, *Bahá'í Focus on Peace*, p. 96.
138. See Tyson, *World Peace and World Government*, pp. 75 and 79-80.
139. Ibid., p. 85. See also pp. 80-7 and 90.
140. 'Mass Conversion and the Golden Age', p. 3.
141. Research Department of the Universal House of Justice, 'Some Extracts from Letters on Behalf of the Guardian on the Subject of the Prophecy of Daniel', comp. Research Department of the Universal House of Justice, unpublished compilation, n.p.
142. Letter from Shoghi Effendi's secretary to a Bahá'í dated 21 November 1949, quoted in International Teaching Centre, letter to the Continental Board of Counsellors in the Americas, p. 4.
143. *Political Non-involvement and Obedience to Government: A Compilation of Some of the Messages of the Guardian and the Universal House of Justice* comp. Peter J. Khan. n.p. [Mona Vale, N.S.W.]: Bahá'í Publications Australia, 1979, p. 5. See also International Teaching Centre, letter to the Continental Board of Counsellors in the Americas, p. 1.

AN ANALYSIS OF THE BAHÁ'Í WORLD ORDER MODEL

144. As 'the catastrophe' or 'calamity' has formed a particular mind-set among certain Bahá'ís and their local communities from time to time in the West, it would be of interest to study the Bahá'í writings on this subject in more depth.

It is clear in Shoghi Effendi's writings that he considered the events surrounding World War II to be the beginnings of the prophesied catastrophe. His secretary wrote, on his behalf, in 1934 to the German National Spiritual Assembly: 'The world is drawing nearer and nearer to a universal catastrophe which will mark the end of a bankrupt and of a fundamentally defective civilization.'(Shoghi Effendi, *The Light of Divine Guidance: The Messages from the Guardian of the Bahá'í Faith to the Bahá'ís of Germany and Austria* (Hofheim-Langenhain, Germany: Bahá'í-Verlag, 1982), p. 55.

In 1936 he wrote to the Bahá'ís of the West:

'We may well believe, we who are called upon to experience the operation of the dark forces destined to unloose a flood of agonizing afflictions, that the darkest hour that must precede the dawn of the Golden Age of our Faith has not yet struck. Deep as is the gloom that already encircles the world, the afflictive ordeals which that world is to suffer are still in preparation, nor can their blackness be as yet imagined. We stand on the threshold of an age whose convulsions proclaim alike the death-pangs of the old order and the birth-pangs of the new. Through the generating influence of the Faith announced by Bahá'u'lláh this New World Order may be said to have been conceived. We can, at the present moment, experience its stirrings in the womb of a travailing age — an age waiting for the appointed hour at which it can cast its burden and yield its fairest fruit.' (Shoghi Effendi, *The World Order of Bahá'u'lláh*, p. 169).

Also in 1936 Shoghi Effendi explained in a letter, published as 'The Unfoldment of World Civilization', that except for world unity, the world had tried every possible system of government and every means to solve its deep-reaching, manifold problems. Humanity was about to enter the worst part of the series of afflictions which would eventually unify it. Society's political and economic structure was almost on 'the point of complete breakdown':

'Nor have these tribulations, grievous as they have been, seemed to have reached their climax, and exerted the full force of their destructive power. The whole world, wherever and however we survey it, offers us the sad and pitiful spectacle of a vast, an enfeebled, and moribund organism, which is being torn politically and strangulated economically by forces it has ceased to either control or comprehend. The Great Depression, the aftermath of the severest ordeals humanity had every experienced, the disintegration of the Versailles system, the recrudescence of militarism in its most menacing aspects, the failure of vast experiments and new-born institutions to safeguard the peace and tranquillity of peoples, classes and nations, have bitterly disillusioned humanity and prostrated its spirits. Its hopes are, for the most part, shattered, its vitality is ebbing, its life strangely disordered, its unity severely compromised.

EMERGENCE: DIMENSIONS OF A NEW WORLD ORDER

'On the continent of Europe inveterate hatreds and increasing rivalries are once more aligning its ill-fated peoples and nations into combinations destined to precipitate the most awful and implacable tribulations that mankind throughout its long record of martyrdom has suffered. On the North American continent economic distress, industrial disorganization, widespread discontent at the abortive experiments designed to readjust an ill-balanced economy, and restlessness and fear inspired by the possibility of political entanglements in both Europe and Asia, portend the approach of what may well prove to be one of the most critical phases of the history of the American Republic. Asia, still to a great extent in the grip of one of the severest trials she has, in her recent history, experienced, finds herself menaced on her eastern confines by the onset of forces that threaten to intensify the struggles which the growing nationalism and industrialization of her emancipated races must ultimately engender. In the heart of Africa, there blazes the fire of an atrocious and bloody war — a war which, whatever its outcome, is destined to exert, through its world-wide repercussions, a most disturbing influence on the races and colored nations of mankind.

'With no less than ten million people under arms, drilled and instructed in the use of the most abominable engines of destruction that science has devised; with thrice that number chafing and fretting at the rule of alien races and governments; with an equally vast army of embittered citizens impotent to procure for themselves the material goods and necessities which others are deliberately destroying; with a still greater mass of human beings groaning under the burden of ever-mounting armaments, and impoverished by the virtual collapse of international trade—with evils such as these, humanity would seem to be definitely entering the outer fringes of the most agonizing phase of its existence.' (Ibid., pp. 188-9.)

In this same letter Shoghi Effendi discusses the important step forward represented by the establishment of the League of Nations, but also explains that, 'This historic step, however, is but a faint glimmer in the darkness that envelops an agitated humanity. It may well prove to be no more than a mere flash, a fugitive gleam, in the midst of an ever-deepening confusion. The process of disintegration must inexorably continue, and its corrosive influence must penetrate deeper and deeper into the very core of a crumbling age. Much suffering will still be required ere the contending nations, creeds, classes and races of mankind are fused in the crucible of universal affliction, and are forged by the fires of a fierce ordeal into one organic commonwealth, one vast, unified, and harmoniously functioning system. Adversities unimaginably appalling, undreamed of crises and upheavals, war, famine, and pestilence, might well combine to engrave in the soul of an unheeding generation those truths and principles which it has disdained to recognize and follow. A paralysis more painful than any it has yet experienced must creep over and further afflict the fabric of a broken society ere it can be rebuilt and regenerated (Ibid., pp. 193-4).

In 1938 Shoghi Effendi further associated World War II with Bahá'u'lláh's predictions of catastrophe, and with scriptural prophecy:

AN ANALYSIS OF THE BAHÁ'Í WORLD ORDER MODEL

'Pregnant indeed are the years looming ahead of us all. The twin processes of internal disintegration and external chaos are being accelerated and every day are inexorably moving towards a climax. The rumblings that must precede the eruption of those forces that must cause "the limbs of humanity to quake" can already by heard. "The time of the end," "the latter years," as foretold in the Scriptures, are at long last upon us. The Pen of Bahá'u'lláh, the voice of 'Abdu'l-Bahá, have time and again, insistently and in terms unmistakable, warned an unheeding humanity of impending disaster.' (Shoghi Effendi, *Messages to America: Selected Letters and Cablegrams Addressed to the Bahá'ís of North America, 1932-1946* (Wilmette, IL: Bahá'í Publishing Committee, 1947), pp. 13-14).

In 1939 he again incorporated quotes of Bahá'u'lláh concerning the catastrophe in a letter to the National Spiritual Assembly of the Bahá'ís of the United States and Canada, associating it with World War II. He also wrote: 'Humanity, heedless and impenitent, is admittedly hovering on the edge of an awful abyss, ready to precipitate itself into that titanic struggle, that crucible whose chastening fires alone can and will weld its antagonistic elements of race, class, religion and nation into one coherent system, one world commonwealth.' (Ibid., p. 27).

In a 1940 cable, Shoghi Effendi stated: 'The stupendous struggle now convulsing the major part of the European continent is progressively revealing the ominous features, and increasingly assuming the proportions, of the titanic upheaval foreshadowed seventy years ago by the prophetic Pen of Bahá'u'lláh.' (Ibid., p. 42).

In another 1940 cable, Shoghi Effendi wrote: 'The long-predicted world-encircling conflagration, essential pre-requisite to world unification, is inexorably moving to its appointed climax.' (Ibid.) In 1941 he cabled: 'The most great convulsion envisaged by the Prophets from Isaiah to Bahá'u'lláh, cataclysmic in violence, planetary in range, is assailing, at long last, the predominating nations of the Asiatic and American continents.' (Ibid., p. 53).

In 1941 Shoghi Effendi again wrote: 'The internecine struggle, now engulfing the generality of mankind, is increasingly assuming, in its range and ferocity, the proportions of the titanic upheaval foreshadowed as far back as seventy years ago by Bahá'u'lláh. It can be viewed in no other light except as a direct interposition by Him Who is the Ordainer of the Universe, the Judge of all men and the Deliverer of the nations. It is the rod of both the anger of God and of His correction. The fierceness of its devastating power chastens the children of men for their refusal to acclaim the century-old Message of their promised, their Heaven-sent Redeemer. The fury of its flames, on the other hand, purges away the dross, and welds the limbs of humanity into one single organism, indivisible, purified, God-conscious and divinely directed.' (Ibid., p. 45).

In this letter Shoghi Effendi states that World War II is the direct continuation of World War I, and that it actually began with the 1937 Sino-Japanese conflict, eventually extending to engulf almost the entire world. He continues: 'The races of the world, Nordic, Slavonic, Mongolian, Arab and African, are alike subjected to its consuming violence. The world's religious systems are no less affected by the universal paralysis which is creeping over the minds and souls of men. The persecution of world Jewry, the rapid deterioration of Christian institutions, the intestine division and disorders of Islám, are but manifestations of the fear and trembling that has seized humanity in its hour of unprecedented turmoil and peril. On the high seas, in the air, on land, in the forefront of battle, in the palaces of kings and the cottages of peasants, in the most hallowed sanctuaries, whether secular or religious, the evidences of God's retributive act and mysterious discipline are manifest. Its heavy toll is steadily mounting — a holocaust sparing neither prince nor peasant, neither man nor woman, neither young nor old.' (Ibid., p. 46).

In *The Promised Day is Come*, written after World War II had begun, Shoghi Effendi refers to this world conflagration as 'the wind of God':

'A tempest, unprecedented in its violence, unpredictable in its course, catastrophic in its immediate effects, unimaginably glorious in its ultimate consequences, is at present sweeping the face of the earth. Its driving power is remorselessly gaining in range and momentum. Its cleansing force, however much undetected, is increasing with every passing day. Humanity, gripped in the clutches of its devastating power, is smitten by the evidences of its resistless fury. It can neither perceive its origin, nor probe its significance, nor discern its outcome. Bewildered, agonized and helpless, it watches this great and mighty wind of God invading the remotest and fairest regions of the earth, rocking its foundations, deranging its equilibrium, sundering its nations, disrupting the homes of its peoples, wasting its cities, driving into exile its kings, pulling down its bulwarks, uprooting its institutions, dimming its light, and harrowing up the souls of its inhabitants.' (Shoghi Effendi, *The Promised Day is Come*, p. 3).

In 1942, commenting on the importance of the entry of the United States into World War II, Shoghi Effendi stated that this invested the war: 'with the character of a truly world-embracing crisis, designed to release world-shaking, world-shaping forces, which, as they operate, and mount in intensity, will throw down the barriers that hinder the emergence of that world community which the World Religion of Bahá'u'lláh has anticipated and can alone permanently establish. (Shoghi Effendi, *Messages to America*, p. 54).

As severe and disruptive as World War II was, it apparently did not produce all the results Shoghi Effendi was expecting from Bahá'u'lláh's prophecies of a calamity. In November 1948 he made what appears to be a speculation that approaching conflicts in Asia (the communist takeover in China took place in 1949 and the Korean War began in 1950) would lead to a further development in the catastrophe prophesied by Bahá'u'lláh. The growth and progress of the Bahá'í community was 'synchronized with a further and still more precipitous decline in the fortunes of a war-torn bleeding society' as was 'every aggravation in the state of a world still harassed by the ravages of a devastating conflict, and now hovering on the brink of a yet more crucial struggle . . .' (Shoghi Effendi, *Citadel of Faith*, pp. 61-2). The Korean War, however, did not take on the proportions of a universal conflagration, and in 1957 Shoghi Effendi's secretary wrote: 'It is our duty to redeem as many of our fellowmen as we possibly can, whose hearts are enlightened, before some great catastrophe overtakes them, in which they will either be hopelessly swallowed up or come out purified and strengthened, and ready to serve. (*A Special Measure of Love: The Importance and Nature of the Teaching Work among the Masses* (Wilmette, IL: Bahá'í Publishing Trust, 1974), p. 18). Although Shoghi Effendi had previously implied that Bahá'u'lláh's many prophecies of a calamity referred to World War II, in 1957 he made clear that in fact he now believed that World War II was just a foretaste of what was to come. Shoghi Effendi wrote of: 'the ominous manifestations of acute political conflict, of social unrest, of racial animosity, of class antagonism, of immorality and of irreligion, proclaiming, in no uncertain terms, the corruption and obsolescence of the institutions of a bankrupt Order.

'Against the background of these afflictive disturbances — the turmoil and tribulations of a travailing age — we may well ponder the portentous prophecies uttered well-nigh fourscore years ago, by the Author of our Faith [Bahá'u'lláh], as well as the dire predictions made by Him Who is the unerring Interpreter of His teachings ['Abdu'l-Bahá], all foreshadowing a universal commotion, of a scope and intensity unparalleled in the annals of mankind.

'The violent derangement of the world's equilibrium; the trembling that will seize the limbs of mankind; the radical transformation of human society; the rolling up of the present-day Order; the fundamental changes affecting the structure of government; the weakening of the pillars of religion; the rise of dictatorships; the spread of tyranny; the fall of monarchies; the decline of ecclesiastical institutions; the increase of anarchy and chaos; the extension and consolidation of the Movement of the Left; the fanning into flame of the smouldering fire of racial strife; the development of infernal engines of war; the burning of cities; the contamination of the atmosphere of the earth — these stand out as the signs and portents that must either herald or accompany the retributive calamity which, as decreed by Him Who is the Judge and Redeemer of mankind, must, sooner or later, afflict a society which, for the most part, and for over a century, has turned a deaf ear to the Voice of God's Messenger in this day — a calamity which must purge the human race of the dross of its age-long corruptions, and weld its component parts into a firmly-knit world-embracing Fellowship . . .' (Shoghi Effendi, *Messages to the Bahá'í World 1950-1957*, p. 103).

145. International Teaching Centre, letter to the Continental Board of Counsellors in the Americas, pp. 1-3.
146. Letter written on behalf of the Universal House of Justice quoted ibid., p. 4. See also pp. 3-5.
147. Communication from the Universal House of Justice to the International Teaching Centre dated 20 February 1984, quoted ibid., p. 7.

148. Letter written on behalf of the Universal House of Justice to a Bahá'í dated 15 April 1976, quoted ibid., p. 6.
149. 'The economic factions, political parties, national hatreds, racial prejudices, and religious antagonisms, will continue to bring about devastating wars until the spirit of the Cause permeates the heart of man, and its universal teachings pull down the existing barriers.' (Letter written by Shoghi Effendi's secretary to the American National Spiritual Assembly dated 24 November 1931, quoted ibid., p. 5).

'There is nothing in the teachings to tell us exactly how much longer the present turbulent state of the world is going to endure; but we do know that humanity must suffer until it becomes spiritually awakened...' (Letter written by Shoghi Effendi's secretary to a Bahá'í dated 26 February 1946, quoted ibid.).
150. The 'Age of Transition' is the Bahá'í term for the transition period to their preferred new world order.
151. The Universal House of Justice, 'Riḍván' message to the Bahá'ís of the World 1990, in *Bahá'í Journal*, vol. 7, no. 3 (June 1990), pp. 2-3.
152. The Universal House of Justice, 'Riḍván' message to the Bahá'ís of the world 1991, in *Bahá'í Journal*, vol. 8, no. 2 (May 1991), p. 1.
153. International Teaching Centre, letter to the Continental Board of Counsellors in the Americas, p. 4.
154. See *Peace*, p. 45.
155. Shoghi Effendi, *Citadel of Faith*, p. 33; Shoghi Effendi, *Messages to the Bahá'í World*, pp. 74-5; and Shoghi Effendi, *The World Order of Bahá'u'lláh*, p. 157. On page 155 of *Messages to the Bahá'í World*, Shoghi Effendi specifies that the advent of the Bahá'í world commonwealth will signalize the establishment of the Kingdom of God on Earth.
156. Shoghi Effendi, *The Promised Day is Come*, p. 116.
157. See Lerche in this book, pp. 101-30. For more information on the basic approaches to world order in the field of international relations, see Richard Falk, 'Contending Approaches to World Order', in Falk, Kim and Mendlovitz, eds., *Toward a Just World Order*, pp. 157-61, and Dolman, *Resources, Regimes, World Order*, pp. 52-8. Hedley Bull prefers to define three different traditions: Hobbesian (realist), Grotian (internationalist) and Kantian (universalist). Bull, *The Anarchical Society*, pp. 24-5. The application of Kant's *Perpetual Peace* to a universalist or cosmopolitan approach to world order is not fully accepted. For descriptions of other preferred world order models see Grenville Clark and Louis B. Sohn, *World Peace Through World Law* 2nd rev. ed. (Cambridge, Mass.: Harvard University Press, 1962); Falk, *A Study of Future Worlds;* Mendlovitz, ed., *On the Creation of a Just World Order;* Galtung, *The True Worlds;* Falk, Kim and Mendlovitz, eds., *Toward a Just World Order*; Dolman, *Resources, Regimes, World Order;* Kothari, *Footsteps into the Future;* and Johansen, *The National Interest and the Human Interest.*
158. Shoghi Effendi, *The World Order of Bahá'u'lláh*, p. 36.
159. This probably refers to the Universal House of Justice.
160. Ibid., pp. 41-3. For further references in the Bahá'í writings to unity and the concept of unity in diversity see, for instance: Bahá'u'lláh, *Epistle*

to the *Son of the Wolf*, pp. 14 and 62-3; Bahá'u'lláh, *The Proclamation of Bahá'u'lláh*, pp. 67-8 and 112; Bahá'u'lláh, *Tablets*, pp. 67, 69, 87-8, 127-8, 129, 166 and 168; Bahá'u'lláh, *Gleanings*, p. 286; Bahá'u'lláh and 'Abdu'l-Bahá, *The Bahá'í Revelation: including Selections from the Bahá'í Holy Writings and Talks by 'Abdu'l-Bahá* rev. ed. (London: Bahá'í Publishing Trust, 1970), p. 219; 'Abdu'l-Bahá, *The Promulgation of Universal Peace*, pp. 4, 12, 19, 63, 69, 150, 153, 158, 181, 228-35, 297-302, and 321-2; 'Abdu'l-Bahá, *Paris Talks*, pp. 21-2, 45-9, 51-4, 129-30, 131, 133-4, and 138-40; 'Abdu'l-Bahá, *'Abdu'l-Bahá in London*, p. 28; 'Abdu'l-Bahá, *The Secret of Divine Civilization*, pp. 39 and 73; 'Abdu'l-Bahá, *Foundations of World Unity*, comp. Horace Holley (Wilmette, IL: Bahá'í Publishing Trust, 1968), pp. 14 and 28; 'Abdu'l-Bahá, *Selections*, pp. 30-1; 52-3; and 291-2; Shoghi Effendi, *The Promised Day is Come*, pp. 118-19; Shoghi Effendi, *Dawn of a New Day: Messages to India, 1923-1957* (New Delhi: Bahá'í Publishing Trust, n.d.), pp. 47-8; Shoghi Effendi, *The World Religion: A Summary of its Aims, Teachings and History* (New York: Bahá'í Publishing Committee, 1938), p. 3; The Universal House of Justice, *Wellspring of Guidance*, p. 131; The Universal House of Justice, *Messages from the Universal House of Justice: 1968-1973* (Wilmette, IL: Bahá'í Publishing Trust, 1976), p. 49; *Peace*, p. 45; *Peace: More Than an End to War*, p. 106; and *The Power of Unity*, pp. 35-6. For an interesting analysis of the dialectical implications of the concept of unity in diversity see Nader Saiedi, 'A Dialogue with Marxism', in Lee, ed., *Circle of Unity*, pp. 244-5.

161. The Universal House of Justice, *Wellspring of Guidance*, p. 134, and *Peace*, p. 40. See, also, Shoghi Effendi, *The World Order of Bahá'u'lláh*, p. 170. The Bahá'í writings emphasize the importance of imbuing humanity with spiritual virtues, as without them, material progress will lead to the creation of destructive technology and aggressive and oppressive behaviour. See 'Abdu'l-Bahá, *Selections*, pp. 283-5, and 'Abdu'l-Bahá, *The Proclamation of Universal Peace*, pp. 12 and 109.

162. See, for instance, Shoghi Effendi, *Messages to America*, p. 15.

163. Shoghi Effendi, *The World Order of Bahá'u'lláh*, pp. 203-4.

164. Shoghi Effendi, *The Advent of Divine Justice*, p. 15 and Shoghi Effendi, *God Passes By*, p. 325.

165. Shoghi Effendi, *The World Order of Bahá'u'lláh*, p. 206. See also Shoghi Effendi, *Citadel of Faith*, pp. 6-7 and Shoghi Effendi, *Messages to the Bahá'í World*, p. 155.

Manifestations of God who will follow Bahá'u'lláh will have as one of their primary missions the further evolution of this world civilization. (Ibid., pp. 155-6.) For more on the Bahá'í doctrine of progressive revelation, especially as it applies to those Manifestations of God who will follow Bahá'u'lláh, see Shoghi Effendi, *The Dispensation of Bahá'u'lláh* (London: Bahá'í Publishing Trust, 1981).

166. See, for instance, Shoghi Effendi, *The World Order of Bahá'u'lláh*, p. 152; Shoghi Effendi, *Messages to America*, p. 96; *Principles of Bahá'í Administration*, 3rd ed. (London: Bahá'í Publishing Trust, 1973), p. 1; and The Universal House of Justice, *The Constitution of the Universal House*

of Justice (Haifa: Bahá'í World Centre, 1972), pp. 7 and 8. For Shoghi Effendi's analysis of the nature of the Bahá'í administrative order in relation to past organizations, see Shoghi Effendi, *The World Order of Bahá'u'lláh*, pp. 152-4.

167. Shoghi Effendi claims that, 'This new-born Administrative Order incorporates within its structure certain elements which are to be found in each of the three recognized forms of secular government, without being in any sense a mere replica of any one of them, and without introducing within its machinery any of the objectionable features which they inherently possess. It blends and harmonizes, as no government fashioned by mortal hands has as yet accomplished, the salutary truths which each of these systems undoubtedly contains without vitiating the integrity of those God-given verities on which it is ultimately founded.' (Shoghi Effendi, *The World Order of Bahá'u'lláh*, pp. 152-3).

Only the pertinent aspects of the Bahá'í administrative order are discussed in this article. For more on the Bahá'í administrative order see 'Abdu'l-Bahá, *Will and Testament of 'Abdu'l-Bahá* trans. Shoghi Effendi, (Wilmette, IL: Bahá'í Publishing Trust, 1968); David Hofman, *A Commentary on the Will and Testament of 'Abdu'l-Bahá*, 4th ed. (Oxford: George Ronald, 1982); Louis Hénuzet, *L'Ordre administratif de Bahá'u'lláh* (Brussels: Maison d'Editions Bahá'íes, 1981); 'The Administrative Order of Bahá'u'lláh' in *The Covenant and Administration: A Compilation* (Wilmette, IL: Bahá'í Publishing Trust, 1969), pp. 44-93; *Principles of Bahá'í Administration;* John Ferraby, *All Things Made New: A Comprehensive Outline of the Bahá'í Faith*, 2nd rev. ed. (London: Bahá'í Publishing Trust, 1987), pp. 262-90; Patricia Plecas and Geoffrey Marks, *The Bahá'í Electoral Process*, Bahá'í Comprehensive Deepening Program (Wilmette, IL: Bahá'í Publishing Trust, 1973); Shoghi Effendi, *Bahá'í Administration;* Shoghi Effendi, *The National Spiritual Assembly* comp. Universal House of Justice, 2nd enlarged ed. (London: Bahá'í Publishing Trust, 1973); *The Establishment of the Universal House of Justice* comp. Research Department of the Universal House of Justice (London: Bahá'í Publishing Trust, 1984); Universal House of Justice *Individual Rights and Freedoms in the World Order of Bahá'u'lláh* (Wilmette, IL: Bahá'í Publishing Trust, 1989); *The Continental Boards of Counsellors* comp. Research Department of the Universal House of Justice. 3rd ed. (London: Bahá'í Publishing Trust, 1981); *The Nineteen Day Feast* comp. Research Department of the Universal House of Justice (London: Bahá'í Publishing Trust, 1989); *Local Spiritual Assemblies* comp. Universal House of Justice (London: Bahá'í Publishing Trust, n.d.); Universal House of Justice, *The Constitution of the Universal House of Justice*; *The Bahá'í World*, vol. 18, pp. 473-80, 536-47 and 554-67; and *The Continental Boards of Counsellors: Letters, Extracts from Letters, and Cables from the Universal House of Justice. An Address by Counsellor Edna M. True*, comp. National Spiritual Assembly of the Bahá'ís of the United States (Wilmette, IL: Bahá'í Publishing Trust, 1981).

168. *Lights of Guidance*, p. 2.

169. An example of this is the relationship between women and men.

AN ANALYSIS OF THE BAHÁ'Í WORLD ORDER MODEL

170. 'The integrity of the family bond must be constantly considered, and the rights of the individual members must not be transgressed. The rights of the son, the father, the mother — none of them must be transgressed, none of them must be arbitrary. Just as the son has certain obligations to his father, the father likewise, has certain obligations to his son. The mother, the sister and other members of the household have their certain prerogatives. All these rights and prerogatives must be conserved, yet the unity of the family must be sustained.' ('Abdu'l-Bahá, *The Promulgation of Universal Peace*, p. 168).
171. In the Bahá'í calendar, a year, which is a solar year, has nineteen months of nineteen days, with four intercalary days (five in a leap year).
172. The Universal House of Justice, *The Nineteen Day Feast*, p. v.
173. Ibid., p. vii; see, also, p. vi.
174. The Universal House of Justice, quoted in *Lights of Guidance*, p. 4.
175. Shoghi Effendi, *Bahá'í Administration*, p. 38.
176. Whether these national spiritual assemblies will continue in their present form, their areas of jurisdiction based on acknowledged national boundaries, is an open question. In fact, their geographical area of jurisdiction has been adapted to different circumstances suited to the development of the Bahá'í community: for example, 'regional' spiritual assemblies administering a number of countries on the same continent, and national spiritual assemblies for the states of Alaska and Hawaii today. The constitution of the Universal House of Justice describes the Bahá'í administrative order as partly being comprised of 'elected councils, universal, secondary and local'. (The Universal House of Justice, *The Constitution of the Universal House of Justice*, p. 8).
177. Shoghi Effendi, *Bahá'í Administration*, p. 39.
178. 'Abdu'l-Bahá, *The Promulgation of Universal Peace*, p. 455.
179. 'Abdu'l-Bahá, *Will and Testament*, p. 20.
180. For more information on the concept of infallibility in the Bahá'í Faith see Juan Ricardo Cole, *The Concept of Manifestation in the Bahá'í Writings*, Bahá'í Studies, vol. 9 (Ottawa: Association for Bahá'í Studies, 1982) pp. 11-14, and Loni Bramson-Lerche, 'Some Aspects of the Establishment of the Guardianship', in Moojan Momen, ed., *Studies in Honor of the Late Hasan M. Balyuzi*, Studies in the Bábí and Bahá'í Religions, vol. 5 (Los Angeles: Kalimát Press, 1988), pp. 255-8.
181. Bahá'u'lláh, *Tablets*, pp. 69-70.
182. Ibid., p. 93.
183. Ibid., p. 125.
184. Bahá'ís sometimes erroneously refer to the rulers as 'the elected arm' and the learned as 'the appointed arm'. For a description and explanation of the development of the institutions of the 'learned arm' see the Universal House of Justice, *Messages*, pp. 91-5.
185. It should be noted that the Bahá'í writings are not completely clear as to the division of executive power. The constitution of the Universal House of Justice states: 'This Administrative Order consists, on the one hand, of a series of elected councils, universal, secondary and local, in which are vested legislative, executive and judicial powers over the Bahá'í

community and, on the other, of eminent and devoted believers appointed for the specific purposes of protecting and propagating the Faith of Bahá'u'lláh under the guidance of the Head of that Faith.' (The Universal House of Justice, *The Constitution of the Universal House of Justice*, p. 8). 'Abdu'l-Bahá, however, is quoted as saying: 'Again I repeat, the House of Justice, whether National or Universal, has only legislative power, and not executive power.' (*Star of the West*, vol. VII, no. 15 (December 12, 1916), p. 139). In 1949 Shoghi Effendi's secretary wrote on his behalf to Peter Mühlschlegel, 'The Hands of the Cause will have executive authority in so far as they carry out the work of the Guardian.' (Shoghi Effendi, *The Light of Divine Guidance: Letters from the Guardian of the Bahá'í Faith to Individual Bewlievers, Groups and Bahá'í Communties in Germany and Austria*, vol. 2 (Hofheim-Langenhain: Bahá'í-Verlag, 1985), p. 82). The Hands of the Cause of God were the individuals first appointed to the 'learned arm' of the Bahá'í administrative order. For more information on this Bahá'í institution, see *The Bahá'í World*, vol. 18, pp. 474-5.

186. See, for instance, 'Abdu'l-Bahá, *Will and Testament*, pp. 12-13. The International Teaching Centre has as its members all the remaining Hands of the Cause of God and certain Counsellors.

The Universal House of Justice has called the branch of the 'learned' one of the unique aspects of the Bahá'í administrative order as the individuals which comprise these institutions have no authority, but because of their knowledge, qualities and rank have a vital role in the administration of the Bahá'í Faith. (The Universal House of Justice, *Messages*, p. 95).

187. *Consultation*, pp. 7-9; 'Abdu'l-Bahá, *The Promulgation of Universal Peace*, p. 183; *Principles of Bahá'í Administration*, p. 20.
188. Quoted in *Consultation*, p. 10.
189. 'Abdu'l-Bahá, *The Promulgation of Universal Peace*, pp. 72-3 and 183.
190. Shoghi Effendi, *Bahá'í Administration*, p. 21.
191. Ibid., p. 22.
192. Ibid.
193. Ibid., p. 63.
194. Ibid., p. 21.
195. Ibid., pp. 21-2.
196. The Universal House of Justice, *The Constitution of the Universal House of Justice*, pp. 14-15 and Ad Hoc Committee, 'Relationship of the Believer to the Institutions of the Bahá'í Faith', Memorandum to the Universal House of Justice, 20 July 1988, p. 5. For more on consultation see Genevieve Coy, *Counsels of Perfection: A Bahá'í Guide to Mature Living* (Oxford: George Ronald, 1978), pp. 144-53; *Consultation*; and the Universal House of Justice, *Individual Rights and Freedoms in the World Order of Bahá'u'lláh*.
197. *Local Spiritual Assemblies*, p. 19.
198. There is a belief amongst some Bahá'ís that the current form of the Bahá'í administrative order will not change in any important way. See, for instance, Robert H. Stockman, 'An Outline of the Heroic and

Formative Ages', unpublished lecture notes, September 1986 p. 11, and Robert H. Stockman, 'Bahá'í Administration: The History of Its Development', unpublished lecture notes, April 1986 p. 25.
199. The Universal House of Justice, *The Promise of World Peace*, p. 24.
200. *Peace*, p. 40.
201. See Farzam Arbáb, 'Development: A Challenge to Bahá'í Scholars' in Association for Bahá'í Studies, ed., *Bahá'í Studies Notebook*, vol. III, nos. 3 & 4, February 1984 pp. 1-18; Holly Hanson Vick, *Social and Economic Development: A Bahá'í Approach* (Oxford: George Ronald, 1989); and Janet Khan, 'The Bahá'í Community as a Model for Social Change' in *Bahá'í News*, no. 682, (January 1988), pages 2-4.
202. One critique some specialists in international relations have in regards to the concept of world government is that they feel it will lead to an excessive and unhealthy centralization. See for instance Hoffmann, *Primacy or World Order*, p. 181.
203. The Universal House of Justice, *Individual Rights and Freedoms in the World Order of Bahá'u'lláh*, pp. 5-6; and Ad Hoc Committee, 'Relationship of the Believer to the Institutions of the Bahá'í Faith', p. 2.

Taking just the democratic forms of government as an example, both use universal, direct and indirect suffrage. In the Bahá'í administrative order universal, direct elections are held for the local level of administration and indirect for the national and international levels. The Bahá'ís tend to use democratic methods in their administration of community affairs. Another example is that both have a constitutional basis. For the Bahá'ís it is their Declaration of Trust and By-Laws (ibid). For a model of the Declaration of Trust and By-Laws, see *Bahá'í World*, vol. 18, pp. 538-45 and 564-7.

There are, however two essential differences between democratic forms of government and the Bahá'í administrative order. The first is that those elected to membership in an assembly do not derive their authority from the people who voted. Rather they are responsible to their own consciences as inspired by the principles of their religion. Furthermore, the elected members do not represent a particular portion of the Bahá'ís, but the entire community (Shoghi Effendi, *The World Order of Bahá'u'lláh*, p. 153; the Universal House of Justice, *Individual Rights and Freedoms in the World Order of Bahá'u'lláh*, p. 10; and Ad Hoc Committee, 'Relationship of the Believer to the Institutions of the Bahá'í Faith', pp. 2 and 9).

The second main difference is in the Bahá'í electoral procedure. The Bahá'ís are to have complete freedom when they vote. There is to be no interference or pressure whatsoever by any institution or individual, so that the voter can choose according to his or her conscience. There are to be no political parties or methods used in party politics, as well as no intrigue or propaganda. No reference is to be made to individual names. There are to be no deceptions, collusion, compulsion, canvassing, electioneering, attempts to influence others, nominations or domination of the proceedings by certain individuals. Secret balloting is used and Bahá'ís are to keep the contents of their votes strictly to themselves. Once the election is completed, the Bahá'ís are morally obligated to accept the results. The individual Bahá'í elects the assembly, has the right to be heard by it and may appeal any decision. The assembly guides and directs community affairs and decides on matters affecting the community or individuals. Once elected it is to be obeyed and supported by the Bahá'ís. Local spiritual assemblies and national spiritual assemblies are currently elected annually so that if the community is dissatisfied with one or more of the members or if other, more qualified people have come to the attention of the electorate, changes can be made. (Shoghi Effendi, *Bahá'í Administration*, p. 136; Shoghi Effendi, *The Light of Divine Guidance: The Messages from the Guardian of the Bahá'í Faith to the Bahá'ís of Germany and Austria*, pp. 67-8; The Universal House of Justice, *Individual Rights and Freedoms in the World Order of Bahá'u'lláh*, pp. 9-10; Shoghi Effendi, *The National Spiritual Assembly*, p. 13; *Local Spiritual Assemblies*, pp. 4-6; *Bahá'í Elections* comp. Research Department of the Universal House of Justice (London: Bahá'í Publishing Trust, 1990), pp. 1, 5, and 7-10.

FROM LEAGUE OF NATIONS TO WORLD COMMONWEALTH
A Bahá'í Perspective on the Past, Present and Future of International Organization
Brian D. Lepard

WHEN Germany and France went to war in the summer of 1870, there was no international organization able to discourage the outbreak of hostilities or help in seeking a peaceful settlement of the conflict once it had begun. A few years earlier, in more peaceful times, if France, Germany and other nations of Europe had wished to discuss their trade relations on a regular basis, they would have found no international body capable of providing a forum for these negotiations. In fact, in 1870, there were no more than a handful of international organizations of any kind in existence. The few organizations operating at that time represented only a tiny number of countries and were limited in their activities to very narrow functions. They had little, if any, practical impact upon the conduct of international relations.

Today, in contrast, there are over 6000 international organizations functioning in the international system.[1] These organizations work in a wide variety of fields and fulfil a broad array of functions, ranging from the co-ordination of international airline routes and the provision of technical developmental assistance to poorer countries, to the promotion of respect for universal human rights and the maintenance of international peace and security. Some organizations, such as the United Nations, represent nearly every State in the world; others, like the European Community (EC), seek to unite members of a particular geographic region. Over 800 international organizations are composed solely of governments, and are properly called 'intergovernmental organizations'; both the UN and the EC are of this type. At the same time, there are more than 5600 international non-governmental organizations (NGOs), representing ordinary people around the world organized in professional leagues, religious groups, and similar associations.[2] This plethora of intergovernmental and non-governmental organizations cutting across national boundaries has made the web of international contacts vastly more intricate and complex, and represents a veritable revolution, within the last century, of the way in which nations and peoples relate to one another.[3]

The teachings of the Bahá'í Faith are directly relevant to this revolution. Bahá'u'lláh brought for the first time in religious history explicit teachings about the need for an international federation capable of harmonizing the affairs of an interdependent world and bringing about world peace. The writings of 'Abdu'l-Bahá, Shoghi Effendi and the Universal House of Justice have expanded upon Bahá'u'lláh's teachings concerning international organization, and have made specific references to international organization's history, present functioning and future.

In *The Promise of World Peace*, the Universal House of Justice describes the development of international organizations as a sign of the progress that has been achieved towards realizing the goal of world peace, and as a favourable portent for the possibilities of building a unified world.

> The tentative steps towards world order, especially since World War II, give hopeful signs. The increasing tendency of groups of nations to formalize relationships which enable them to co-operate in matters of mutual interest . . . prepare the path to world order.[4]

The Universal House of Justice — and the Bahá'í teachings in general — ascribe to international organizations a central role in the development of the future global social order. Therefore this article attempts to explore, from a Bahá'í perspective, the significance and potential of international organizations in this century. Of necessity, it can only provide a broad-brush sketch of certain fundamental issues. Furthermore, it focuses on the role of inter-governmental organizations that are potentially universal in membership, rather than on the work of non-governmental organizations or limited-membership organizations such as the European Community.

Three Factors Affecting International Organization

Bahá'í writings suggest that three major factors have shaped and will continue to shape the development and growth of international organization. The first is the *de facto* interdependence of nations in the political, economic and social spheres. The Bahá'í writings emphasize that one of the distinguishing characteristics of this age is the ever-increasing contact between peoples of different nations and regions. According to 'Abdu'l-Bahá, 'means of communication have multiplied, and the five continents of the earth have virtually merged into one.'[5] Indeed, these contacts have become an indispensable part of life in this century. Moreover, the factors giving rise to global interdependence — such as the development of instantaneous worldwide communication — have made possible, for the first time in human history, the unification of the world and the development of institutions of global scope.

The second major factor affecting international organization is the problem of war and conflict. This problem reflects a larger disintegrative process at work in the world. The Universal House of Justice quotes Bahá'u'lláh in describing this process:

> 'The winds of despair', Bahá'u'lláh wrote, 'are, alas, blowing from every direction, and the strife that divides and afflicts the human race is daily increasing. The signs of impending convulsions and chaos can now be discerned, inasmuch as the prevailing order appears to be lamentably defective.' This prophetic judgement has been amply confirmed by the common experience of humanity.[6]

The threat of nuclear war, the numerous civil and regional wars still being fought, and the build-up of weapons by major powers and impoverished countries alike are evidence of the intensity of violence in our era. The conflict that has been so rampant in the twentieth century has influenced the development of international organizations primarily by inspiring in their founders the desire to put an end to war. At the same time, the very persistence of international conflicts has limited the progress that has been achieved by these organizations towards realizing the goal of world peace.

While acknowledging the reality of conflict, Bahá'í writings recognize the simultaneous development of an emotional and spiritual awareness of world community as a third factor shaping international organization. The Universal House of Justice states that the disintegrative forces at work in the world represent but 'immature stages in a vast historical process and that the human race is today experiencing the unavoidable tumult which marks its collective coming of age.'[7] These forces are a prerequisite to undertaking the stupendous enterprise of building a peaceful world. That such an enterprise is possible, that the necessary constructive forces do exist, that unifying social structures can be erected, is the theme we urge you to examine.[8]

Clearly, one constructive force that exists in the world today is the gradual development, within the last century, of a realization that all the peoples of the world are citizens of one planet, and that the problems facing the human race today demand co-operation on a global scale. This realization has emerged among people of varied nationality, race, religious persuasion and economic circumstance. The Universal House of Justice cites, as signs of the positive forces at work, the

> vast increase in co-operation among hitherto isolated and antagonistic peoples and groups in international undertakings in the scientific, educational, legal, economic and cultural fields; the rise in recent decades of an unprecedented number of international humanitarian organizations; the spread of women's and youth movements calling for an end to war; and the spontaneous spawning of widening networks of ordinary people seeking understanding through personal communication.[9]

To this list of hopeful signs can be added the rapid and unprecedented rise of democracy in Eastern Europe and the resulting drive to re-evaluate old strategic alliances and develop new avenues for co-operation between East and West.

Historical Development

International organizations have developed in response to all three of the factors described above — the need to manage the new interdependence, the desire to prevent war and the drive to improve international co-operation in recognition of the existence of an emerging global community. These factors are listed in the approximate order in which they came to exert an important influence, and help to distinguish three unique periods in the growth of international organization.

The first period began in the early nineteenth century and lasted until the outbreak of war in 1914. The early nineteenth century also witnessed unprecedented revolutions in technology and industrial development, and a rapid expansion in international contacts utilizing the new technologies and coping with the new developments. The very first permanent organizations whose membership cut across international boundaries — such as the International Telegraphic Union, founded in 1865, and the Universal Postal Union, established in 1874 — emerged, according to international relations scholar Inis Claude Jr, in response to 'the difficulties posed and the opportunities offered by the unprecedented international flow of commerce in goods, services, peoples, ideas, germs and social evils.'[10] Very soon these specialized inter-governmental organizations were functioning in a seemingly limitless number of fields, dealing with subjects as diverse as health, railroads and prison conditions.[11] In the political arena, the Great Powers of Europe — Austria, France, Great Britain, Prussia and Russia — first met in 1815 to consult upon means for co-ordinating their policies and coping with shared concerns. This so-called 'Concert System' produced international congresses in 1856, 1871, 1884-5 and 1906.

This initial period of international organization, while primarily a realistic reaction to the new facts of interdependence, also drew inspiration from the growing concern with deterring and limiting war. In 1899, and again in 1907, worldwide conferences were convened at the Hague to discuss disarmament and the peaceful settlement of disputes. According to Claude, these conferences, in spite of their ultimate failures, 'represented the climax of a century of development in which attention shifted more and more to the possibilities of international institutions as instruments of world peace.'[12]

The second period in the development of international organization coincided with the life of the League of Nations and was characterized, above all, by the search for ways of preventing war.[13] World War I brought to a powerful climax the concern of statesmen with reducing the likelihood of global hostilities. For the first time, the average citizen and leaders alike experienced the devastation of 'total war' and the enormous destructive power of modern weapons. During the war, scores of popular associations emerged all over the world calling for an end to all wars and for the establishment of an international organization that would have the power to preserve peace.

The League of Nations was established primarily in response to this universal call for an end to war. The centrepiece of the League Covenant — adopted in April 1919 — was its provision for the creation of a collective security system along the lines advocated by President Woodrow Wilson. Every member was to commit itself to regard an aggression against any one State as an attack upon the whole community, and, once remedies such as arbitration and conciliation had been exhausted, to implement financial, economic and diplomatic sanctions against the aggressor State, with the option of contributing to a military force should military action be necessary. As part of this collective security machinery, the League established, for the first time, a standing international court — the Permanent Court of International Justice.

The doctrine of collective security, which had suddenly acquired intellectual respectability during the war, had been enunciated by Bahá'u'lláh nearly 50 years before. Bahá'u'lláh had written to the world's leaders: 'Should any one among you take up arms against another, rise ye all against him, for this is naught but manifest justice.'[14] In the late 1860s and early 1870s, the time when Bahá'u'lláh was proclaiming these principles in letters addressed to the kings and rulers of the world, only a few so-called 'idealists' were taking them seriously.[15] By 1919, however, the principle of collective security was accepted, at least as an ideal, by the major leaders of the world. As Shoghi Effendi wrote in 1936, 'For the first time in the history of humanity the system of collective security, foreshadowed by Bahá'u'lláh and explained by 'Abdu'l-Bahá, has been seriously envisaged, discussed and tested.'[16]

The League also built upon mechanisms for managing interdependence that had been devised in the previous period. Most importantly, the League established for the first time permanent political organs: the League Council and League Assembly. It set up an international secretariat, administered by a Secretary-General, which drew its membership from many member States but which was politically neutral and independent of any government. The League also established the International Labour Organization — still operating today — to help improve working conditions around the world.

The League of Nations also made progress towards universal recognition that the establishment of world peace requires a global effort. But this progress was limited. While, on paper, the doctrine of collective security expressed an admirable ideal of world community, attempts to apply it in practice failed due to a lack of will to implement the League Covenant's provisions. Moreover, the League was never universal. At its peak of membership, it had 60 members, but the United States — already at that time one of the most powerful countries in the world — never joined due to isolationist sentiment in the US Senate, Germany withdrew in 1933 as a result of Hitler's rise to power, and the Soviet Union was expelled after its invasion of Finland in 1939. Shoghi Effendi noted this weakness in the League: 'The League of Nations, its opponents will observe, still lacks the universality which is the prerequisite of abiding success in the efficacious settlement of international disputes.'[17]

Nevertheless, the League exemplified a growing popular movement involving people around the world in attempts to establish peace, and reflected, perhaps unconsciously, the unifying forces then active in the world. Shoghi Effendi viewed these forces as destined to triumph in the long run, and accordingly applauded the League's accomplishments in a 1936 communication:

> Though the great outcry raised by post-war nationalism is growing louder and more insistent every day, the League of Nations is as yet in its embryonic state, and the storm clouds that are gathering may for a time totally eclipse its powers and obliterate its machinery, yet the direction in which the institution itself is operating is most significant. The voices that have been raised ever since its inception, the efforts that have been exerted, the work that has already been accomplished, foreshadow the triumphs which this presently constituted institution, or any other body that may supersede it, is destined to achieve.[18]

World War II effectively dissolved the League, but it was not long before a third chapter in the history of international organization was opened, signalled by the establishment of the United Nations.[19] To Bahá'ís it is significant that as long ago as 1912, 'Abdu'l-Bahá made a prophetic reference to the creation of the United Nations. He stated at a public talk in Sacramento, California: 'May the first flag of international peace be upraised in this state.'[20] Thirty-three years later, at the 1945 San Francisco Conference on International Organization, that vision became reality.

The United Nations, like the League, was born out of a great war and the corresponding intense desire to eliminate wars once and for all. The UN tried again to eliminate war in a number of ways. Most importantly, it strengthened the collective security system envisaged in the League Covenant by giving it more 'teeth'. In the League Covenant, there was no obligation to undertake joint military action. The UN Charter, in contrast, established a Security Council with broadly-ranging powers to maintain peace, including the power to take enforcement action against breaches of the peace and to require Member States to contribute military forces for this purpose. Furthermore, the UN recognized the importance of Great Power co-operation (which had been lacking in the League because of the US's absence), by providing the five Great Powers — the United States, the Soviet Union, the United Kingdom, France and China — with permanent seats on the fifteen-member Security Council. Each of these five States had the power to veto any substantive resolution, so that any decision would have the benefit of the Great Power agreement which was seen as essential for its successful implementation. Finally, the UN Charter conferred upon the Secretary-General more power than the League had done, and gave him a more active and visible role in seeking the settlement of international political disputes.[21]

In all these ways, the UN built upon the peace machinery of the League. The UN, however, was different in one very important respect. Much more that its predecessor, it aspired to the ideal of world community. First, it sought to be universal in its membership. With a few exceptions, it has largely realized this ideal, now representing 159 countries out of approximately 170 independent nations in the world.[22] Moreover, the UN has inspired and supervised, starting in the 1950s, the process of decolonization and the granting of independence to over 75 countries in the Third World.

Second, the UN attempted from its inception to involve ordinary people in its operation. Not only did non-governmental organizations participate in its creation at the 1945 San Francisco Conference, but over 600 NGOs continue to maintain a working relationship with the United Nations, including for some (such as the Bahá'í International Community) the right to express their views in certain UN meetings.

Third, the UN, while recognizing the importance of efforts to combat aggression, held to the belief that co-operation to promote economic and social well-being, including human rights, is an equally important component in the quest for world peace. The UN accordingly established an Economic and Social Council (ECOSOC) and numerous bodies dealing with economic development, social issues such as drug abuse, the status of women, and human rights. The UN adopted a Universal Declaration of Human Rights in 1948 and, in 1966, two legally-binding covenants incorporating the human rights set forth in the Universal Declaration.[23] On the basis of these human rights documents, the UN firmly established the principle that a State's treatment of its own citizens is a legitimate concern of the international community.

Finally, the UN created an international secretariat that sought not only to be independent of any national influences in fulfilling primarily administrative functions, as the League Secretariat had done, but to promote a distinct internationalist vision, more world-inclusive than the policies of any particular government.[24]

The United Nations, in keeping with its emphasis on world community, developed still further institutions for managing global interdependence. Alongside the UN proper, numerous specialized agencies were created under the UN umbrella to co-ordinate activities in specific fields — organizations such as the International Monetary Fund, the World Bank and the World Health Organization. These fundamentally autonomous organizations have their own secretariat and staff, undertake technical assistance activities in their respective fields, and hold periodic conferences bringing together governments as well as NGOs to discuss pressing world issues. Today, the UN's activities in these technical fields constitute the bulk of its overall work. While these ongoing and frequently low-key activities are often ignored because of an overemphasis on the UN's discussion of highly visible political issues, they represent one of the UN's most important contributions to fostering greater co-operation among the nations of the world.

Thus, the history of international organization has reflected a steady evolution towards higher and higher forms of unity and towards the development of a new awareness that the diverse peoples of the earth together constitute a single world community. The League of Nations and its successor the United

Nations — the two great experiments in international organization — have built upon previous achievements and edged humankind closer to the realization of the ideal of unity.

Accomplishments and Failures of International Organizations in the Contemporary World

International organizations, as they have developed during the course of the last century, have more accomplishments to their credit than many people realize. These accomplishments should be welcomed and supported. At the same time, it should be recognized that barriers still exist to the establishment of universal and lasting peace, and that these organizations as they function today have a number of shortcomings.

On the positive side, international organizations have made substantial progress in coping with world problems through co-operative efforts. They have developed international programmes and strategies for eradicating disease in Third World countries; reducing infant mortality rates through the education of mothers in proper ante- and post-natal care; regulating the use of the seas and their natural resources more equitably; reducing barriers to trade and commerce through the work of the General Agreement on Tariffs and Trade (GATT); and, through the activities of UNESCO, improving world literacy and primary education.

In addition to their activities in these fields, international organizations have further refined mechanisms, such as the independent multinational secretariat, that help to manage interdependence. The Universal House of Justice has welcomed the United Nations's development of this institution:

> The army of men and women, drawn from virtually every culture, race and nation on earth, who serve the multifarious agencies of the United Nations, represent a planetary 'civil service' whose impressive accomplishments are indicative of the degree of co-operation that can be attained even under discouraging conditions.[25]

In all these areas, international organizations have scored notable successes, and their efforts have helped to lay the foundation for a more peaceful world. As the Universal House of Justice notes:

> The increasing attention being focused on some of the most deep-rooted problems of the planet is yet another hopeful sign.... all such

measures, if courageously enforced and expanded, will advance the day when the spectre of war will have lost its power to dominate international relations.[26]

International organizations have had considerably less success in eliminating the problem of war — a problem not so susceptible as (for example) disease to specialized and scientific solution. Nevertheless, the League of Nations, the United Nations and other organizations have succeeded in mitigating some of the negative effects of international conflicts.[27] They have developed a number of mechanisms to help reduce the likelihood of war, and to keep conflicts contained once initiated. For example, the UN Secretary-General has exercised his 'good offices', as an independent representative of the international interest, in attempting to mediate disputes and to find mutually-agreeable solutions.[28]

The UN has also pioneered the technique of interposing 'peace-keeping' forces in troubled areas. These forces, which are armed but not allowed to fight except in self-defence, are placed in buffer zones with the consent of hostile parties in order to keep their forces apart and reduce the likelihood of direct confrontation, thereby providing the opportunity for negotiation. They have served at one time or another in such places as the Congo, Cyprus, the Golan Heights, the Sinai and southern Lebanon.[29] In all these cases, while the UN has not succeeded in preventing conflict entirely, it is not hard to envisage how these situations would have been far worse without its involvement.

In addition, the UN has served as a forum in which conflicts can be discussed by the international community as a whole, with the goal of seeking appropriate and impartial solutions. It has attempted to educate public opinion about the paramount need for peace and disarmament through its publications, periodic conferences and the designation of international 'decades' and 'years' such as the International Year of Peace, observed in 1986.

Perhaps most importantly, the United Nations and other international organizations have succeeded in offering the world a vision of one human family. The UN stands as a symbol of the ideal of a united humanity and a world in which everyone enjoys certain fundamental human rights. It has established international human rights standards, such as the Universal Declaration of Human Rights and the two human rights covenants, that have been accepted, at least in principle, by all the nations of the world. This is an extraordinary achievement in a world of increasingly numerous and culturally diverse States. The Universal House of Justice welcomes these initiatives as a source of hope for the world's peoples:

> Despite the obvious shortcomings of the United Nations, the more than two score declarations and conventions adopted by that organization, even where governments have not been enthusiastic in their commitment, have given ordinary people a new lease on life.[30]

The United Nations, in addition, has trained greater attention on the plight of the poorest countries, and has articulated at the very least a moral obligation to come to the aid of the less well-off.[31] Indeed, its extensive developmental assistance activities in the Third World — in the fields of agriculture, nutrition and education, among others — have become a familiar and indispensable part of life for millions of poor peasants, farmers and slum dwellers. In many parts of the world, these people have come to rely on the UN for their everyday subsistence, and look to it and its ideals as a source of hope for their future. The Food and Agriculture Organization, for example, has provided technical experts to assist rural populations in improving the production and distribution of their agricultural products. UNICEF has led a worldwide campaign to fight infant mortality by educating mothers in techniques for oral rehydration, and the World Health Organization has conducted vaccination campaigns in rural villages, one result of which has been the virtual eradication of smallpox. All these activities of the United Nations and other organizations have helped to draw the world closer together in spirit and in conscience.

Shortcomings of International Organizations

While they have achieved the gains outlined above, international organizations have nonetheless failed to resolve the fundamental problems still confronting the human race in this age. This failure is due to a number of factors. On the one hand, the problems of our time are deeply-rooted, and international organizations have neither been designed nor given the authority to address the root causes of these problems. As the Universal House of Justice notes:

FROM LEAGUE OF NATIONS TO WORLD COMMONWEALTH

Flaws in the prevailing order are conspicuous in the inability of sovereign states organized as United Nations to exorcise the spectre of war, the threatened collapse of the international economic order, the spread of anarchy and terrorism, and intense suffering which these and other afflictions are causing to increasing millions.[32]

On the other hand, even when, on paper, international organizations have been given the authority to act, the reality is that their members have all too frequently clung to the protection of their perceived national interests. They have failed to endorse policies which, while involving some element of self-sacrifice in the short run, would help ameliorate global conditions and therefore improve the well-being of every nation in the long run. For example, the General Agreement on Tariffs and Trade, established to promote free trade and the elimination of most trade restrictions, has encountered great difficulties in coaxing States to eliminate non-tariff trade barriers (for example, customs restrictions). Nations have often found it in their own short-term political interest to place these restrictions on imports, failing to recognize that their own economies, and the world economy as a whole, would be much stronger if such barriers were removed.

This example highlights the failure of international institutions to resolve many of the problems created by global interdependence. Yet another example is the failure of the pertinent international institutions — in this case the International Monetary Fund and the World Bank — to ameliorate the continuing debt crisis among numerous Third World countries. Discussions in the UN on this issue have manifested a distinct lack of co-operation between northern (creditor) countries and southern (debtor) countries. Alongside the debt crisis, millions around the world are still starving from a lack of basic necessities. The progress made by such agencies as the UN Development Programme has only touched the surface of a deep and persistent problem.

In all these areas, a lack of co-ordination among national policies is evident, as is a virtually universal resistance to creating a 'higher authority' to harmonize such policies and address these international problems resolutely and efficiently. At the same time, in their operational responses to these problems, the secretariats of international organizations have at times manifested a lack of co-ordination among their own activities and a tendency towards bureaucratic inefficiency and delay.

Moreover, the United Nations has not eliminated war. According to the Universal House of Justice:

> The League of Nations, the United Nations, and the many organizations and agreements produced by them have unquestionably been helpful in attenuating some of the negative effects of international conflicts, but they have shown themselves incapable of preventing war. Indeed, there have been scores of wars since the end of World War II; many are yet raging.[33]

Contemporary wars and conflicts, such as the ongoing tensions in the Middle East, reflect the persistence of extreme nationalism and racial, ethnic and religious prejudices, prejudices that international organizations have been powerless to overcome.

In part because of national and other prejudices, States have been reluctant to utilize the peace and security machinery of the United Nations. Disputes are frequently brought to the UN only after they have reached the boiling point and the parties are unwilling to back down. In many cases, the UN Security Council — the primary UN body responsible for maintaining peace — has been stymied because of disagreements among its members. In particular, the Charter's 'veto' provisions have blocked Security Council action on many important issues. As long ago as 1955, the Bahá'í International Community United Nations Office suggested that the United Nations amend its Charter to rescind this veto provision in order to permit the UN's collective security machinery to function even in the absence of unanimity among the Great Powers.[34] The veto — and disagreement in general — have, until the recent crisis in the Middle East, prevented the UN from undertaking the collective security action envisaged in the UN Charter.

Lastly, the United Nations and other international organizations, while making important strides towards the ideal of world community, have not succeeded in bringing about a universal, deeply-rooted change of attitudes in favour of this ideal. Nationalism is a very persistent force in the United Nations, and the newly-created States in Africa and Asia seem to be just as adamant as the larger powers in proclaiming their independence and refusing to accede to internationally-formulated policies that they perceive as conflicting with their own national interests.

Furthermore, most of the world's leaders remain staunch defenders of the principle of absolute State sovereignty. They have, to date, declined to relinquish any portion of State sovereignty in favour of a world government, and are quick to emphasize that the UN and other international organizations are voluntary associations of sovereign and independent States. The UN's Charter is based on the concept of the sovereign equality of all its members, and upholds the principle of non-interference in matters falling within the 'domestic jurisdiction' of member States.[35] Furthermore, national leaders have often found support for their defence of absolute sovereignty in the nationalistic attitudes of their own citizens, who are frequently suspicious of any dealings with foreigners, or of any attempt to create a supranational organization.

For all these reasons, international organizations have fallen short in their attempts to create the unified and peaceful world that has been the ultimate goal of their efforts. Yet there is hope for the future. According to the Bahá'í viewpoint, the weaknesses of international organizations can be overcome. Indeed, international organizations are destined to play a prominent role in the establishment of universal peace. The next section explores this aspect of the Bahá'í teachings in greater depth.

The Future of International Organization: From United Nations to World Commonwealth

Developing a Sense of World Community

Bahá'ís emphasize that universal recognition of the oneness of the human race is the cornerstone of peace, and of the success of international organization. Awareness that the world constitutes a single community is the most recent factor in the growth of international organization. It reflects a new maturity that must be strengthened as the primary pillar supporting global institutions. A new resolve is required to break the shackles of greed, ambition and prejudice that have divided and enslaved humankind in old patterns of conflict. Notions of superiority based on class, race, ethnic origin, religion or nationality must be dispelled through recognition that all people are members of one human race:

World order can be founded only on an unshakeable consciousness of the oneness of mankind, a spiritual truth which all the human sciences confirm. . . . Acceptance of the oneness of mankind is the first fundamental prerequisite for reorganization and administration of the world as one country, the home of humankind. Universal acceptance of this spiritual principle is essential to any successful attempt to establish world peace.[36]

Such a recognition, if perhaps emerging, is still limited among peoples and leaders. Many still subscribe to the view that people will never be able to consider all others on the planet equally as brothers and sisters — that, for example, a Frenchman will never feel the same sympathy for an African as for a fellow Frenchman. Yet the Bahá'í teachings are not only optimistic on this point; they indicate the means by which such a new attitude can be achieved. In particular, such a transformation requires education in the principle of human unity, at all levels and for individuals of all ages and backgrounds, with particular emphasis on the youngest children. This principle should 'be universally proclaimed, taught in schools, and constantly asserted in every nation as preparation for the organic change in the structure of society which it implies.'[37]

Programmes of education designed to foster this awareness should focus on examining all the findings of the biological, social, economic and political sciences that testify to the oneness of the human race. They could include, in particular, study of the biological unity of the human race as one human species; the basic needs, desires and emotions shared by all human beings; the quest by each individual for self-identity; the universal institution of the family as the building block of society; the shared need to develop a sense of cultural identity; the social, economic, cultural and political interdependence of all peoples; and the universal search for spiritual progress through religion.[38] The goal of these studies would be not only to create an intellectual awareness of human unity and interdependence, but also to foster in each individual a more deeply-rooted sense of kinship with all other members of the human race.

Religion has an essential role to play in this educational process. According to the Universal House of Justice, 'No serious attempt to set human affairs aright, to achieve world peace, can ignore religion.'[39] On this theme Bahá'u'lláh wrote: 'Religion is the greatest of all means for the establishment of order in the world and for the peaceful contentment of all that dwell therein.'[40]

All the great religions of the world have brought eternal spiritual teachings — such as the teaching to love one's neighbour as oneself — that have helped to lay the foundation for peaceful social life. All too often humankind has ignored these fundamental teachings of love and social harmony, has abused religion for selfish ends, and fought bloody wars in its name. The passages cited above clearly refer to the essential spiritual teachings of the great world religions, and not to their abuse and distortion for selfish ends. Such transcendent, humane and altruistic principles have demonstrated their power to lift people above their materialistic and parochial quarrels, and provide them with a more world-inclusive vision — a vision powerful enough to alter their conduct and direct it toward the welfare of others.

While education in the principle of human oneness may offer the best hope for a solution to the contemporary problems of disunity and conflict, the Bahá'í writings point out that in the more immediate future the lesson of unity may well have to be learned through suffering. According to Shoghi Effendi, 'That the forces of a world catastrophe can alone precipitate such a new phase of human thought is, alas, becoming increasingly apparent.'[41]

Such a catastrophe might take many forms — including an ecological disaster, world economic collapse, or even another world-engulfing war. It is a sad but accurate commentary that humankind in recent history has turned its thoughts to peace only because it has experienced the horrors of war. Nevertheless, humankind at the present historical juncture does have a choice: 'Whether peace is to be reached only after unimaginable horrors precipitated by humanity's stubborn clinging to old patterns of behaviour, or is to be embraced now by an act of consultative will, is the choice before all who inhabit the earth.'[42]

Building a World Commonwealth of Nations

Whichever path is chosen, the Bahá'í writings state unequivocally that human beings will eventually recognize their unity. The inevitable result of this transformation of attitudes will, in the Bahá'í view, be the creation of a commonwealth of nations designed to embody, perpetuate and foster that unity. The reality of human unity makes such a commonwealth a necessity for ordering and regulating world affairs. Shoghi Effendi writes:

> Some form of world super-state must needs be evolved, in whose favour all the nations of the world will have willingly ceded every claim to make war, certain rights to impose taxation and all right to maintain armaments, except for purposes of maintaining internal order within their respective dominions. Such a state will have to include within its orbit an International Executive adequate to enforce supreme and unchallengeable authority on every recalcitrant member of the commonwealth; a World Parliament whose members shall be elected by the people in their respective countries and whose election shall be confirmed by their respective governments; and a Supreme Tribunal whose judgement will have a binding effect even in such cases where the parties concerned did not voluntarily agree to submit their case to its consideration.[43]

The League of Nations and the United Nations have represented important strides towards the realization of a world federal commonwealth. They have laid the groundwork for the patterns of co-operation and co-ordination upon which such a commonwealth would rely. The Bahá'í concept of world commonwealth possesses certain similarities to the underlying characteristics of the United Nations, yet it also differs in several important ways.

Most importantly, while the United Nations operates within the framework of the contemporary system of completely sovereign States, in which states are subject to no higher authority able to compel them to abide by international law, the world commonwealth envisioned in the Bahá'í writings would, of necessity, limit the sovereignty of States in areas judged to be properly of international jurisdiction, such as in matters of war and peace. A jealous protection of unlimited State sovereignty has severely constrained the progress that organizations such as the UN have been able to make. In the Bahá'í view, peoples and States must accordingly reject this doctrine on the basis of a broader concern for the welfare of humanity as a whole:

> Nation-building has come to an end. The anarchy inherent in state sovereignty is moving towards a climax. A world, growing to maturity, must abandon this fetish, recognize the oneness and wholeness of human relationships, and establish once and for all the machinery that can best incarnate this fundamental principle in its life.[44]

At the same time, it would be incumbent on the constituent representatives of the world commonwealth to think in planetary terms and to be generally willing to accede to policies that would promote the interests of humanity as a whole, rather than strictly national interests. As the UN experience has demonstrated, a constitutional structure alone can never substitute for broader vision and the sincere will to co-operate.

Many people have rejected the idea of world government because they fear — and not without reason — the potential for world dictatorship. They are apprehensive that any form of supranational control would undermine the legitimate role of States, lead to cultural uniformity and impinge on human rights and personal liberty.

In recognition of this danger, the Bahá'í teachings make clear that the future world commonwealth must safeguard 'the autonomy of its state members and the personal freedom and initiative of the individuals that compose them.'[45] Furthermore, the world parliament foreseen in the Bahá'í writings would be based on the principle of federalism. While possessing certain legislative powers akin to those of a national federal system, it would leave fundamental rights and responsibilities to independent agencies and to States themselves, thus achieving a balance of authority between all levels of government — local, national and international. Such a commonwealth would retain 'the system of national autonomy so essential if the evils of excessive centralization are to be avoided';[46] at the same time, it would permit and even encourage 'the diversity of ethnical origins, of climate, of history, of language and tradition, of thought and habit, that differentiate the peoples and nations of the world.'[47] In this respect, the world commonwealth foreseen by Bahá'ís would protect one of the United Nations's most valued characteristics — its preservation and encouragement of diversity among States and cultures.

A world commonwealth, would, like the United Nations, need to be universal in national membership, but it would also need to make appropriate provision for the participation of ordinary people, for whose benefit it would ultimately exist.[48] For example, the Bahá'í standard requires that citizens and governments both play a role in selecting their representatives to the future world parliament, in contrast to the UN General Assembly in which national representatives are selected exclusively by governments.[49]

Finally, the Bahá'í approach, like that of the United Nations, recognizes that peace has many components and cannot be realized solely through preventing warfare. The establishment of universal and lasting peace is also dependent on progress towards such social goals as the eradication of all forms of discrimination, including racial and religious discrimination; the elimination of extremes of wealth and poverty; the implementation of the principle of the equality of the sexes; the greater economic development of all peoples; the establishment of universal education in all countries, with priority placed on the poorest; and the eventual use of a universal auxiliary language.

Preventing War: the Bahá'í Concept of Collective Security

Bahá'u'lláh — and later 'Abdu'l-Bahá — called for a system of collective security designed to deter war. The theory and practice of collective security has been a thorny issue in the development of international organization, and is of particular significance at the present time. The Universal House of Justice has referred to the use of military force in the Gulf as demonstrating the importance of the principle of collective security, while illustrating how far the nations have to go before they can be said to have met the standard prescribed in Bahá'u'lláh's writings.

> The forces which united the remedial reactions of so many nations to the sudden crisis in this region demonstrated beyond any doubt the necessity of the principle of collective security prescribed by Bahá'u'lláh more than a century ago as a means of resolving conflict. While the international arrangement envisioned by Him for the full application of this principle is far from having been adopted by the rulers of mankind, a long step towards the behaviour outlined for the nations by the Lord of the Age has thus been taken. How illuminating are Bahá'u'lláh's words foreshadowing the future reorientation of the nations: 'Be united, O concourse of the sovereigns of the world,' He wrote, 'for thereby will the tempest of discord be stilled amongst you, and your peoples find rest. Should any one among you take up arms against another, rise ye all against him, for this is naught but manifest justice.'[50]

FROM LEAGUE OF NATIONS TO WORLD COMMONWEALTH

While the Bahá'í teachings indicate that a collective security system is not on its own sufficient to attain world peace, they do stress that it is necessary for its establishment and maintenance. 'Abdu'l-Bahá has described the broad outlines of such a system, which would be initiated through a binding covenant agreed by all the leaders of the world.

According to 'Abdu'l-Bahá, this covenant, first of all, should fix international boundaries — a matter still the subject of controversy in many parts of the world. It should lay down generally-agreed principles of international relations, such as, one might infer, the principle of *pacta sunt servanda* ('treaties are to be observed') and the prohibition of the use of force by a State except in self-defence. It would also establish specific international obligations, which could include the obligation to refrain from the use of force, to reduce levels of armaments in accordance with a universal plan, to participate in collective security action, and to submit disputes to binding arbitration or judgement by a world court.

If a government violate any of the provisions of this treaty, as determined by an international court, all other governments would be obliged to oppose it.[51] According to Shoghi Effendi, this covenant 'shall have as its sanction the instant and coercive intervention of the combined forces of the federated units.'[52] Such intervention would be made possible through the operation of a 'world executive, backed by an international Force', which would 'carry out the decisions arrived at, and apply the laws enacted by' the world legislature, and would 'safeguard the organic unity of the whole commonwealth.'[53]

These ideas resemble in some respects the principles incorporated in the Covenant of the League of Nations and in the United Nations Charter. How then, one might ask, is the Bahá'í concept of collective security different?

First, the Bahá'í teachings affirm that no collective security system can function unless there is a new resolve among the peoples and leaders of the world to make it work, resulting from a more profound awareness of the oneness of humankind. In this regard the Universal House of Justice has stated clearly that 'Based on political agreements alone, the idea of collective security is a chimera.'[54] Fostering this awareness is of primary importance.

Second, the Bahá'í concept goes a step further than the UN system by calling for the creation of a binding security pact among all nations, enforceable by an international executive and if necessary by an international military force. The machinery of an international military force was proposed by the French during the discussions leading to the creation of the League of Nations, and was later incorporated in principle in Chapter VII of the UN Charter. The task at hand now, according to the Bahá'í position, is to create such a force based on universal agreement, and to endow it with sufficient power to deter any contemplated act of aggression, or to repel actual aggression if necessary. Moreover, the system proposed in the Bahá'í writings leaves open the possibility that *any* violation of the obligations defined in the covenant — not only aggression as under the UN Charter — could be met with enforcement action. Thus, for example, nation-States could be compelled to submit their disputes to binding arbitration, or to disarm, in accordance with their international commitments. The various decisions and laws enacted by the world parliament (for example, concerning human rights violations) would likewise be enforceable.

Third, alongside the question of enforcement, the Bahá'í approach emphasizes that a system of collective security cannot function effectively unless States agree to relinquish a portion of their arms. In the Bahá'í view, disarmament must be universal, simultaneous and supervised by the world commonwealth, in order to ensure that it is fair, just and effective — in contrast to the demands sometimes heard in the United Nations and elsewhere for unilateral disarmament, or for disarmament only by certain States. Clearly, a number of intermediate steps may be necessary before a fully operational system of universal, supervised disarmament can be implemented and much more work is required to develop effective techniques for monitoring armaments levels.

Finally, the Bahá'í writings foresee the establishment of a world court that would 'adjudicate and deliver its compulsory and final verdict in all and any disputes that may arise between the various elements constituting this universal system.'[55] Such a court — whose members would be elected from among those who are 'well informed concerning international laws' by national parliaments — would have the authority to rule on conflicts between States even without their consent, and to enforce its decisions.[56] In this respect, it would differ significantly from the present International Court of Justice established under the United Nations. The International Court of Justice can only decide cases in which the parties involved have consented, either directly or indirectly, to its jurisdiction, and its decisions are often ignored by one or more of the parties.

While possessing a 'strong arm' in the last resort, the international court foreseen by the Bahá'í writings would, like the mechanisms that have been developed by the United Nations, provide for flexibility and negotiation in the settlement of international disputes. It would attempt first to promote conciliation, mediation and arbitration. Thus, the collective security system envisaged in the Bahá'í writings would exhibit both force and flexibility:

> . . . for this system of collective security to be effectively established strength and elasticity are both essential — strength involving the use of an adequate force to ensure the efficiency of the proposed system, and elasticity to enable the machinery that has been devised to meet the legitimate needs and aspirations of its aggrieved upholders.[57]

Managing Interdependence: the Need for New Instruments of Co-operation

New institutions and modes of co-operation are required to manage global interdependence. The world parliament mentioned above would, through the enactment of appropriate legislation in matters of international concern, be able to co-ordinate more effectively the world's response to the pressing problems of our age. At the same time, while the world parliament would have ultimate authority over certain domains, it would be essential to involve individuals and all levels of government to avoid the stifling effects and inefficiencies of over-centralization.

One can envisage, alongside this world parliament, the further and accelerated development of a complex transnational network of individuals, private organizations and international agencies, all operating in unique ways and with relative autonomy to foster harmony among nations, yet functioning under the umbrella of the world commonwealth. In this respect, the Bahá'í vision seeks to retain the advantages of decentralization inherent in the UN's system of independent specialized agencies, but would at the same time ensure greater co-ordination of efforts. Such agencies would rely on the services of an international civil service like the one developed by the United Nations. The UN experience has already shown that such an independent civil service can be created and can function effectively.[58]

Other mechanisms for facilitating co-operation will also need to be devised. According to Shoghi Effendi, among the tasks to be carried out are the continued improvement of world intercommunication; the development of an international language taught as an auxiliary to mother tongues; and the evolution of a uniform system of currency and of weights and measures in order to facilitate international commerce and scientific discourse.[59] The perfection of these instruments of co-operation would assist humankind in building a more just and unified world social order. In particular,

> economic barriers and restrictions will be completely abolished, and the inordinate distinction between classes will be obliterated. Destitution on the one hand, and gross accumulation of ownership on the other, will disappear. The enormous energy dissipated and wasted on war, whether economic or political, will be consecrated to such ends as will extend the range of human inventions and technical development, to the increase of the productivity of mankind, to the extermination of disease, to the extension of scientific research, to the raising of the standard of physical health, to the sharpening and refinement of the human brain, to the exploitation of the unused and unsuspected resources of the planet, to the prolongation of human life, and to the furtherance of any other agency that can stimulate the intellectual, the moral, and spiritual life of the entire human race.[60]

Conclusion: From the Present to the Future

We have seen that contemporary international organizations have developed as the result of the interaction of three historical forces: the need to cope with increasing interdependence through international collaboration; the desire to prevent and eliminate war; and a growing awareness of world unity. These are the same forces which, Bahá'ís believe, will propel humankind further into an era of more integrated and extensive international organization.

FROM LEAGUE OF NATIONS TO WORLD COMMONWEALTH

The need to manage interdependence is already widely accepted, and commitment to the implementation of new mechanisms to foster co-operation is steadily growing. With respect to the desire for peace, many people around the world — and their leaders — are mobilized to end the nuclear arms race and to reduce the levels of biological, chemical and conventional weapons currently stockpiled. It is not yet clear, however, whether these initiatives alone will be sufficient finally to lead humanity to the implementation of a system of collective security. As already suggested, yet more conflict may be required before the desire to eliminate war becomes sufficiently acute to bring about this change. Finally, an awareness of world unity is gradually developing. The recent 'peaceful revolutions' in many parts of the world have sparked a new optimism about the possibilities for positive social change throughout the globe. They have fostered a new sense of shared destiny between the peoples of the East and West. Yet the persistence of extreme nationalism and parochial ways of thinking may well limit the impact of these developments.

The Bahá'í writings unequivocally state — and the world-wide Bahá'í community upholds the view — that these forces will continue to grow in strength and will produce, 'in God's due time, the Lesser Peace, the political unification of the world.'[61] This political peace will result in a unity of nations which, 'Abdu'l-Bahá indicates, 'in this century will be securely established, causing all the peoples of the world to regard themselves as citizens of one common fatherland.'[62] Accordingly, the establishment of a world commonwealth is not an ideal postponed to some indefinite future, but rather a reality that is just around the corner. According to the Bahá'í writings, the achievement of this political unity will be followed, eventually, by the establishment of what Bahá'u'lláh calls the 'Most Great Peace,' characterized by a spiritual as well as social and political understanding of world unity.

The course of developments predicted in the Bahá'í writings indicate that the world commonwealth will be founded by the agreement of the world's leaders. As already mentioned, Bahá'u'lláh, and later 'Abdu'l-Bahá, called upon the leaders of the world to hold an international consultation for this purpose. Recently the Universal House of Justice has re-iterated this call:

With all the ardour of our hearts, we appeal to the leaders of all nations to seize this opportune moment and take irreversible steps to convoke this world meeting. All the forces of history impel the human race towards this act which will mark for all time the dawn of its long-awaited maturity. Will not the United Nations, with the full support of its membership, rise to the high purposes of such a crowning event?[63]

If the history of international organization is any guide, we can infer that the leaders who will gather to establish the machinery of a world federal system will most probably be inspired by the model of the United Nations. They will draw upon the valuable lessons and knowledge gleaned from the world's accumulated experience in promoting co-operation through global organization. They might well choose to accomplish their goal through a revision of the existing UN Charter. Whatever form the world commonwealth ultimately takes, its creation will represent a new stage in an evolutionary process that began over 100 years ago, rather than a miraculous, new creation that is totally detached from the past and present of international organization.

People of all persuasions and outlooks can contribute to this process by educating their fellow citizens in the reality and implications of global interdependence. Such organizations as the World Federalists, the World Constitution and Parliament Association, Planetary Citizens and Parliamentarians for World Order are already carrying out important work in this area.

At the United Nations, the Bahá'í International Community United Nations Office is attempting to share these ideals with international officials and to help strengthen the UN. This office, which represents the worldwide membership of the Bahá'í community, has contributed the Bahá'í viewpoint to United Nations discussions on such issues as peace and disarmament, human rights, the promotion of the status of women and the enhancement of social and economic development.

There is also much work to be done by scholars in raising the consciousness of their colleagues and in formulating suggestions for the organization of a future unified world community. Leaders who will take the momentous step of establishing a world commonwealth will, after all, be in need of serious suggestions regarding the practical issues they will confront.[64]

In the Bahá'í view, international organization does have a future, and a glorious future at that. Whatever the immediate trials humankind may face, the significant advances represented by such organizations as the League of Nations and the United Nations will not be lost. Rather, they will lead to the creation of even more successful organizations. Most importantly, through the efforts of every human being, the ideals of world peace and unity which international organizations seek to promote can become a living reality.

NOTES

1. The *Yearbook of International Organizations*, 2nd ed., 1985/86, vol. 1 (New York: K. G. Saur, 1985) lists 6497 intergovernmental and non-governmental organizations which it classifies as 'conventional organizations' or 'organizations of special form.' Depending on the definition used for the term 'international organization,' the figure calculated can vary considerably (See *Yearbook*, p. 1586).
2. For statistics on the number of international non-governmental organizations, see ibid., p. 1586.
3. Scholarly but readable accounts of the history and contemporary functioning of international organizations can be found in Harold K. Jacobson, *Networks of Interdependence: International Organizations and the Global Political System*, 2nd ed. (New York: Alfred A. Knopf, 1984) and Inis L. Claude, Jr., *Swords Into Plowshares: The Problems and Progress of International Organizations*, 4th ed. (New York: Random House, 1971).
4. The Universal House of Justice, *The Promise of World Peace: A Statement by the Universal House of Justice* (London: Bahá'í Publishing Trust, 1985), p. 12.
5. 'Abdu'l-Bahá, *Selections from the Writings of 'Abdu'l-Bahá*, comp. Research Department of the Universal House of Justice, trans. Marzieh Gail and others, rev. ed. (Haifa: Bahá'í World Centre, 1982), pp. 31-2.
6. The Universal House of Justice, *The Promise of World Peace*, p. 2.
7. Ibid., pp. 3-4.
8. Ibid., p. 4.
9. Ibid., pp. 1-2.
10. Claude, *Swords*, p. 34.
11. See ibid.
12. Claude, *Swords*, p. 32. 'Abdu'l-Bahá referred to the list of arbitrators prepared by the first Hague Conference (known as the 'Permanent Court of Arbitration') in observing that a true world court 'would be more far-reaching than the Hague tribunal.' ('Abdu'l-Bahá, *The Promulgation of Universal Peace: Talks Delivered by 'Abdu'l-Bahá during His Visit to the United States and Canada in 1912*, comp. H. MacNutt, 2nd ed. (Wilmette, IL: Bahá'í Publishing Trust, 1982), p. 389).
13. On the League of Nations generally, see F.P. Walters, *A History of the League of Nations* (New York: Oxford University Press, 1960).
14. Shoghi Effendi, *The World Order of Bahá'u'lláh: Selected Letters*, 2nd rev. ed. (Wilmette, IL: Bahá'í Publishing Trust, 1974), p. 192.

15. Bahá'u'lláh addressed these letters to, among others, Napoleon III, Queen Victoria, Czar Alexander II and King William I of Prussia. See Bahá'u'lláh, *The Proclamation of Bahá'u'lláh to the Kings and Leaders of the World* (Haifa: Bahá'í World Centre, 1972). On acceptance of the principle of collective security, see Claude, *Swords*, pp. 261-4.
16. Shoghi Effendi, *The World Order of Bahá'u'lláh*, pp. 191-2.
17. Ibid., p. 193.
18. Ibid., p. 191.
19. For a general review of the United Nations and its activities, see *Basic Facts About the United Nations* (New York: United Nations, 1984) and Peter R. Baehr and Leon Gordenker, *The United Nations: Reality and Ideal* (New York: Praeger, 1984).
20. 'Abdu'l-Bahá, *The Promulgation of Universal Peace*, p. 377.
21. See Chapter XV of the UN Charter.
22. *Countries of the World and Their Leaders Yearbook 1986* (Detroit: Gale Research Company, 1989) lists 169 independent nations as of 26 July 1988 (p. 121). There are no standard criteria for determining whether or not a country is independent, since this is primarily a political question. As a result, figures for the number of independent countries may vary.
23. See *The United Nations and Human Rights* (New York: United Nations, 1984).
24. On this point, see Claude, *Swords*, pp. 206-11.
25. The Universal House of Justice, *The Promise of World Peace*, p. 24.
26. Ibid., p. 12.
27. See also footnote 33 below. Apart from a brief reference to collective security action, this essay does not attempt to grapple with the ramifications of the Gulf War and its aftermath. It is too early to make a dispassionate assessment of the effects of the conflict on the development of international organization, although it clearly has enormous implications for the future of the United Nations.
28. For a broad account of the Secretary-General's role in the maintenance of peace and security, see Leon Gordenker, *The United Nations Secretary-General and the Maintenance of Peace* (New York: Columbia University Press, 1967).
29. UN peacekeeping efforts are described in *The Blue Helmets: A Review of United Nations Peacekeeping* (New York: United Nations, 1985).
30. The Universal House of Justice, *The Promise of World Peace*, p. 12.
31. For example, the UN General Assembly has called upon the developed States to contribute 0.7 per cent of their annual Gross National Product to the developing countries. So far, this goal has been met by only a few Scandinavian countries.
32. The Universal House of Justice, *The Promise of World Peace*, p. 2.
33. Ibid., p. 18.
34. 'Proposals for Charter Revision Submitted to the United Nations by the Bahá'í International Community' (1955), in The Universal House of Justice *The Bahá'í World*, vol. XIII, 1954-1963 (Haifa: Bahá'í World Centre, 1970), pp. 795-802.
35. Articles 2(1) and 2(7) of the UN Charter. This, of course, is mitigated by the Universal Declaration of Human Rights and its two binding

covenants, and particularly by the Convention on the prevention of genocide.
36. The Universal House of Justice, *The Promise of World Peace*, p. 17.
37. Ibid., p. 17.
38. See the written statement submitted by the Bahá'í International Community to the United Nations Second World Conference to Combat Racism and Racial Discrimination, held in Geneva, 1-12 August 1983.
39. The Universal House of Justice, *The Promise of World Peace*, p. 5.
40. Quoted ibid., p. 5.
41. Shoghi Effendi, *The World Order of Bahá'u'lláh*, p. 46.
42. The Universal House of Justice, *The Promise of World Peace*, p. 1.
43. Shoghi Effendi, *The World Order of Bahá'u'lláh*, pp. 40-1.
44. Ibid., p. 202.
45. Ibid., p. 203.
46. Ibid., p. 41.
47. Ibid.
48. For an explanation of the role of the individual in the future commonwealth foreseen in the Bahá'í writings, see the 'Revised submission by the Bahá'í International Community to the questionnaire prepared by the Special Rapporteur, Mrs. Erica-Irene Daes, in connection with her study on the status of the individual and contemporary international law.' (1985)
49. See Shoghi Effendi, *The World Order of Bahá'u'lláh*, pp. 40-1.
50. The Universal House of Justice, 'Riḍván' message to the Bahá'ís of the world, 1991, in *Bahá'í Journal*, vol. 8, no. 2 (May 1991).
51. See 'Abdu'l-Bahá, *The Secret of Divine Civilization* trans. Marzieh Gail, 2nd ed. (Wilmette, IL: Bahá'í Publishing Trust, 1970), pp. 64-5.
52. Shoghi Effendi, *The World Order of Bahá'u'lláh*, p. 41.
53. Ibid., p. 203.
54. The Universal House of Justice, *The Promise of World Peace*, p. 15. Claude has pointed out that loyalty to the world community is a fundamental 'subjective' requirement for the effective functioning of collective security (Claude, *Swords*, p. 251).
55. Shoghi Effendi, *The World Order of Bahá'u'lláh*, p. 203.
56. 'Abdu'l-Bahá, *Selections*, p. 306.
57. Shoghi Effendi, *The World Order of Bahá'u'lláh*, p. 192.
58. The Universal House of Justice, *The Promise of World Peace*, p. 24.
59. Shoghi Effendi, *The World Order of Bahá'u'lláh*, pp. 203-4.
60. Ibid., p. 204.
61. The Universal House of Justice, *Wellspring of Guidance: Messages 1963-1968* (Wilmette, IL: Bahá'í Publishing Trust, 1970), p. 133.
62. Shoghi Effendi, *The World Order of Bahá'u'lláh*, p. 39.
63. The Universal House of Justice, *The Promise of World Peace*, pp. 21.
64. For an example of a thoughtful attempt to address, from a Bahá'í perspective, some of the practical issues involved in establishing a world federation, see J. Tyson, *World Peace and World Government: From Vision to Reality* (Oxford: George Ronald, 1986).

EMERGENCE: DIMENSIONS OF A NEW WORLD ORDER

HUMAN NATURE AND THE PROBLEM OF PEACE
Charles Lerche

THE Universal House of Justice, in *The Promise of World Peace*, stresses the importance of a 'fundamental' and 'paralysing' contradiction in human affairs:

> On the one hand, people of all nations proclaim not only their readiness but their longing for peace and harmony, for an end to the harrowing apprehensions tormenting their daily lives. On the other, uncritical assent is given to the proposition that human beings are incorrigibly selfish and aggressive and thus incapable of erecting a social system at once progressive and peaceful, dynamic and harmonious, a system giving free play to individual creativity and initiative but based on co-operation and reciprocity.[1]

The statement goes on to illustrate how this contradiction can be resolved, developing, in a unique way, themes which those familiar with the literature of the Bahá'í Faith will recognize.

Clearly, an individual's understanding of human nature and the purpose of human existence has a very strong, if not determining, influence on his or her general attitudes towards social life, and particularly on expectations about the possibility of universal and lasting peace. Thus, the existence of such a basic contradiction and its relationship to the problem of peace are of special interest. What follows is an attempt to explore this relationship in some depth.

The sweeping and fundamental changes necessary for world peace as envisaged in Bahá'í literature and as recently restated by the Universal House of Justice have often been described as 'utopian', meaning that they represent an unattainable state of perfection in social life. A careful reading of *The Promise of World Peace* suggests, however, that a pessimistic attitude toward the possibility of peace stems from a misunderstanding of human nature and history, and that, rather than being at odds with the true nature of the human person, social change toward peace in our age represents the truest expression of the human spirit. Thus, the pursuit of peace and unity, from this perspective, is not utopian but realistic, in that it accords completely with the needs of the age and, in itself may well provide the means through which the social, psychological, and spiritual qualities necessary for a New Age can be developed.

To more fully appreciate the Bahá'í position we must ask ourselves how the 'falsehood that human beings are incorrigibly selfish and aggressive'[2] came to play such a major role in our self-evaluation. How for instance, in the theory and practice of statecraft, with which this essay is particularly concerned, did it become the foundation for what is known as the theory of political 'realism', which has dominated thought on international affairs since World War II? We will explore this issue and illustrate how various thinkers — theologians, philosophers, political theorists, natural scientists — have contributed to the rise and persistence of this negative image of human nature. We will also try to provide some examples of why, as the Universal House of Justice argues, an alternative, positive image is an essential prerequisite for any peace proposal or plan to be truly successful.

Roots of the Negative Image

As suggested above, belief in the inherent aggressiveness and selfishness of humankind comes from many sources. Prominent among these are those writers who, in trying to explain the continuing occurrence of ever more destructive wars, have suggested that the basic nature of the individual human being is so constituted as to generate aggressive behaviour in pursuit of self-interest. The characteristic argument goes on to assert that it is vain to wish people to be otherwise than individually aggressive and that it is more profitable to attempt to formulate social arrangements whereby this quality can be controlled to some degree and diverted into harmless pursuits — but certainly not eliminated, or even substantially curbed.[3]

St Augustine in *The City of God* put forth an early version of this position which has had a major influence on Christian thought — and western thought in general — through the centuries. Augustine saw in humanity's fall from grace through original sin the explanation of our inability to both perceive and act according to the dictates of true reason. As one commentator has summed up Augustine's conception: 'Reason accurately interpreting the true interest of each would lead all people to live harmoniously in society with no need for a political authority to control and direct them.'[4]

Such an ideal society, though in fact an anarchy, would be peaceful, since, as Augustine wrote, 'with the good, good men, or at least perfectly good men, cannot war.'[5] This, however, is not the case because people do not understand their condition in terms of the need to work for collective progress and security but rather, their inherently flawed vision can only lead them to think in terms of self-preservation in an obviously competitive and hostile environment. Furthermore, Augustine felt that humankind was prone to the 'love of so many vain and hurtful things' which went beyond the basic requirements of life, and whose acquisition provided a rationale for the mayhem, such as quarrels, robberies, murder, and wars,[6] which characterizes the 'city of man.'

From the traditional Christian perspective, of course, so dramatic an improvement in human affairs as the elimination of warfare between nations is impossible until the return of Christ and the establishment of his Kingdom on earth, one of the signs of the coming of which is to be 'wars and rumours of wars.' According to Augustine only very little can be done to minimize these violent manifestations of human nature until the City of God comes to replace the city of man as promised in the scriptures. As one of the great books in western religion and philosophy, *The City of God* has been understood to give great support to the negative image, and subsequent writers have made use of it to this end.

In the philosopher Benedict de Spinoza we find an argument similar to Augustine's but without the same belief in human defects being determined by original sin.[7] Spinoza develops the concept of reason in more detail, by arguing first that the basic goal of every human act is self-preservation. A person of reason will try to ensure personal self-preservation by co-operative behaviour, because 'mutual assistance, the division of labour, is necessary to his own sustenance and preservation.'[8] The ideal for Spinoza is also a kind of anarchy:

> ... that all should so in all points agree, that the minds and bodies of all should form, as it were, one single mind and one single body, and that all should, with one consent, as far as they are able, endeavour to preserve their being, and all with one consent seek what is useful to them all.[9]

Here Spinoza puts forth an argument which reappears in many forms in western intellectual history: a collectivity of individuals freely pursuing their true interests will naturally be in harmony. This contributed to what was known as 'liberalism', and gave rise to such concepts as the 'invisible hand' which could adjust a market of freely competitive privately owned firms, and the 'balance of power' which was conceived of as working spontaneously to keep the States-system in equilibrium.[10]

Thus, Spinoza posited a standard whereby the rationality of human action can be judged, and clearly what one finds in the world does not meet this standard. He therefore concluded that people are defective because they allow themselves to be led by their passions rather than their reason, and passion leads them into various forms of conflict. Rather than contribute to a general condition of reciprocity and co-operation they seek the prurient pleasure of domination which, ironically, contributes less to their own self-preservation than would harmonious interaction. Spinoza acknowledged that the passions can to some extent be brought under the control of reason, but felt that this is so arduous that very few people will ever achieve it. Hence, humankind's defective nature is a given, and must be taken into account in all social considerations. For instance, he argues that States must always be on guard against each other because, though international relations may at times be characterized by good faith and co-operation which is in the true interests of States, this condition can always deteriorate under the mischievous influence of passion.[11]

An early, specifically political, thinker whose name has been linked with a cynical view of human nature is the Renaissance Italian Nicolo Machiavelli. Though it has been debated whether or not Machiavelli's thought was really 'machiavellian' in the way that term is usually employed, there is little doubt that the approach to government outlined in *The Prince* and *The Discourses* takes as given the pervasiveness of certain negative qualities in humankind. For example, he wrote, 'One can generally say this about men: they are ungrateful, fickle, simulators and deceivers, avoiders of danger, greedy for gain.'[12]

Also, he felt that these qualities in people necessitated a strong, in fact authoritarian, style of government to keep order in society. Otherwise people would engage in conflict for the least of motives:

Ancient writers were of the opinion that men are wont to get annoyed with adversity and fed up with prosperity, both which passions give rise to the same effects. For whenever there is no need for men to fight, they fight for ambition's sake, and they never relinquish it, not matter how far they have risen. The reason is that nature has so constituted men that, though all things are objects of desire, not all things are attainable, so that desire always exceeds the power of attainment.[13]

Finally, Machiavelli believed that he had described the perennial characteristics of human nature. He believed that it had not changed since classical times and it was not likely to change in the future. Thus, it was essential to reckon with it when considering the political system for a State.

Thomas Hobbes, the seventeenth century English political philosopher, put forth a similar view in his classic treatise on the foundations of the State, *Leviathan*. Hobbes's basic point was that, lacking a central power to keep men in order, a general war of all against all — the so-called 'state of nature' — would prevail, which is, in fact, but another way of expressing the belief that people are naturally aggressive. The following passage is illustrative:

Again, men have no pleasure, but on the contrary a great deal of grief, in keeping company when there is no power able to overawe them all. For every man looks that his companion should value him at the same rate he sets upon himself; and upon all signs of contempt or undervaluing naturally endeavours, as far as he dares (which among them that have no common power to keep them in quit is far enough to make them destroy each other), to extort a greater value from his contemners by damage and from others by the example.[14]

One noteworthy characteristic of the work of Machiavelli, and particularly Hobbes, is the lack of any argument, such as we found in Augustine and Spinoza to the effect that if only people could see clearly, that is, could follow right reason, they would seek co-operation rather than conflict. Machiavelli was simply too practical to concern himself with a course of action pursued by so few of the prince's subjects; while Hobbes, on the other hand, suggests that the expression of aggressiveness in a state of nature is not blameworthy but rather a correct pattern of action which is dictated by the conditions in which the individuals find themselves. It only acquires a moral stigma in the context of a hierarchically organized political system with a powerful ruler, because such behaviour disturbs the organic order of the State.

Augustine, Spinoza, Machiavelli and Hobbes, as sketched above, give us some idea of the historical antecedents of contemporary pessimism about the possibility of the members of the human race ever living together in peace. However, to more fully appreciate the depth of modern despair over this matter we have to review, at least superficially, the more immediate intellectual and historical events which have influenced thinking in our era. There has been tension for centuries in western intellectual circles between what, for lack of a better term, can be called 'pacifist' and 'bellicist'[15] theories of international life. The pacifists — who include among others Erasmus, More, Comenius, Cruce, Fenelon, Penn, Voltaire, Rousseau and Bentham — were very sceptical about the utility of the military to society, often contrasting the productivity of the merchant with the parasitic qualities of the professional soldier, and they regarded the abolition of force from international society as the ultimate goal of political life.[16] This school of thought also fostered the modern variety of pacifism as a refusal on moral grounds to participate at all in a societal war effort. Bellicism, whose intellectual forebears were, among others, Machiavelli, Hobbes and Bacon, developed in the nineteenth century partially in reaction to the influence of pacifism. The Bellicist position, as represented by such writers as Clauswitz, Hegel, Nietzsche, Treitschke and Bernhardi, accepted an unbridgeable gap between people's professions about their conduct and the form which that conduct actually took. Therefore, no matter how intensely one might deplore the fact of war, it is a fact and should be regarded as such. Some, like Hegel, in the course of eulogizing the State, saw war as a force which could contribute positively to national unity. Nietzsche of course was an extremist even in this camp, and went so far as to assert that the negation of all Christian virtues such as love and mercy was necessary to release human creativity and develop the 'superman'.[17]

In this regard the 'social Darwinist' thinkers deserve a special mention, since they promoted a philosophy directly antecedent to the fascist movements which in the 1930s and 1940s terrorized and demoralized humanity. Two prominent thinkers were General Friedrich von Bernhardi and Alfred Thayer Mayan, who both subscribed in one form or another to the view that Darwin's principle of the 'survival of the fittest' was applicable to the understanding of international relations. Nations were in competition and it was war that provided the means by which the weak, (therefore inferior) groups were 'selected out' of the human evolutionary process, and the strong, superior groups persisted and reproduced, thus strengthening and perfecting the human race. From this perspective war is something positive, though harsh, in that it contributes to human progress; and war is inevitable, since it is the manifestation of a law which applies to all of nature.

World War I and the trauma it induced was, in a sense, the logical outcome of bellicist thinking. Though the causes of the war are still under discussion it would probably be fair to say that one reason the war occurred was that none of the prominent European leaders was committed to, or saw the necessity for, a resolution of the contemporary crisis which stopped short of violent conflict.[18] War was very much a part of their repertoire of State behaviour, and something to which one might resort to redress even very minor slights to national prestige (an attitude promoted by the spokesman of the Prussian military caste, the historian Treitschke).[19] However, as the conflict developed it became obvious to the participants, and to the world in general that this war was different and that international society would never be the same after it was over. Thus, when the armistice was reached and the peace negotiations got under way there appeared what was known as 'new diplomacy', whose central advocate was the American president Woodrow Wilson.

The advocates of new diplomacy felt that the old European practice of *raison d'etat* in international relations, characterized by secret diplomacy and indifference to the claims of smaller States, was largely responsible for the devastation of the war and should be replaced by a new international order based on international law and organization and the principle of self-determination of nations. Thus, with the various treaties signed at the Paris Peace Conference (most prominent among them being the Treaty of Versailles), and the founding of the League of Nations, there dawned a new era in international thought. Scholars of international relations began to play the role of activists concerned with propagating the idea that strong international organization could resolve the problems of international conflict. In other words, the liberal, fundamentally optimistic view that humankind's aggressive nature, as expressed collectively through expansionist policies of States, could be either controlled or altered sufficiently to ensure a more peaceful future was generally upheld. It was further believed that once the new order was in place the integrating effects of free trade would demonstrate to all members of the international community that peaceful interaction was of more benefit than the costly and disruptive practice of war.[20]

The rise of fascism in the 1930s and the inability of the League of Nations to restrain the dictators in their aggression shattered this new found reformist attitude, and, particularly as the true face of German national socialism revealed itself, a new commitment to the negative image emerged in western thinking about human nature and world affairs.

> Cynicism and disappointment overtook the academic community, particularly in the United States during World War II. The reformist approach to the study of international relations was jettisoned. The prevailing academic judgment was that the faith of the reformers had been misplaced; individuals were neither perfect nor perfectible; reason and morality had no role to play in the study or practice of international relations: institutions could never be reformed nor war eliminated. Power — usually identified as military strength — was considered the only absolute in the affairs of nation-states, and power politics was thought to be neither immoral nor irrational, only inevitable.[21]

Thus, the school of political 'realism' was born, and the fact that such a position was termed 'realistic' is in itself instructive. The title indicates an overriding belief that what was revealed to the world by the conduct of the fascist nations represents what is somehow real (or most real) about human beings at least insofar as their relations as organized States is concerned. Such thought is highly critical of Wilson, who in his commitment to nineteenth century liberal reformism is said to have paid insufficient attention to the reality of power in human affairs.[22]

The work of Reinhold Niebuhr has been seminal in this intellectual development. Niebuhr was a theologian and not a political analyst or theorist as such, but he had a great deal to say on major trends in twentieth century world affairs. In the tradition of Augustine, Niebuhr believed that human beings are tainted by original sin, and therefore capable of evil. However, his thought is definitely modern, inasmuch as he argues that humanity's sinfulness is also a result of fundamental, existential anxiety. This anxiety arises from the contradiction between recognition of our finiteness and our aspiration to be unlimited — in effect, to usurp the place of God.[23] In the effort to fulfil this aspiration, people inevitably attempt to subordinate others, which is in itself unjust. To bolster this self-interested enterprise, economic and political theories are invented which claim to be universal, but which can never be so, due to the human limitations of their authors. When adopted by societies, such theories give rise to conflicts over power and prestige which are much more intense and tragic than conflict over mere self-preservation, as Niebuhr himself explained:

> They are conflicts in which each man or group seeks to guard its power and prestige against the peril of competing expressions of power and pride. Since the very possession of power and prestige always involves some encroachments upon the prestige and power of others, this conflict is by its very nature a more stubborn and difficult one than the mere competition between various survival impulses in nature.[24]

Thus the individual is evil and aggressive because he/she is proud, and this pride finds expression in a 'will to power'.

While he agrees with Spinoza that moral behaviour is difficult, Niebuhr at least concedes to the individual its possibility, although he considers it very unlikely in groups, since the individual in modern society projects his will to power onto the nation-State, and the collective expression of individual wills is what is generally understood as national power. Thus the tendency for nations to go to war finds its origins in 'dark, unconscious sources in the human psyche,'[25] and cannot easily be wished away through dreaming up schemes of ideal world order, or relying on enlightened self-interest to guide countries away from aggression. In passing we should also note that Niebuhr was highly critical of the notion of world government as a path to peace, since he argued, as many realists have done, that truly instructive political theory comes from political practice, and not, as the idealists would have had it, vice versa. Thus, world institutions could not create a global community. Rather, only if global cohesiveness were substantially stronger than it was at the time of his writing would a theory of world government acquire relevance. To deny the reality of political practice and advocate the practicability of world government is from his point of view to be truly guilty of utopian thinking, and this sort of utopianism is particularly dangerous because it tends to underestimate the evil of which the 'sons of darkness' are capable.[26]

Hans Morgenthau, who acknowledged being influenced by the work of Niebuhr was perhaps the single most influential writer on international relations since World War II, and his famous textbook on the subject, *Politics Among Nations*, is considered a classic and is still widely used. Though his statements relevant to our theme are found in many places (including *Politics Among Nations*) they are very succinctly and trenchantly put forth in his shorter work *Scientific Man Versus Power Politics* in which he argues that human affairs will inevitably be plagued with conflict because of two aspects of human nature. First is human selfishness, which derives from efforts to meet material needs. Morgenthau argues that even though social life would ideally demand complete unselfishness from the individual, fear of poverty alone is enough to make unalloyed selflessness very rare. He brings to light what he feels is a basic paradox in morality: complete unselfishness would lead to the destruction of the individual (through hunger if nothing else), so a certain amount of selfishness must be sanctioned in order to guarantee the practice of even moderate unselfishness.[27] He continues:

> Once the very logic of the ethics of unselfishness has thus put its stamp of approval on selfishness, individual egotisms, all equally legitimate, confront each other; and the war of every man against every man is on. . . . What the one wants for himself, the other already possesses or wants, too. Struggle and competition ensue . . . Man cannot hope to be good but must be content with being not too evil.[28]

The other root of conflict and the evil it brings in its wake is the lust for power, which Morgenthau calls (after Augustine) the *animus dominandi*, manifesting itself 'as the desire to maintain the range of one's person with regard to others, to increase it, or to demonstrate it.'[29] Though closely related to the issue of selfishness, the *animus dominandi* is significantly different from it, since most of the goals of selfishness derive from the demonstrable biological and social needs of the individual which are essential to his survival; whereas the desire for power is more concerned with status and cannot be satisfied, at least in principle, until all people and things have become objects of domination. Thus Morgenthau argues that the desire for power, in its extreme form the longing to be god-like, is akin to other great longings in the human spirit such as the mystic's quest to be one with the universe.[30] He goes further to argue that the *animus dominandi* plays a part in all social life for in all interaction there is at least some element of a desire to prevail over one's fellow creatures. He concludes this part of his argument by stating:

> It is this ubiquity of the desire for power which, besides and beyond any particular selfishness or other evilness of purpose, constitutes the ubiquity of evil in human action. Here is the element of corruption and of sin which injects even into the best of intentions at least a drop of evil and thus spoils it. On a grand scale, the transformation of churches into political organizations, of revolutions into dictatorships, of love of country into imperialism, are cases in point.[31]

Morgenthau also believed that the individual projects the will to power onto the State. The State, which in the name of public order, discourages the individual's expression of this drive for purely personal ends, does however, encourage him or her to support the power-seeking of the State in the name of patriotism and good citizenship. Furthermore while the individual is restrained by the higher authority of the State, the State is, in the context of modern international society which lacks any higher central authority, limited only by its own means in the expression of its *animus dominandi*. Also, the national drive for power can in reality (not just in imagination) have the whole world — or at least a substantial part of it — as its object, as the careers of various historical conquerors have demonstrated. Morgenthau's point is that in the transference of the will to power from the individual to the national level, the corruption, which he argues taints all human action, is greatly intensified. He consequently promoted the view that States acted in all situations to maximize their national interests narrowly defined as power, which is in sharp contrast to the prevalent view that power was merely a means to higher ends in statecraft. He called this outlook political realism since, to him, the essential aspect of political life, the factor which determined the significance of all others, was the largely irrepressible expression of the will to power.

So far in our treatment of the evolution of the negative image, or what world order theorist Richard Falk calls the 'pessimistic inevitability' school of thought about international affairs, we have limited our inquiry to the fairly closely related fields of religion, philosophy, and political science. However, in the twentieth century support for this position has come from sources generally regarded to be even more reliable and convincing since they are thought to represent the findings of natural science. Specifically we are referring to psychology and biology, and we will trace briefly some of the arguments made by Sigmund Freud and Konrad Lorenz, who, though by no means alone in their ideas, are representative and well known.

Freud believed, and wrote in a famous letter to Einstein, that people carry within them 'an active instinct for hatred and aggression.'[32] He saw the root of this drive in the death impulse, a concept which emerged in his later work. Freud's earlier work had suggested that aggression was a result of frustration of the individual's libidinal urges, but subsequently he evolved a dualistic image of the human psyche which had both a life instinct, *eros*, and a death instinct which he called *thanatos*. Freud argued that instincts caused people to act so as to reduce tension, and that death represented, in a sense, the ultimate release. However, the drive to live leads the individual to redirect the destructive impulse away from himself towards other objects, i.e., 'enemies'.

In this way aggressive action allows for the expression of the *thanatos* which could, in other circumstances lead to suicide. So, as one commentator has written, 'the recurrence of war and conflict becomes a necessary periodic release by which groups preserve themselves through diverting their self-destructive tendencies to outsiders.'[33]

This view seems to suggest that there is always an accumulation of negative energy in society which must either be diverted outward or used to the detriment of the individual or the society as a whole.[34] Whether or not Freud's analysis is correct, the very familiarity of the term 'death wish' is testimony to the influence which this aspect of his theory has had on the popular imagination. It seems to strongly imply that the most basic forces operative in our inner being are the sources of violent conflict, and that as long as these forces exist, some unspecified level of aggressive behaviour must be accepted as inherent in the human condition.

Konrad Lorenz's conceptualization of human aggression, though very different from Freud's, has also contributed significantly to the negative image. Lorenz viewed humanity as one biological species among many in the world, and his research on various lower species such as fish, dogs and birds, convinced him that rather than being the expression of a death wish, human aggression is an instinct like other instincts, and has been 'imprinted' on our genetic make-up in order to preserve the species.[35] Aggression expressed between members of the same species is, according to him, related to the necessity of ensuring that too many members of the species don't settle in one area, exhaust its resources, and cause a precipitous reduction in the numbers of the species which might even lead to its extinction. Animals stake out a territory, and try to prevent others, through threat or use of force, from encroaching on it. This concept was made popular some years ago by another writer, Robert Ardrey, as the so-called 'territorial imperative'. Lorenz felt that aggression was fundamentally a good thing and noted that particularly strong animals, or animals unusually well-equipped for killing, evolved aggression-inhibiting mechanisms to prevent the species from destroying itself. For instance, a defeated wolf bares its neck to its conqueror who will acknowledge its defeat without going on to kill the opponent. However, weaker animals who could not do so much damage had no need for such rituals, and did not evolve them; and herein lies the problem for humans. As a rather weak biological species in physical terms, we lack such aggression-inhibitors, but our more sophisticated brain has put us in a rather dangerous situation. Lorenz explained it in this way:

> In human evolution, no inhibitory mechanisms preventing sudden manslaughter were necessary, because quick killing was impossible anyhow; the potential victim had plenty of opportunity to elicit the pity of the aggressor by submissive gestures and appeasing attitudes. No selection pressure arose in the pre-history of mankind to breed inhibitory mechanisms preventing the killing of conspecifics until, all of a sudden, the invention of artificial weapons upset the equilibrium of killing potential and social inhibitions.[36]

Thus, Lorenz is saying that humankind is innately aggressive but that this is only natural, and should be taken into account in the political realm. He feels it is possible for humanity to evolve relatively quickly the needed inhibitors, and he feels it must be a social priority to do so, even though it took lower species countless centuries to develop theirs. Such a rapid step is possible through the medium of culture, which can ensure that important lessons for the species are passed on to the next generation.[37]

However, there are several fairly serious implications of Lorenz's analysis of aggression which should not be missed. He can be understood to be saying that since human aggressive action is the outcome of the operation of a 'natural' force, i.e., an instinct, people are in some sense not responsible for their aggressive behaviour. This premise has been seen by some critics (among them the psychologist Erich Fromm) as undermining morality, as suggesting that real peace is unlikely if not impossible, and as lending support to traditionally conservative political thought that accepts humanity's negative qualities as dominant, and seeks to limit the effects of anti-social inclinations — rather than actually try to improve human beings — primarily by trying to maintain the status quo rather than work towards an ideal of a better society.

What ideas, if any, do these various writers share in regard to our subject? First of all, whether the analysts have adopted a primarily religious or secular perspective, they all believe that aggressive behaviour is not learned, but comes directly from something innate. Thus it cannot be simply unlearned, or not learned, by a subsequent generation. This sets very definite limits on the forms that human civilization can safely take, i.e., it is not 'realistic' to hope that there ever could be a social order that would be based on a marked decrease in the level of domestic and international conflict. Furthermore they generally posit that what most would call evil in human character, i.e., selfishness and the drive to dominate, is the strongest aspect of our reality; and there is little hope that any higher nature, if such a thing exists, could ever become strong enough to control these qualities. With this summary in mind we can briefly consider a few critiques which have been made of the negative image.

The Negative Image Critiqued

The proposition that violence is a part of human nature and that this quality explains the prevalence of war in human history receives little support in more contemporary research and commentary. In fact, when one looks at the evidence to the contrary, one wonders why the negative image has had such influence on thinking in our age. Starting with the notion that violence is innate, social-psychologist Otto Klineberg pointed out, in a paper presented at a UNESCO symposium on violence, that contemporary social science generally doesn't take the proposition seriously since the human being requires both a biological capacity to act, and enough social experience to know the meaning and significance of violent action, which includes components of both formal and informal learning.[38] Furthermore, while it should probably be admitted that violence can be easily learned,

> it has never been demonstrated that it is easier to learn than, for example, co-operative, friendly and neighbourly behaviour. It is after all only a minority of people, even in situations of social upheaval, who engage in violent, anti-social behaviour. This was true in the case of student violence even at its height, as well as in the 'ghetto riots' in the United States. As for individual violence, no matter how high the homicide rates go, they never reach a majority of the population.[39]

Further along this line, the well-known study *Violence in America*, commissioned to investigate the causes for the problems of the American inner cities to which Klineberg referred, came to the conclusion that, 'nature provides us only with the capacity for violence: it is social circumstance that determines whether and how we exercise that capacity.'[40]

Henri Laborit, making use of recent findings in cerebral chemistry, argues that current knowledge in that field indicates that humanity's innate behaviour is very limited and not particularly violent,[41] and even what is called 'innate' can be modified over the long term through certain forms of learning. He also rejects the concept of 'territorial' behaviour as a set of acquired characteristics which cannot be found in some societies, and suggests that the same learning processes which transmit violent behaviour could also be used to create and reinforce patterns of non-violent action in society.[42]

Also, as we have seen, the human tendency to be aggressive is supposed to be the root cause of violent conflict between countries. Thus, nation-States as collectives of individuals should be inherently aggressive, but this premise also finds very little confirmation. For instance, Lewis F. Richardson, regarded as one of the leading analysts of international conflict behaviour, concluded that the participation of nation-States in wars has been so varied that 'none can be properly characterized as inherently belligerent or inherently pacific.'[43] Another quantitative study of 652 different societies found that only 33 per cent of them could be said to be belligerent in the sense that 'they were found to have engaged in aggressive warfare for economic and political exploitation.'[44] Furthermore, this same study found a positive correlation between a society's level of modernization and its level of belligerence, which would seem to run counter to the notion that aggression is somehow primal and should find freer expression in less differentiated social contexts. The final, and perhaps most compelling criticism at this level is that the link between individual human aggression and war organized and carried out by the nation-State has never been conclusively demonstrated.[45] Its assertion is not its proof. If, for example, humans are naturally aggressive, why is it necessary to provide such extremes of compulsion and indoctrination to obtain large enough numbers to become soldiers in time of national need?

These criticisms of the negative image of human nature are of great significance with respect to the contradiction in human affairs referred to by the Universal House of Justice. No single dark period of human history, such as the fascist era in Europe — as horrifying as it proved to be — can be considered sufficient proof of the basic tenets of political realism as described above. It is certainly true that people in organized society are capable of extremes of violence, as well as other evils; but, as the Universal House of Justice points out, it does not follow that this behaviour should be taken to represent the true nature of either the individual person or of human collective life; neither can this be a justification for rejecting the possibility of world peace and the eventual emergence of a more closely knit global community. There is, in fact, as we have tried to show, good reason to believe otherwise.

Another Image

The literature of the Bahá'í Faith presents an alternative conceptual framework in which to understand human selfishness and aggression. A survey of the writings of the Báb, Bahá'u'lláh and 'Abdu'l-Bahá — the central figures of the Bahá'í Faith — the interpretations and guidance of Shoghi Effendi, and the letters of the Universal House of Justice provides an extensive range of relevant passages. For our present purposes we will confine our selection to a few of the basic themes referred to above, to demonstrate that there exists at least one positive alternative which can contribute to the resolution of the contradiction under consideration.

The Bahá'í writings depict the human being as having an inner nature which is neither inherently good nor evil, but which has the potential for development in either direction. In this regard 'Abdu'l-Bahá has explained:

> In man there are two natures; his spiritual or higher nature and his material or lower nature. In one he approaches God, in the other he lives for the world alone. Signs of both these natures are to be found in man. In his material aspect he expresses untruth, cruelty and injustice; all these are the outcome of his lower nature. The attributes of his Divine nature are shown forth in love, mercy, kindness, truth and justice, one and all being expressions of his higher nature. Every good habit, every noble quality belongs to man's spiritual nature, whereas all his imperfections and sinful actions are born of his material nature. If a man's Divine nature dominates his human nature, we have a saint.[46]

To Bahá'ís the purpose of individual human existence is, through the exercise of volition, to learn to control physical drives and desires and to come to exemplify spiritual qualities and virtues. In his brief, epigrammatic volume *The Hidden Words*, Bahá'u'lláh calls humanity to this effort in verses such as these:

> O Son of Man!
> Upon the tree of effulgent glory I have hung for thee the choicest fruits, wherefore hast thou turned away and contented thyself with that which is less good? Return then unto that which is better for thee in the realm on high.[47]
>
> O Son of Spirit!
> Noble have I created thee, yet thou has abased thyself. Rise then unto that for which thou wast created.[48]

The Baháʼí teachings argue that religion in its true form has provided the means through which individuals, and whole societies, have experienced this sort of transformation. ʻAbduʼl-Bahá repeatedly made a distinction between material and spiritual civilization, the latter being the goal and purpose of revealed religion:

> Baháʼuʼlláh teaches that material civilization is incomplete, insufficient and that divine civilization must be established. Material civilization concerns the world of matter or bodies, but divine civilization is the realm of ethics and moralities. Until the moral degree of the nation is advanced and human virtues attain a lofty level, happiness for mankind is impossible. The philosophers have founded material civilization. The Prophets have founded divine civilization.[49]

In another passage he uses the rise of the nation of Israel as described in the Old Testament as an example of the transforming power of true religious teaching:

> When a movement fundamentally religious makes a weak nation strong, changes a nondescript tribal people into a mighty and powerful civilization, rescues them from captivity and elevates them to sovereignty, transforms their ignorance into knowledge and endows them with an impetus of advancement in all degrees of development (this is no theory, but historical fact), it becomes evident that religion is the cause of manʼs attachment to honor and sublimity.[50]

Furthermore, through the virtually universal teaching that the earthly life is but one stage of our existence, and that true happiness and fulfilment now, and in those further stages, depends on developing a sense of detachment from the constantly changing milieu of material circumstances in which one finds oneself, religious instruction serves to help regulate human acquisitiveness and the aggression to which it has often given rise. On this theme of detachment Baháʼuʼlláh has written:

> O Son of Man!
> Should prosperity befall thee, rejoice not, and should abasement come upon thee, grieve not, for both shall pass away and be no more.[51]
>
> O Son of Man!
> Thou dost wish for gold and I desire thy freedom from it. Thou thinkest thyself rich in its possession, and I recognize thy wealth in thy

sanctity therefrom. By My life! This is My knowledge, and that is thy fancy; how can My way accord with thine?[52]

These passages suggest, among other things, that human acquisitiveness is based on a wrong set of values, on a conception of wealth which, in light of the instability of material possessions, proves to be an illusion. In another passage, 'Abdu'l-Bahá explains that it is just such an understanding which enables a truly religious person to overcome his or her natural acquisitiveness:

> ... it is impossible for a human being to turn aside from his own selfish advantages and sacrifice his own good for the good of the community except through true religious faith. For self-love is kneaded into the very clay of man, and it is not possible that, without any hope of a substantial reward, he should neglect his own present material good. The individual, however, who puts his faith in God and believes in the words of God — because he is promised and certain of a plentiful reward in the next life, and because worldly benefits compared to the abiding joy and glory of future planes of existence are nothing to him — will for the sake of God abandon his own peace and profit and will consecrate his heart and soul to the common good.[53]

Religious martyrdom is a most dramatic instance of how commitment to spiritual ideals can inspire behaviour quite contrary to the negative image. Bahá'í martyrs in Iran, who chose to die rather than recant their faith, have certainly been an inspirational example to their fellow Bahá'ís around the world since the birth of the Bahá'í Faith in the mid-nineteenth century. Not all people are potentially martyrs, but the same dynamic of inner change can find expression in other ways such as the desire to help those less fortunate than oneself through charitable activity, or to give one's time in non-remunerative work in service to the community. Furthermore, when spiritual inspiration has been lacking in a particular society for some time those dark qualities which lend credence to the negative image have reasserted themselves with a distressing but instructive regularity. In this regard Shoghi Effendi wrote:

> No wonder, therefore, that when, as a result of human perversity, the light of religion is quenched in men's hearts, and the divinely appointed Robe, designed to adorn the human temple, is deliberately discarded, a deplorable decline in the fortunes of humanity immediately sets in, bringing in its wake all the evils which a wayward soul is

capable of revealing. The perversion of human nature, the degradation of human conduct, the corruption and dissolution of human institutions, reveal themselves, under such circumstances, in their worst and most revolting aspects.[54]

When a society reaches this stage of decadence, Shoghi Effendi states, it must be reborn or perish.

Such a cyclical pattern in social life, moving from spiritual-mindedness to materialism and back again, has been demonstrated in the macro-sociological work of P. A. Sorokin.[55] The Universal House of Justice has further stated: 'Most particularly, it is in the glorification of material pursuits . . . that we find the roots which nourish the falsehood that human beings are incorrigibly selfish and aggressive.'[56]

Thus it is precisely during the more materialistic historical eras, such as our own, that the negative image acquires particular influence, but this development is understood by Bahá'ís as a loss of vision and perspective rather than as an insight.

From the foregoing it should be clear that religion as a vehicle of social change and development is distinguished from secular ideologies because it postulates and caters for that in the human spirit which reaches 'towards transcendence . . . towards an invisible realm, towards the ultimate reality . . .';[57] and though we live in what is generally thought of as a secular age, most people in the world do have some sort of religious or spiritual conviction, however vague and unformalized, or in some sense share in the great desire to transcend the merely material and transient in life. It is also evident that both the religious attitude in humankind and the institutions we build to give it expression are subject to decay and distortion. However, this in itself cannot justify ignoring or discounting the centrality of humanity's spiritual life to its history. The works of such great scholars as Toynbee, Sorokin, and deChardin in fact make the case that to a large extent the story of humanity is the story of religion.

The real potency of any alternative positive image of human nature which includes the possibility of world peace, however, can only be demonstrated by the behaviour of those who uphold it: can they, individually and collectively, control their acquisitiveness and aggression, and exemplify peacefulness in all its manifold aspects? Only a dynamic example of this kind can erode people's belief in the negative image, which persists, we would suggest, because nothing more compelling has yet appeared to replace it in the prevalent world-view. It is perhaps for this reason that the Universal House of Justice has offered the Bahá'í community as just such a 'model for study.'[58]

Peace Proposals

As stated at the beginning of this essay, the Universal House of Justice has described the conjunction of the virtually universal recognition of the necessity for world peace, and the general belief in the negative image as a 'paralysing contradiction' in human affairs which hinders the progress towards such a peace. In this last section we will examine this situation more closely: specifically how does the negative image inhibit peace efforts, and how would a more positive concept of human nature, similar to that described above, contribute to their success? As in many areas of human endeavour, preconceptions and prejudices can often take on the character of self-fulfilling prophecies.

Though manifold in their variations, there are really only a few basic approaches to world peace. The one most often put forward in our century is probably that of some form of world government, and the argument in its favour characteristically blames the prevalence of war on a States-system which upholds the principle of the unlimited sovereignty of each member nation. This, in effect, makes for anarchy in international relations since there is no central overriding authority in the system to keep the members in order. One solution to this problem is to create a set of world institutions, preferably on a federal model,[59] to provide the necessary law and order at the global level. The argument has the force of simplicity, and also in its favour is the fact that to date the federal model has proven itself to be an effective system of administration in States of great internal diversity such as the United States, Germany, Canada, India and Nigeria, among others.

However, today the concept of world government, or more specifically, world federalism, is much less popular than in the immediate post-World War II period. Why should this be? One analyst of world federalism as a movement has argued that the movement was 'chilled' by such developments in world affairs as the Cold War, the nuclear arms race, and the war in Vietnam, all of which demonstrated the weakness of the United Nations organization, the base from which, according to the Federalist plan, a new world government should develop.[60] Thus, once again the world witnessed a divergence between the ideals which States had committed themselves to uphold in their interactions, and the ways in which they actually behaved. This gap between theory and practice is, as we have discussed, precisely what gives rise to cynicism, despair, and 'realist' thinking. Paradoxically, such international problems as those listed above both highlight the need for more control at the global level and, by demonstrating the force of the national drive to dominance and hegemony (whether motivated by ideology, economic gain, or national prestige), serve to reinforce people's worst suspicions about human nature.

Furthermore, if one believes in the *animus dominandi*, world government doesn't necessarily represent a comforting prospect. Realist writers have a tendency to argue that in light of the perpetual pursuit of selfish interest defined simply as power, a world government could easily deteriorate into a world tyranny. It becomes increasingly urgent to answer such arguments when from all quarters evidence is mounting that humanity is facing an ever increasing agenda of problems which cannot effectively be dealt with by national governments acting in isolation,[61] or even within the existing frameworks of international organization, or international regimes.[62] The argument that we are better off tinkering with the status quo would be merely shortsighted if the status quo were in fact stable, but there are numerous signs that the international order is deteriorating with rather alarming speed, as Richard Falk has observed:

> No amount of tinkering can fix up the present international system. Too many fundamental pressures exist: continuing demographic pressures (increasing population and even more rapidly increasing urbanization), increasing destructiveness and instability of the weapons environment, waste of economic resources to fuel the arms race and to sustain affluent life-styles, sterility of an economistic vision that identifies progress with material growth and societal fulfilment with entry into the middle classes, moral backwardness of an overall economic and political system that imposes 'order' rather than orients investment and production around the satisfaction of basic needs, and short-sightedness of growth patterns that are not ecologically sustainable. These interrelated pressures are cumulative, and their eventual impact could inflict irreversible damage, foreclosing future options.

The logic that controls the state system is no longer tolerable. It is too dangerous, wasteful, and stultifying. It inhibits the sort of economic, political, and cultural development that fulfils individual and collective potentialities at various stages of industrialization.[63]

Increasingly harsh conditions and increasingly limited resources tend to aggravate the already existing tendencies to aggression in international relations, even further reinforcing belief in the negative image and making a new step forward in international co-operation that much more difficult. Thus, the need for a new image is critical.

In recent years there has been a resurgence of the belief that disarmament is, in itself, a path to peace. Though generally discredited after the collapse of the inter-war effort to improve international relations through international law-making, in the wake of the contemporary arms race between the superpowers, significant elements in the populations of western Europe and north America were mobilized in a peace movement whose central goal was the reduction and ultimate elimination of the stockpiles of weapons (principally nuclear) in both East and West. Despite the current signs that such concerns have been acknowledged by the superpower leadership, grave fundamental problems remain. Both sides in the East-West conflict have, until recently, clung to their own variations of the negative image, and articulated official views of each other which portrayed a belief in the implacable aggressiveness of the 'enemy'. Even now, in an era of supposed co-operation, any slight deviation from the rather narrow path of peaceful co-existence which the superpowers have mapped out for themselves revives the bombastic rhetoric of both sides. Marxist philosophy, of course, views all history as the history of class struggle, though the roots of conflict are not so much in the individual as in the inevitable social clash over the control of the means of production during a particular period of history.[64] The contemporary form of this conflict, according to the kind of thinking which, although currently eclipsed, was for decades the orthodox line in Soviet policy-making, shifted after the Russian revolution from rivalry among the major European imperialist powers to a confrontation between the forces of socialism and the forces of capitalism, the latter being led in the post-World War II period by the United States.[65] For their own part, the western camp put forth what is basically a neo-Kantian argument that 'closed' societies (i.e., those which do not consider popular opinion in the formulation of public policy, including foreign policy), are likely to be more aggressive in international relations, because decision-making elites are free to do as they like. The converse of this is that democracies, in the western sense, are more peace-loving precisely because the people generally want peace and when their views are heard they will be able to influence their government's policy in this direction.

The fact that the historical truth of neither of these arguments can be demonstrated conclusively — i.e., that class struggle has determined the course of history, or that western democratic States have been more peace-loving — does not seem to have had much effect on their hardline proponents, although the recent revolutions in Eastern Europe and internecine strife among the republics of the Soviet Union has clearly revealed the instability of the structure reared upon marxist analysis of human nature and society.

Of course, it is necessary for the government of a nation-State to take every precaution to preserve the security of that State, and no real threat should be underestimated; but it has also been demonstrated through analysis of the decision-making styles of certain key leaders that their own images of human nature — and of their opponents — have so influenced their evaluation of each others' actions as to rule out, on occasion, even the slightest chance that the other side might be taking genuinely constructive or conciliatory action.[66] Again, the vicious cycle is complete: one is not prepared to perceive a peace-oriented gesture by one's rival as being sincere, so rivals are left only with more coercive means to try and achieve their ends, and these, in turn strengthen one's belief in the other side's baleful intentions. This is a common enough behaviour pattern in human affairs, which has been extensively researched by social-psychologists.[67] It also helps to explain why some elements in the West have taken so long to accept the contemporary changes in Eastern Europe and the Soviet Union at face value.

A prevalence of negative 'mirror images' also makes disarmament very difficult. The process of disarmament, as it advances, will offer all who are involved at least some opportunities to 'cheat' if they should be so inclined. The opportunities will be greater in the early stages, and will become less as the overall number of weapons is reduced and the inspection network is fully operational and gains experience. There must be a certain minimum level of good faith among the parties involved to get the process through the initial period of uncertainty, and this is precisely what is lacking in a world committed to a general belief in innate human aggressiveness.

In this regard the Universal House of Justice has forcefully called on ideologues of both the East and West to give account of their actions, and, if they find themselves wanting, to admit the need for a new vision and a new beginning. The western world has looked with approval on the leaders of Eastern Europe and the Soviet Union being called to account by their own people over the past few years, but consideration of the global community shows that this is not a matter which affects only those on one side of the political fence. Neither capitalist nor socialist ideologies have delivered the new society which both have long promised.

> The intolerable conditions pervading society bespeak a common failure of all, a circumstance which tends to incite rather than relieve the entrenchment on every side. Clearly, a common remedial effort is urgently required. It is primarily a matter of attitude. Will humanity continue in its waywardness, holding to outworn concepts and unworkable assumptions? Or will its leaders, regardless of ideology, step forth and, with a resolute will, consult together in a united search for appropriate solutions.[68]

The Universal House of Justice goes on to articulate more fully the Bahá'í proposal for peace which calls for a universal gathering to fix the constituent elements of a more highly integrated new world order that should include on its agenda the realization of such vital social goals as the equality of men and women, universal education, elimination of all forms of prejudice, eradication of the extremes of wealth and poverty, and the adoption of a universal auxiliary language, among others. As the foregoing discussion has demonstrated, real progress in any of these avenues would require commitment to the belief that human society *can* be made more just, more enlightened, more progressive and secure. Otherwise the agenda put forth as a challenge to the world's leaders, and to humanity in general, seems overwhelming. With regard to the starting point for this agenda, the Bahá'í outlook includes the belief that, as Bahá'u'lláh wrote, we have been created noble, that we have abased ourselves not least of all by grossly underestimating human potential, and that all have a role to play in carrying forward an ever advancing civilization in this critical epoch.

Conclusion

In the foregoing, we have demonstrated the roots of the negative image of human nature as it has evolved through the writings of some of the greatest thinkers of many ages. This image was, in most cases, largely justified by the data to which they had access. People did show themselves to be violent and selfish with such regularity as to indicate that these qualities were basic aspects of their nature. Examining such ideas helps one to understand better the reasons why the negative image is so potent. But Bahá'ís consider that this image is inhibiting the successful completion of what they believe is the next step of human social development — the establishment of the normative framework and technical infrastructure for world unity. Bahá'ís consider that the negative image is, as the Universal House of Justice has argued, incompatible with most imaginable paths to this ever more critically needed social condition, and that a positive image such as that found in the Bahá'í writings is necessary for its achievement.

Having made this argument, Bahá'ís do not underestimate the difficulties that stand in the way of accepting a positive image of human nature and the vision of a new world order that can give it form. Rather, they consider that the trauma of our age is bringing into being an audience increasingly receptive to this very idea. This, they believe, will bring ever closer the crowning goal of 'the unification of all the peoples of the world in one universal family.'[69]

NOTES

1. The Universal House of Justice, *The Promise of World Peace: A Statement by the Universal House of Justice* (London: Bahá'í Publishing Trust, 1985), p. 3.
2. Ibid.
3. This section makes use of Kenneth W. Waltz's classic essay *Man, the State, and War* (New York: Columbia University Press, 1959). Chapters one and two are of particular relevance.

4. Ibid., p. 23.
5. St. Augustine, *The City of God* (New York: Hafner Publishing Co., 1948), translated by Marcus Dods (2 vols.) Book XV, ch. V. (cited in Waltz).
6. Waltz, *Man, the State and War*, p. 23.
7. Spinoza more or less equated God with nature, and from this there followed a rather unorthodox theology.
8. Cited in Waltz, p. 23.
9. Benedict de Spinoza, *Ethics*, Part IV, Prop. XVIII, note, in: *The Chief Works of Benedict de Spinoza*, translated by R. H. M. Elwes, 2 vols. (New York: Dover Publications, 1951), cited in Waltz.
10. See: M. Howard, *War and the Liberal Conscience* (New Brunswick, N.J.: Rutgers University Press, 1978).
11. Waltz, *Man, the State and War*, p. 25.
12. Nicolo Machiavelli, *The Portable Machiavelli*, edited and translated by Peter Bondanella and Mark Musa (New York: Viking Press, 1979), p. 25. I am grateful to James A. Donnelson for bringing this and the next passage to my attention.
13. Nicolo Machiavelli, *The Discourses of Machiavelli* translated from the Italian with an Introduction and Notes by Leslie J. Walker (London and Boston: Routledge and Kegan Paul, 1975), p. 295.
14. Thomas Hobbes, *Leviathan* (New York: Liberal Arts Press, 1958), p. 106.
15. J. E. Dougherty, and R. L. Pfaltzgraff Jr., *Contending Theories of International Relations*, 2nd ed. (New York: Harper & Row, 1981), chapter 5.
16. Ibid.
17. Ibid.
18. See: John G. Stoessinger, *Why Nations Go to War*, 3rd ed. (New York: St. Martin's Press, 1982), chapter one.
19. Dougherty and Pfaltzgraff, op. cit.
20. This attitude is described in detail and sharply critiqued in E. H. Carr, *The Twenty Years' Crisis: 1919-1939* (New York: Harper & Row, 1964).
21. Charles O. Lerche Jr., and Abdul A. Said, *Concepts of International Politics* (Englewood Cliffs, N.J.: Prentice-Hall, 1979), p. 4.
22. This was hardly a fair criticism as shown by Inis Claude in chapter three of his award-winning study: *Power and International Relations* (New York: Random House, 1962).
23. Dougherty and Pfaltzgraff, p. 94.
24. H. K. Davis and R. D. Good, ed.'s, *Reinhold Niebuhr on Politics* (New York: Charles Scribner's Sons, 1960), p. 77.
25. Reinhold Niebuhr, *Beyond Tragedy* (New York: Charles Scribner's Sons, 1938), p. 158 (cited in Waltz).
26. See on this theme Niebuhr's *The Children of Light and the Children of Darkness* (New York: Charles Scribner's Sons, 1944).
27. Hans J. Morgenthau, *Scientific Man Versus Power Politics* (Chicago: Phoenix Books, 1967), p. 191.
28. Ibid, p. 192.
29. Ibid.

30. Ibid, p. 194.
31. Ibid, pp. 194-5.
32. 'Why War?', from a letter written by Freud and sent to Einstein in 1932. The text can be found in Robert A. Goldwin et. al. (ed.'s) *Readings in World Politics* (New York: Oxford University Press, 1959). Freud goes on to say: 'The upshot of these observations . . . is that there is no likelihood of our being able to suppress humanity's aggressive tendencies.' (cited in Dougherty and Pfaltzgraff).
33. Dougherty and Pfaltzgraff, p. 258.
34. Ibid.
35. Ibid., p. 251.
36. Konrad Lorenz, *On Aggression*, translated by Marjorie Kerr Wilson (New York: Bantam, 1967), p. 233.
37. Dougherty and Pfaltzgraff, p. 264.
38. Otto Klineberg, 'The Causes of Violence: A Social-Psychological Approach' in *Violence and its Causes* (Paris: U.N.E.S.C.O., 1981), p. 113.
39. Ibid.
40. T. R. Gurr, *Violence in America. Report to the National Commission on the Causes and Prevention of Violence* (New York: Signet Books, 1969), p. 177 (cited in Klineberg).
41. Henri Laborit, 'The Biological and Sociological Mechanisms of Aggressiveness: in *Violence and its Causes*.
42. Ibid.
43. Lewis F. Richardson, *Statistics of Deadly Quarrels* (Pittsburgh: The Boxwood Press, 1960), p. 176.
44. T. Brock and J. Galtung, 'Belligerence Among the Primitives: A Re-Analysis of Quincy Wright's Data' *Journal of Peace Research*, vol. 3 (1966), pp. 33-45.
45. R. Falk, S. S. Kim, and S. H. Mendlovitz, *Toward a Just World Order* (Boulder, Colorado: Westview Press, 1982), p. 220.
46. 'Abdu'l-Bahá, *Paris Talks: Addresses Given by 'Abdu'l-Bahá in Paris in 1911-1912* 11th ed. (London: Bahá'í Publishing Trust, 1971), p. 60.
47. Bahá'u'lláh, *The Hidden Words of Bahá'u'lláh* trans. Shoghi Effendi with the assistance of some English friends, rev. ed. (Wilmette, IL: Bahá'í Publishing Trust, 1970), p. 9.
48. Ibid.
49. 'Abdu'l-Bahá, *The Promulgation of Universal Peace: Talks Delivered by 'Abdu'l-Bahá during His Visit to the United States and Canada in 1912* comp. H. MacNutt, 2nd ed. (Wilmette, IL: Bahá'í Publishing Trust, 1982), p. 375.
50. Ibid, p. 363.
51. Bahá'u'lláh, *The Hidden Words*, p. 16.
52. Ibid, pp. 16-17.
53. 'Abdu'l-Bahá, *The Secret of Divine Civilization* trans. Marzieh Gail, 2nd ed. (Wilmette, IL: Bahá'í Publishing Trust, 1970), pp. 96-7.
54. Shoghi Effendi, *The World Order of Bahá'u'lláh: Selected Letters*, 2nd rev. ed. (Wilmette, IL: Bahá'í Publishing Trust, 1974), pp. 187-8.
55. The theory is fully expounded and documented in Sorokin's landmark work in four volumes: *Social and Cultural Dynamics* (New York: American Books, 1937).

56. The Universal House of Justice, *The Promise of World Peace*, p. 8.
57. Ibid., p. 5.
58. Ibid., p. 24.
59. This is also the Bahá'í proposal.
60. George A. Codding, Jr. 'Federalism: The Conceptual Setting' in P. Taylor, and A. J. R. Groom ed.'s, *International Organization: A Conceptual Approach* (London: Francis Pinter, 1978), p. 340.
61. See, C. O. Lerche, 'The Global Agenda' in Lee, ed., *Circle of Peace: Reflections on the Bahá'í Teachings* (Los Angeles: Kalimát Press, 1986).
62. For more on international regimes see: R. O. Keohane, and J. S. Nye, *Power and Interdependence* (Boston: Little, Brown, and Co., 1977).
63. Richard Falk, 'Satisfying Human Needs in a World of Sovereign States: Rhetoric, Reality, and Vision' in Falk, ed., *The End of World Order: Essays on Normative International Relations* (New York: Holmes & Meier, 1983).
64. The marxist perspective was not discussed in the first section precisely because it argues that is society, rather than the individual, that is inherently conflictual and, therefore, often violent.
65. 'The Economic Foundations of Wars: A Soviet View', in *Marxism-Leninism on War and Army (A Soviet View)* (Moscow: Progress Publishers, 1972).
66. See O. R. Holsti, 'The Belief System and National Images: A Case Study' *The Journal of Conflict Resolution*, VI (1962), 244-52.
67. See H. C. Kelman, ed., *International Behavior: A Social Psychological Analysis* (New York: Holt, Rinehart, and Winston, 1965).
68. The Universal House of Justice, *The Promise of World Peace*, p. 8.
69. Ibid., p. 23.

EMERGENCE: DIMENSIONS OF A NEW WORLD ORDER

A UNIVERSAL POLITICAL THESIS

Peter A. Mühlschlegel

THE United Nations designated 1986 'International Year of Peace'. Much was said and written about peace in that year, and Bahá'ís contributed to it with their usual optimism. But was the dedication of a special 'year', and an outpouring of well-intentioned statements sufficient to advance the cause of world peace? The years since 1986 have been as conflict-filled as any other period in modern times, and recent events have shown that war is certainly not out of fashion.

What can be done to more actively promote universal peace within the development of Bahá'u'lláh's world order? Can Bahá'ís establish a middle way between the gentle and gradual path of personal teaching by word and by example, and revolutionary agitation, which Bahá'u'lláh strictly forbids? Is there a third path, which, running counter to current political philosophy, would define the ethical parameters with which to judge the contemporary scene?

I would venture to express the universal political thesis of the world-wide Bahá'í community as follows:

> Any foreign policy which serves goals other than the immediate transformation of the United Nations into a fully functioning world federation, bears within it the seeds of future world wars and is equivalent to a crime against humanity.

This thesis is at once a harsh judgement and a vital discriminating statement, derived from the two-fold process of creation and destruction delineated by Shoghi Effendi in 1936.

> The former, as it steadily evolves, unfolds a System which may well serve as a pattern for that world polity towards which a strangely-disordered world is continually advancing; while the latter, as its disintegrating influence deepens, tends to tear down, with increasing violence, the antiquated barriers that seek to block humanity's

---

This essay is translated from the German by Hugh Featherstone Blyth.

progress towards its destined goal. The constructive process stands associated with the nascent Faith of Bahá'u'lláh, and is the harbinger of the New World Order that Faith must erelong establish. The destructive forces that characterize the other should be identified with a civilization that has refused to answer to the expectation of a new age, and is consequently falling into chaos and decline.[1]

Shoghi Effendi describes the events of our time as a titanic spiritual struggle. We have certainly learned much in the years since this statement was made, more than half a century ago, particularly in the art of human co-existence. Only in the field of co-existence among nation-States has the situation remained largely unchanged. The obsolete philosophy of alliances, the rusty strategy of deterrence, the same old armaments madness: all these still prevail, and far too many people profit from their continuation. Those who feel the need to cling to their political mandate, power or honour demonstrate the least positive will to mitigate the chaotic anarchy of more than 160 sovereign nations through the development of an all-encompassing world order.

The Sovereign Will of God

This, however, is precisely what Bahá'u'lláh, whom Bahá'ís regard as the Manifestation of God and the Lord of the Age, proclaimed as the will of God more than 125 years ago in his pronouncements to the generality of the human race and its rulers.

> The Great Being, wishing to reveal the prerequisites of the peace and tranquillity of the world and the advancement of its peoples, hath written: The time must come when the imperative necessity for the holding of a vast, an all-embracing assemblage of men will be universally realized. The rulers and kings of the earth must needs attend it, and, participating in its deliberations, must consider such ways and means as will lay the foundations of the world's Great Peace amongst men. Such a peace demandeth that the Great Powers should resolve, for the sake of the tranquillity of the peoples of the earth, to be fully reconciled among themselves. Should any king take up arms against another, all should unitedly arise and prevent him. . . . That one indeed is a man who, today, dedicateth himself to the service of the entire human race. The Great Being saith: Blessed and happy is he that ariseth to promote the best interests of the peoples and kindreds of the earth. In another passage He hath proclaimed: It is not for him

to pride himself who loveth his own country, but rather for him who loveth the whole world. The earth is but one country, and mankind its citizens.[2]

'Abdu'l-Bahá, in *The Secret of Divine Civilization*, contrasts the exterior and superficial characteristics of the civilization of the day with 'true civilization'. With great clarity he explains the influence of the sovereign divine will on the nature of true diplomacy.

True civilization will unfurl its banner in the mid-most heart of the world whenever a certain number of its distinguished and high-minded sovereigns — the shining exemplars of devotion and determination — shall, for the good and happiness of all mankind, arise, with firm resolve and clear vision, to establish the Cause of Universal Peace. They must make the Cause of Peace the object of general consultation, and seek by every means in their power to establish a Union of the nations of the world. They must conclude a binding treaty and establish a covenant, the provisions of which shall be sound, inviolable and definite. They must proclaim it to all the world and obtain for it the sanction of all the human race. This supreme and noble undertaking — the real source of the peace and well-being of all the world — should be regarded as sacred by all that dwell on earth. All the forces of humanity must be mobilized to ensure the stability and permanence of this Most Great Covenant... Should this greatest of all remedies be applied to the sick body of the world, it will assuredly recover from its ills and will remain eternally safe and secure.

A few, unaware of the power latent in human endeavor, consider this matter as highly impracticable, nay even beyond the scope of man's utmost efforts. Such is not the case, however. On the contrary, thanks to the unfailing grace of God, the loving-kindness of His favored ones, the unrivaled endeavors of wise and capable souls, and the thoughts and ideas of the peerless leaders of this age, nothing whatsoever can be regarded as unattainable. Endeavor, ceaseless endeavor, is required. Nothing short of an indomitable determination can possibly achieve it. Many a cause which past ages have regarded as purely visionary, yet in this day has become most easy and practicable. Why should this most great and lofty Cause — the day-star of the firmament of true civilization and the cause of the glory, the advancement, the well-being and the success of all humanity — be regarded as impossible of achievement? Surely the day will come when its beauteous light shall shed illumination upon the assemblage of man.[3]

This was written in 1875 for the attention of a ruling elite to whom such thoughts were utterly alien. In 1936 Shoghi Effendi's description of the future world commonwealth ('inasmuch as we can envisage it') closed with the following sentence:

> A world federal system, ruling the whole earth and exercising unchallengeable authority over its unimaginably vast resources, blending and embodying the ideals of both the East and the West, liberated from the curse of war and its miseries, and bent on the exploitation of all the available sources of energy on the surface of the planet, a system in which Force is made the servant of Justice, whose life is sustained by its universal recognition of one God and by its allegiance to one common Revelation — such is the goal towards which humanity, impelled by the unifying forces of life, is moving.[4]

Humankind on its way to the Kingdom of God on earth, no less. Bahá'u'lláh and 'Abdu'l-Bahá have, with infinite patience and unequalled clarity, drawn the attention of not only their followers but also the rulers of their times to this interpretation of the evolution of our social lives.[5] The question which those who adhere to their vision today must address is: how can we convince those in authority, after a lapse of four generations and untold damage, to recognize this as the sovereign will of God, or at least as a valid alternative to the current international chaos?

The Varieties of Sovereignty

The Bahá'í position is considerably clarified when we view the emergence of a world federal State as representing the will of God, the goal of political history on this planet. Bahá'ís see no alternative. Political science cannot bring us much further than our present parlous state. Despite a highly developed methodology, it lacks a truly constructive goal-orientation, and lurks dangerously close to the domain of sciences which Bahá'u'lláh condemned as those 'that begin with words and end with words.'[6] Political science can't see the wood for the trees, or the State for the states. It needs to be illumined by the 'light which shineth in the darkness' even though 'the darkness comprehendeth it not.'[7] The clear prescriptions of Bahá'u'lláh and 'Abdu'l-Bahá are what is required in order to develop a new understanding of the concept of sovereignty which State philosophy created some five hundred years ago, but which it has grossly perverted ever since.[8]

The French adjective *souverain* comes from the ecclesiastical Latin *superanus* which means 'placed upmost', 'the highest', 'the most glorious', and 'independent'. Clearly this term fulfilled an important theoretical function in the development of the centralized national authority of the monarch in the face of feudal territorial claims, particularly those of the nobility — a struggle which went as much awry in the Holy Roman Empire as it was successful, after much conflict, in England, France, and other European sovereign States between the fifteenth and eighteenth century.

Primary to the concept of sovereignty is the distinction between an all-encompassing authority and a majority of subjects who give it their allegiance. Additional to this distinction is the territory itself in which this relationship applies, which must be distinguished from the outside world, and, if necessary, defended. As part of the process of democratization, an elected legislative body to whom the executive is responsible has taken the place of a single ruler. Definitions of sovereignty are as diverse as those of any other universal abstractions; some even go so far as to emphasize the capacity to condemn people to death, either through legal process or in war.

Originally sovereignty was seen to depend on the will of God. Even today, monarchs like to use the expression 'by divine grace'. Bahá'u'lláh repeatedly confirms this as an important aspect of divine world order:

> Know thou that We have annulled the rule of the sword, as an aid to Our Cause, and substituted for it the power born of the utterance of men. Thus have We irrevocably decreed, by virtue of Our grace. Say: O people! Sow not the seeds of discord among men, and refrain from contending with your neighbour, for your Lord hath committed the world and the cities thereof to the care of the kings of the earth, and made them the emblems of His own power, by virtue of the sovereignty He hath chosen to bestow upon them. He hath refused to reserve for Himself any share whatever of this world's dominion. To this He Who is Himself the Eternal Truth will testify. The things He hath reserved for Himself are the cities of men's hearts, that He may cleanse them from all earthly defilements, and enable them to draw nigh unto the hallowed Spot which the hands of the infidel can never profane. Open, O people, the city of the human heart with the key of your utterance. Thus have We, according to a pre-ordained measure, prescribed unto you your duty.[9]

From this we may understand that there exists a pre-eminent divine sovereignty, which gradually becomes manifest in the course of history and through the force of conviction of its adherents. Most eschatological beliefs, all expectations of a final Judgement, Return, or Resurrection point in this direction.

If we are trying to define the limits of State sovereignty, the matter does not end with the claim of divine sovereignty. We can see aspects of sovereignty in contexts other than the State, such as, for example, in multinational corporations. Who is more powerful: Paraguay or IBM? We must expand the meaning of 'sovereignty' from a national or territorial term to an institutional one. Institutional sovereignty, or the power to make decisions, is exercised by every institution in its legally defined sphere of action, and often beyond.

Finally, so many limits to the power of the State in the sphere of individual privacy have emerged in the last 200 years, that it would not be incorrect in this context to speak of personal sovereignty.

We have now three positions (divine, institutional and personal) from which the outmoded dogmas and misjudgements based on territorial sovereignty in traditional foreign policy, particularly in regard to the insanity of deterrence and armaments, may be criticized. As once the Old Testament prophets arose to proclaim to their kings the sovereign will of the Lord, should not Bahá'ís now draw the attention of foreign policy officials and leaders of opinion to the divine sovereignty, the command of God, which Bahá'u'lláh unmistakably reveals? On the other hand, the chaotic exercise of economic, financial and/or cultural rights that transcend national borders will be gradually regulated by more and stronger institutions. The interaction of the different administrative levels at which power is exercised plays an important role here. Federated States, provinces, and municipalities can only gain in power and influence when the power of sovereign territorial States is limited in favour of a world State. The misery of a world without peace leads more and more citizens to the conclusion that there should be something approaching a 'third generation' of human rights — i.e., the right to ensure peaceful and rational exercise of power by political leaders, particularly in the international field.

Petty-mindedness and Immaturity

What prevents humankind from comprehending such inter-relationships and pursuing such goals? Firstly, the desire for immediate success, wealth, power and prestige, rather than meaning. Even when these needs are satisfied, and the need for self-realization is pursued through political or social service, this is still insufficient to provide an adequate model for building the future. Bahá'u'lláh wrote of the 'petty-mindedness of such souls as tread the valley of arrogance and pride.'[10] From the point of view of cultural behaviour, this petty-mindedness is none other than a sign of immaturity. Expressions such as national sovereignty, territorial integrity, national self-determination, and so on, today have a similar meaning to the cult of the divinity of the emperor in ancient Rome. From the modern point of view such an imperial cult is an absurdity. At the time however, it represented considerable progress over such city gods as the child-devouring Moloch of the Phoenicians and Carthiginians. In the same way, national State sovereignty is a considerable step forward in thought from the barbaric feudal structures of the late middle ages. However, just as both the cult of the emperor and the worship of Moloch are seen, in the eyes of enlightened monotheism, as culturally damning blasphemies, so the cult of State sovereignty is an affront to the will of God today. Bahá'ís take their lead from the words of Bahá'u'lláh:

> Of old it hath been revealed 'Love of one's country is an element of the Faith of God.' The Tongue of Grandeur hath, however, in the day of His manifestation proclaimed: 'It is not his to boast who loveth his country, but it is his who loveth the world.' Through the power released by these exalted words He hath lent a fresh impulse, and set a new direction, to the birds of men's hearts, and hath obliterated every trace of restriction and limitation from God's holy Book.[11]

The believers in the Lord of the Age should now rush to the aid of the times, and renouncing all use of force but armed 'with the sword of wisdom and utterance,'[12] their gaze fixed upon a goal worthy of their effort, counter the current false conceptions which lead the human race toward the ruin which is the only end of disunity.

The Repressed Tradition

Those who are concerned to practise forward-looking, constructive and open politics need not, necessarily, begin with the prescriptions of Bahá'u'lláh. The intellectual tradition provides noteworthy examples, which have been forced into philosophical limbo by the irredeemable nationalists. Immanuel Kant wrote in 1795 in his monograph *On Perpetual Peace*, 'Seek ye first the kingdom of pure practical reason and its righteousness, and your end (the blessing of eternal peace) shall be added unto you.'

This great philosopher, having first defined 'pure' and then 'practical' reason did not shirk from the risk of being misunderstood as a blasphemer by substituting in the Sermon on the Mount (Matt. 6:33) the words 'pure practical reason' for 'God'.

How sad that those whom this great thought most concerned have either unwittingly neglected or knowingly repressed it in the 200 years since its articulation. This treatment of such an important and challenging philosophical statement gives credence to Marx's description of intellectual production as largely the expression of material interests.

Enlightened western thinkers of the last 400 years have failed to make key distinctions in two areas central to the theme of this discussion: The first is the inability to differentiate between 'religion' and Christianity. The other, which concerns our theme more directly, has been the virtually universal refusal to conceive of the State as an abstraction, free from physical, territorial or national limits, as the State-in-itself, and accessible at every level. How much less capable must they be of imagining a world State?

This is certainly a sign of the apocalyptic nature of our situation. Clearly we have arrived, not only in the physical and natural sciences, but also in our political science at the borders of our conventional consciousness. As in the time of Noah, as in the times of the prehistoric prophets to whom Muhammad refers in the Qur'án, the human race, including our most learned scientists and philosophers, is no longer capable of further advancement without reference to the new, all-encompassing, future-defining, Manifestation of God.

Curiously, the connections are so obvious that one is forced to recall the expression, 'where there's a will there's a way.' In 1912 'Abdu'l-Bahá advised an important official of the United States government, who asked in what way he could best promote the interests of his country:

You can best serve your country if you strive, in your capacity as a citizen of the world, to assist in the eventual application of the principle of federalism underlying the government of your own country to the relationships now existing between the peoples and nations of the world.[13]

Everyone concerned for the destiny of their own country must recognize the challenge and the hope in 'Abdu'l-Bahá's advice.

Incorrect Programming

The desire to create an all-encompassing and supranational order as an instrument of our will to peace, as the highest and most pervasive motive of our thoughts and actions, is already frustrated in our day-to-day human relationships at work and at home. If those in authority represent the political system to us, a system that we experience as aggressive and unhealthy, as something unavoidable and necessary, then our own ability to conceive of an alternative is hindered.

Bahá'ís would contend that the basic thesis of those in power is false, inasmuch as their foreign policy goals run counter to the declared sovereign will of God. Here we need a new touchstone, a revolution in thought. This new thinking must be radical, must come from the roots, from the depths of our humanity. That it be further immunized against all blinkered thinking and behaviour, necessitates the application of the uncompromising premise formulated in our original thesis, which describes traditional foreign policy as a 'crime against humanity.'

Already in the 1930s Aldous Huxley, the great utopian and peace activist, wrote: 'The collective mentality of nations is that of a fourteen year old boy with criminal tendencies: simultaneously deceitful and childish, evil and imaginative, manically egotistical, over sensitive and greedy, and withal pitifully boastful and conceited.'[14] What would a badly brought-up fourteen year old not do to secure a measure of recognition or status in that which he perceives as his rightful interest? One can with certainty say that neither the criminal teenager nor the sovereign national State can be effectively rehabilitated without the beneficent influence of personal and institutional educators who seek patiently to inculcate a sense of orderly values, examples and goals.

Who are, within the parameters of our universal thesis, these 'criminals'? As in the days of absolute monarchy, a small group of politicians, diplomats and military officers do not wish to recognize that a radically new era has begun, that 'Some form of a world super-state must needs be evolved',[15] and that the State itself as a pure principle must form part of our conceptual vocabulary. Spiritual immaturity in this context may also be described as criminal: that adolescent aberrance in contemporary foreign policy which Huxley so pithily presented, the twisted undeveloped image of humanity held by the power-hungry as described in MacGregor's X-Y theory,[16] the collapse of normal rules of human conduct caused by the jingoism of 'my country, right or wrong', the whole lie and deception of 'big' politics that wells over us from the pages of every newspaper and every television news bulletin. Equally irresponsible is the lack of will to consensus, a product of the mischievous influence of particular interests, the sheer inability to think beyond the limits of one's own territorial State and its petty power plays. Furthermore, the narrow legal framework which circumscribes political thought is just as culpable. As each and every actor on the international political stage owes his allegiance to just one of the 160 sovereign territorial States, upon which depends his personal security and the advancement of his career, the first utterance which trips over the border of national interest leads to a limbo from which the 'utopian' and aberrant speaker can rarely escape. As Karl Jaspers wrote, 'Childishly idealistic politics conducts itself as if the envisaged goal were already realized. Childishly realistic politics conducts itself as if the new vision could never be realized. Both are irresponsible.'[17]

Irresponsibility in the field of international politics, where the continuance or extinction of the human race are at issue, is criminal. One clear manifestation of this criminal tendency is the fact that, 80 years after 'Abdu'l-Bahá's advice to that US official, so little progress has been made by social and political institutions in the application of the principle of federalism to international relations.

Military, Economic and Monetary Sovereignty

In concrete terms we are concerned with the three most elementary claims of the citizen on his State; the right to security, to thrifty, orderly and consistent governance, and to a stable currency. The 160 sovereign States are no longer capable individually of sufficiently satisfying these claims. To this end, we shall have need in future, not only of international co-operation, but also of a supreme State concept, of the world super-State as the highest governing body. Anything less would be constitutionally insufficient.

To this 'form of world super-state . . . all the nations of the world will have willingly ceded every claim to make war, certain rights to impose taxation and all rights to maintain armaments, except for purposes of maintaining internal order within their respective dominions.'[18] The world super-State must stand on a solid financial basis with its own tax structure, unlike the United Nations which has to go begging for every penny from its member-States. Finally it is important for the reconstruction of the world economy, especially for the elimination of poverty and of world-wide inflation, that monetary unification play an early role in the process of international integration. This could perhaps be achieved through the transformation of the International Monetary Fund into a world central bank that would be independent of State influences, as is the Bundesbank in Germany.[19]

Ceaseless Endeavour is Required

How can this necessary breakthrough be achieved? In the contest against irresponsible development of national sovereignty through misconceived foreign policy, Bahá'ís may be able to see a number of 'natural' partners who can be activated, through consciousness-raising, to work for the creation of a world State. Such a partnership would embrace all who would benefit from a truly global policy, including enlightened prominent and influential people concerned for human and citizens' rights, such as the intellectual elite, independent political observers, and journalists; those local and regional authorities exploited by the State, who with the development of a world State would regain some of the functions which have been, directly or indirectly for reasons of defence, assumed by national government; multinational corporations whose development is hindered by the short-sightedness, wilfulness and contradictory nature of national interests, the entangling influence of national regulations on entrepreneurial decision-making, and the diversity of social/regional conditions which impede the optimal combination of the factors of production; international financial institutions whose field of action and prospects of profit could be increased through the orderly harmonizing of currency and capital markets; and the poor, small, powerless emergent nations, who seek to defend themselves against rich, big, powerful established nations.

In a word, it is all a matter of comprehensive enlightenment, of 'ceaseless endeavor',[20] as 'Abdu'l-Bahá put it. By making this issue one of the central themes of Bahá'í activity, this universal political thesis will prevail.

NOTES

1. Shoghi Effendi, *The World Order of Bahá'u'lláh: Selected Letters*, 2nd rev. ed. (Wilmette, IL: Bahá'í Publishing Trust, 1974), p. 170.
2. Bahá'u'lláh, *Gleanings from the Writings of Bahá'u'lláh* trans. Shoghi Effendi, 2nd rev. ed. (Wilmette, IL: Bahá'í Publishing Trust, 1976), pp. 249-250.
3. 'Abdu'l-Bahá, *The Secret of Divine Civilization* trans. Marzieh Gail, 2nd ed. (Bahá'í Publishing Trust: Wilmette, 1970) pp. 64-7.
4. Shoghi Effendi, *The World Order of Bahá'u'lláh*, p. 204.
5. See ibid.
6. Bahá'u'lláh, *Tablets of Bahá'u'lláh revealed after the Kitáb-i-Aqdas* comp. Research Department of the Universal House of Justice, trans. Habib Taherzadeh and others, rev. ed. (Haifa: Bahá'í World Centre, 1982), p. 52.
7. John 1:5.
8. For example Max Weber's absurd distinction between *gesinnungsethik* and *verantwortungsethik*.
9. Bahá'u'lláh, *Gleanings*, pp. 303-4.
10. Ibid., p. 18.
11. Ibid., pp. 95-6.
12. Ibid., p. 296.
13. Shoghi Effendi, *The World Order of Bahá'u'lláh*, p. 37.
14. Aldous Huxley, *Wissenschaft, Freiheit und Frieden* (Zürich, 1947) p. 67.
15. Shoghi Effendi, 'The Goal of a New World Order', in *The World Order of Bahá'u'lláh*, p. 40.
16. Douglas McGregor, *The Human Side of Enterprise* (New York: McGraw-Hill, 1960). McGregor describes the syndrome of negative opinions about people which underlie, consciously or unconsciously, the decisions of businessmen as 'theory X' and attributes to this opinion syndrome the lack of success in overcoming critical situations. He opposes theory X with theory Y, not as a contrast but as an expansion and cultivation of a limited image of mankind through selective conformity, dialogue, goal orientation, functional control and the integration of interests.

17. Karl Jaspers, *Die Atombombe und die Zukunft der Menschheit* (Munich, 1961) p. 351.
18. Shoghi Effendi, 'The Goal of a New World Order' in *The World Order of Bahá'u'lláh*, p. 40.
19. Peter Mühlschlegel, *Der Weltzentralbank-Präsident. Versuche zur Erweiterung unseres ökonomischen Bewusstseins* (The World Central Bank President: Essays in the Enlargement of our Economic Consciousness) (Rosenheim: Horizonte Verlag, 1989).
20. 'Abdu'l-Bahá, *The Secret of Divine Civilization*, p. 66.

EMERGENCE: DIMENSIONS OF A NEW WORLD ORDER

BAHÁ'Í DEVELOPMENT STRATEGY
A Meeting of Social Ideologies
Holly Hanson

PERHAPS the philosophical divide between capitalist and socialist ideologies is not as great as it once appeared. If we consider the attitudes of capitalists and socialists towards their own social and economic systems, we see that few have good reason to be fully satisfied with what they believe. Neither ideology has created well-being and prosperity for all members of society; no system has delivered an impartial and encompassing justice; policy makers in both camps are abandoning basic aspects of ideology in order to make their economic and social systems work.

Socialist economies, which were supposed to be communities of producers bound together by fraternal solidarity, have in many cases collapsed and been forced to introduce initiatives which create profits for the individual. The new profit motive, with which even the Chinese have experimented, which allowed farmers to sell a portion of what they produced instead of turning everything over to the collective, was not called 'anti-communist', but 'primary socialism.' Capitalist economies, which claim to support the freedom and rights of the individual, expand government control when the invisible hand of capital plucks out an uncomfortably large number of workers, and allows them to be unemployed and living on the street. The American economy swings from a strict laissez-faire capitalism to a desire for more public control and planning in predictable cycles.

Dramatic changes to the economy of many socialist countries, and the constant fluctuation from 'socially responsive' to 'fiscally prudent' policies in western democracies obscure the fact that both capitalist and socialist systems are basically flawed. If we examine social economic theory in terms of what each system believes about the individual, the goals of society, and the forces that lead to social progress, we see that socialist ideology has grasped a fundamental truth about the functioning of human society, and capitalist ideology has grasped a fundamental truth about the motivation of the individual, but both systems fall short of their goals through failing to understand the reality of human nature.

The concept of social and economic progress which we find in the Bahá'í revelation combines the truths of both ideologies with an awareness of the transcendent potentialities inherent in humanity. This is a profound difference. A social system based on the premise that God created the human race to step forth out of nothingness for the betterment of the world has a unique positive dynamic.[1] It motivates people to change, to grow, to depend on each other. This is more than capitalist economics with the 'fat cats' being 'nice guys,' or socialist economics with 'comrades' preying on the collective. The whole system is different because the animating principles on which it is based are different. They are spiritual principles. The mystical bond which unites a person with God has powerful, and practical consequences. By channelling this force in society, Bahá'ís believe it is possible to create a 'social system at once progressive and peaceful, dynamic and harmonious, a system giving free play to individual creativity and initiative but based on co-operation and reciprocity.'[2]

We can establish a foundation for thinking about ideologies by briefly sketching how each one functions in practice in social and economic development. Everyone involved in development wants to replace poverty, illiteracy, and economic stagnation with prosperity, education, and well-being; but the techniques they employ and the choices they make are largely determined by ideology. What can people do for themselves? How can they be motivated to do it? What actions will create wealth? What kind of a society is the goal? What will get us there? Development strategy provides a clear basis for comparison because it distils fundamental beliefs about social progress.

Capitalist Development Strategy

The fundamental goal of a capitalist development strategy (which is not always acknowledged) is to make poor countries more like rich countries. The process of development is understood as moving communities from a condition of having less to a condition of having more; i.e., moving up a well-defined hierarchy of socio-economic prosperity. At the top of this hierarchy are the United States, Germany and other highly industrialized, consumer societies, which are thought of as 'developed.' Nations

BAHÁ'Í DEVELOPMENT STRATEGY

which are successfully imitating them are 'developing'; and nations which are the most different from them are 'least developed.'

The immediate objectives of development work may be improved agriculture or health care or housing; but the aspiration, confirmed both by the subsistence farmer drinking Coca Cola and the World Bank official negotiating the terms of a loan, is to bring the qualities and conditions of a western economic system to the Third World.

Thus, capitalist development strategy seeks to shape Third Word economies into the pattern of western nations by providing the poorer countries with all the ingredients which have contributed to industrialization in Europe and America. Prosperity, according to the theory of capitalism, comes from individual entrepreneurs acting in their own self-interest in a favourable environment. It follows, then, that the capable, competent entrepreneurs of the Third World will be able to create prosperity for their nations if only they are given the right tools. They need education in order to realize their own capacity to create wealth. They need appropriate technology to stimulate the rural economy, and decent roads and communications in order to build markets. Enterprising Third World elites need industry to stimulate development. The process of social and economic development, from this perspective, is a series of 'inputs' which are added to a 'less-developed' community to create conditions similar to those that led to economic growth in more developed communities.

One practical example of capitalist ideology in development would be a functional literacy project. Functional literacy teaches reading through information which is chosen because it will be useful to the learner. Lessons are built around things like information on child health, the printing on a medicine bottle, and instructions for applying fertilizers or operating machinery. The goal is to make people more modern, to expose them to new ideas, to make them more efficient in their work and more able to absorb development information. Since traditional attitudes about life, and lack of awareness of technology are thought to retard social progress, literacy education is supposed to make people more willing to change.

The goal of development projects is to launch less developed nations into western-style economic success. People are the agents of this development process, and self-interest is the force that motivates them. There is no element of 'evil' in this system: the assumption of capitalist ideology is that people are good, wealth is good, and people will use the tools they are given to create wealth for themselves, which will be good for society.

Socialist Development Strategy

Development inspired by socialism is an entirely different process. The goal is not a gradual increase in material prosperity, but a total transformation of society. Hunger, illiteracy, disease and economic stagnation are seen as symptoms of injustice, and overcoming that injustice has to be the first step in development. Labourers on a sugar plantation, for example, are malnourished and desperately poor because the landlord wants them to be afraid to leave the plantation; and urban slum dwellers have few employment options because industrialists want a large number of people to be unemployed so that wages remain low. These peasants and workers are not poor because they lack modern attitudes or the tools for economic progress; they are poor because the capitalist system only works when someone is on the bottom.

Socialists see underdevelopment as a result of the class structure of world society, and socialist development seeks to break down the division between the powerless — workers and peasants — and the powerful — industrialists and landlords. When human capacities are not blocked and frustrated by the evil which is a part of capitalist class relationships, people will be able to create more equitable patterns for social, economic and personal life.

Socialist-oriented development activities seek to redistribute power to oppressed people by giving them confidence in their own capacity, and the means to control their own lives. Oppression dehumanizes people: it destroys their self-esteem and makes them passive and inarticulate. Radical development uses anger and indignation to awaken a sense of power and dignity among people who have suffered injustice. The agents of radical development are people who are aware of their oppression and believe in their own capacity to transform their lives. They educate themselves, create their own health-care networks, organize co-operatives for their own benefit, and fight for their rights.

We can see socialist ideology in action in development by considering, again, a literacy campaign. A radical development worker begins literacy instruction by involving peasants or workers in discussions, using pictures which illustrate their condition. People gain confidence and learn to think for themselves by talking about the pictures. Reading and writing lessons are based on the students' own statements expressing anger at the injustice in their lives. The goal of literacy instruction is to make people believe that they have the capacity to overcome the evil in society.

In summary, development inspired by socialist ideology has as its goal the elimination of the oppressive social structures of capitalism, and the evolution of just and wholesome social patterns. There is a definite demarcation of good and evil in this system: the evil is the class structure, which by its very nature prevents social progress, and the good is human capacity. Social and economic development happens when oppressed, underprivileged people become empowered and assume control of their own lives. The tools used are people's anger at oppression and their articulate protest against it, their awareness of the power of human endeavour, and their ability to co-operate and sacrifice for the benefit of social transformation.

Bahá'í Development Strategy

Development based on a Bahá'í outlook begins with a different perception of the world. It's not a capitalist world of individuals pursuing their own interest and gratification; neither is it a socialist world in which liberated human beings create culture out of nature; it is God's world, in which women and men carry forward an ever-advancing civilization using the capacities given to them by their Creator.

Awareness of the spiritual dimension of human reality pervades the Bahá'í approach to social and economic development. A total transformation of society is also the goal for Bahá'ís, but the process of social change is a positive one, in which the fundamental elements of a more mature civilization, such as the nobility of human nature, the elimination of all forms of prejudice, the equality of the sexes, and the importance of selflessness in economic relationships are demonstrated in society, and gradually accepted by people as more effective and workable than current social practices. Bahá'ís believe that social transformation is a gradual process, and that a visible model of a more refined and exalted behaviour is critical to social evolution. The Bahá'í vision of a peaceful, dynamic, and unified world society comes form the laws and teachings of Bahá'u'lláh. For Bahá'ís, accepting these principles and trying to put them into practice in the world is not only a strategy for social change, but also a religious obligation.

The agents of this long-term development process are again individual people, but they are people who consciously try to develop moral strengths, and whose goal in life is service to humanity as well as individual success. The strategy of Bahá'í development is to demonstrate the practical value of the principles of the Faith and, more generally, of such spiritual qualities as love, courage, and self-sacrifice which are inculcated in its scriptures. Bahá'ís believe that these principles and virtues not only have transcendent effects on society, but are also the source of material well-being. For instance, eradication of racism generates prosperity; love and concern in the work environment improve productivity; acting on the principle of equality and sending girls to school helps to reduce rates of infant mortality.

Most Bahá'í development activities are initiated by rural local spiritual assemblies, and are attempts to use the resources of the community to meet its own needs. Simple schools have been arranged in the homes of Bahá'ís; communities have raised funds to send one of their members to a health educator training course; youth have organized tree planting and other service projects.

Intangible qualities are vital to these activities. When a village builds itself a water reservoir, it hasn't just used shovels: the people also needed to consult, to trust each other, to motivate 100 citizens to take their turn digging, and to have confidence in their own capacity. The way things are done is as important to Bahá'ís as the results. Development activities should be conducive to human honour, they should increase a community's solidarity; they should help people learn to consult effectively.

Literacy projects inspired by Bahá'í principles may begin with a group of believers deciding that they want to learn to read because acquiring an education and reading the Bahá'í scriptures are obligations for Bahá'ís. The teacher is usually a volunteer, and basic Bahá'í scriptures are often used as texts. The Iranian Bahá'í community organized classes like this in the early 1900s before public education had been established in Iran, and locally organized literacy activities can be found in many Bahá'í communities around the world. The purpose of literacy education is to give people access to Bahá'u'lláh's writings, which are a source of encouragement, inspiration, and insight for Bahá'ís, and to give them the means to acquire further education.

In summary, to Bahá'ís, spiritual principles are crucial to social progress. The Bahá'í assumption in development is not that humankind is good and wealth is good and that the best possible society will result when everyone acts in his own self-interest; nor is it that all the wrong in the world would disappear with elimination of capitalists and capitalism. Bahá'ís would argue, rather, that human beings have the potential to be good and to make the world a better place through each person submitting his or her individual will to the will of God. People can build societies that maintain the honour and dignity of every member; they can establish economic systems that allow everyone to prosper. They are capable of establishing forms of government that encourage individual expression and maintain stability and order: but they cannot do it alone. The vision of how society can and should develop, and strategies to move it in that direction, come from the teachings of the Messenger of God. The motivation to work towards goals that are difficult and the discipline to curb the individual ego for the benefit of society require an inspiration derived from a relationship with God.

Comparing Development Strategies

How do these ideologies work as development strategies? Each approach has caused improvement in the standard of living of some communities in some developing countries, but none of them has achieved its most basic objectives. For example, in the case of literacy education, we see that all across the ideological divide people have learned to read. Some of the 'budding capitalists' who learned to read medicine bottles and fertilizer instructions ran out of things to read and forgot how, but functional literacy programmes have raised literacy levels and have had some positive side effects. Unfortunately, while people received more education and more health care and more appropriate technology, they also became poorer. The gap between rich and poor nations has become wider in the past 20 years; and per capita incomes in Africa and Latin America have declined dramatically as nations have struggled to repay their debts.[3] Adding development inputs alone did not launch people into prosperity.

Radical development specialists succeeded in teaching people to read by unlocking their anger and frustration at injustice, and significant improvements in literacy and health care delivery have often followed immediately after a revolution. Unfortunately, the sense of pride and power that radical literacy education awakens, and the material benefits which people may have won for themselves, often deteriorate when the revolutionary Party tightens control in order to make the State function. Universal human emancipation does not arrive when the State owns all the means of production and has all the power.

It is not easy to evaluate Bahá'í development activities, because they are only just beginning. Bahá'ís expect civilization-building to be a gradual and evolutionary process; and it seems to take a long time for the impulse towards development to build from the core of a person's faith outward into concrete actions. For Bahá'í development to have a visible impact, the Bahá'í community will have to become more confident about expressing its principles in social action, and the number of Bahá'ís will have to increase.

Whether one is convinced that capitalist or socialist ideologies succeed depends on where one looks for evidence. The newly developed countries of Asia are the models of capitalist success; but child workers under the age of 15 — and sometimes as young as 7 — make up 11 per cent of the work-force, providing cheap labour in sweat-shop garment factories and other industries. Nicaragua, Tanzania, and other socialist governments attempted to provide networks of social services unmatched by other governments; but the standards of living have declined.[4]

Comparing Ideologies

If we take the basic elements of these ideologies revealed by application in their respective development strategies, and consider how they function in the world, it is apparent that each one offers part of the solution, but also that both contain obvious deficiencies. One of the first observations usually made in such a comparison is that capitalist and socialist systems each contain elements which are lacking in the other. However, just as neither ideology alone can cause real social progress, neither can any system which merely combines parts of them, because they define reality in strictly material terms.

The strength of capitalism is its recognition that people need freedom to develop their natural capacities; that each individual has an innate desire to strive, to work, and to enjoy the benefits of his or her own labour. This creative self-interest is inherent in human nature. It is absolutely necessary for human progress, and it is a good thing.[5] But it is not the only aspect of human nature. People also have to transcend themselves, to be generous, to sacrifice themselves for others and to recognize that they are part of an interdependent human race. Capitalist ideology promotes initiative and wealth-creation, but it also promotes greed. It has caused tremendous suffering largely because it focuses on the individual and ignores humanity. In a successful and prosperous economy such as that of the United States, 7 per cent of the population — 17 million people — are chronically unemployed, 33 million are malnourished and the infant mortality rate in its inner-city slums is higher than that of most developing countries.[6]

Capitalism does not create prosperity and well-being for a society: it creates a few extremely rich people, who often emerge from the battle morally compromised and unhappy, and it leaves behind most of the population, all of whom are distracted by materialism and many of whom live in want. Its ethic of over-consumption destroys the natural environment, and a corollary of the economic disparities are huge social divisions which undermine the stability of society.

Socialist ideology, on the other hand, recognizes the mutual obligations that bind the members of a society, and assumes that people will be willing to sacrifice their individual desires for the good of society. Human beings *do* long for justice, they *do* want to be noble. Socialist ideology attracts people because it appeals to these transcendent aspects of human nature. However, socialist-inspired attempts at government or social change cannot deliver the new society which they promise. The evil which is supposed to be inherent in the class structure lingers on in the behaviour of the 'liberated' after the capitalists are gone, and sooner or later the loyal Party faithful get tired of making sacrifices for society when it is obvious that they will not benefit. The anger and hatred which are used to destroy class oppression also develop their own momentum, and revolutionary movements tend to splinter and fight among themselves.

Socialist thought inspires people to want to change the world but it cannot actually get them to do it. People are often egotistical and do not co-operate: enthusiasm runs dry. People lose their revolutionary consciousness and start to think about themselves instead. The Party apparatus, which in theory cannot do evil because evil was a characteristic of the class structure, often becomes more coercive than its predecessor in its efforts to motivate people. The result is a deadening of individual responsibility and commitment to work, economic stagnation, and social paralysis.

Capitalist ideology provides a spark for individual initiative which is lacking in socialist economies, and socialist ideology offers an ethic of social interdependence which is lacking in capitalism. Can the workable parts of both systems be combined to make something that really does promote social progress? The result of this effort is the contemporary welfare State, and it has much to recommend it. Unfortunately, all too often this system creates a society in which the successful are motivated to cheat on their taxes, the poor are motivated to remain unemployed, the economy supports increasing social benefit payments of all kinds, and the very wealthy are motivated to move to Monaco. A mixed economy is really no more effective than either ideological extreme: personal responsibility is eroded, social tensions grow, and although everyone is taken care of, no one feels they are being treated fairly.

The Spiritual Dimension of Economic Theory

The difficulty with capitalism, socialism, and any combination of the two is that they perceive reality as something less than it really is. Life is not just people, things, and the culture that men and women create. The real world includes the creative force that people call God, and the transcendent aspect of human nature that people call the soul. This spiritual reality cannot be stored away for special occasions: it is an integral part of human life, and an essential part of economic activity. There is a distortion and a dysfunction when economists and social thinkers try to force a three dimensional reality — one that is spiritual, human, and material — into a two dimensional framework. It does not work. People and things, by themselves, cannot create social progress. It takes people, things, and the spiritual resources that God gives humankind.

The individual person is the agent of social change in each of these ideologies, and we can visualize the individual as a vehicle, driving humanity towards a better society. For Bahá'ís, the fuel for that vehicle is the love of God. That fuel, constantly replenished by prayer and study of the Bahá'í writings, moves the individual past frustrations with people, through bad spots where the ego asserts itself, pulls the individual forward when he or she is discouraged and does not feel motivated to work for social change; it gives people a clear sense of direction. Individual people moving toward God move the world with them.

Socialist thought also asks each individual to move society forward through his or her own actions. The vehicle of the individual is supposed to sacrifice for the benefit of the ideal socialist State, he or she is supposed to obey the Party and put its interests first; but after a while the revolutionary 'fuel tank' runs dry. People get disillusioned, irritated by doing without things and worried about their future, and they have no more motivation to sacrifice. The vehicle of social progress stops; the individual does not want to contribute any more. When the Party uses force to make the vehicle move forward again, the individual gets battered. In many efforts at collectivization, the revolutionary party seems like a tank, shoving the stalled and uncooperative units of revolution, forcing them to move. Peasants could join the collective or be shot; they could choose to move into the collective village or to forfeit their crops.

The capitalist vehicle analogy is a little different: society will advance when each person builds the most luxurious vehicle he or she possibly can and drives it in exactly the way he or she wants. The most successful society is the one with the most flashy cars. Every entrepreneur has to assemble his or her own vehicle for social progress, and the people who are around first get all the parts they want. Those on the edge of the crowd probably only find the materials to put together a motor scooter, and the ones who arrive late have to walk because there are no materials left.

The man who puts together a stretch limousine with a bar and video may feel that it is a pretty good system, but his overconsumption steals resources from his children and grandchildren, and the people who are forced to walk are probably tempted to do him in and steal his car.

The actions of the individual enable society to progress, and spiritual forces enable the individual to act effectively. The pervasive and animating power of each person's connection with God has both a stimulating and regulating influence on economic life. Love of God inspires the individual to develop virtues and to be creative, to seek excellence, to make maximum use of his or her talents and abilities. At the same time, other dimensions of spirituality motivate people to seek contentment, to avoid excessive consumption, and to share their resources with the poor. True religious belief disciplines the ego, enables people to be selfless, and creates a climate for willing social co-operation. Acknowledging this spiritual dimension of economic and social life would enable socialist and capitalist ideologies to achieve their own goals.

Achieving Socialist and Capitalist Goals for Society

The socialist aspiration that people will transcend their natural selfishness and serve the good of all society can be accomplished when people are conscious of spiritual reality, and recognize that there are rewards for material sacrifice.[7] These rewards may be intangible, but they are real enough. People will not sacrifice for nothing, and religion gives them a logical, convincing and attractive reason to be willing to do it.

The exhilaration of liberation is supposed to make revolutionaries patient, kind, trusting and humble, but these qualities do not come naturally to most people, or are worn away through the frustration of working in groups. Transforming society through the actions of the individual is slogging hard work, and the energy, discipline, and patience to carry on with it come from faith and reliance on God.

The capitalist expectation that individuals making wealth for themselves will eventually create a prosperous society can be realized if the right of the individual to work and enjoy the fruits of his or her own labour is tempered with the spiritual law that personal happiness comes from selflessness and service to other people. The application of spiritual values enables people to distinguish what is important from what is not, and what leads to human happiness.[8] Such values also help people discover what their wealth is good for: by spending it for the advantage of society they can achieve personal fulfilment, and the whole community prospers.

A Meeting of Ideologies

The 'socialist moral conscience' and the 'Protestant work ethic' meet in the Bahá'í concept of social progress. The conviction that God wants people to work hard and to use their talents to create wealth is accepted; on the condition, which finds echoes in socialism, that people should give their wealth away for the benefit of society. 'Wealth is praiseworthy in the highest degree, if it is acquired by an individual's own efforts and the grace of God, in commerce, agriculture, art and industry, and if it be expended for philanthropic purposes.'[9] Individuals can follow the 'capitalist' impulse and profit from their own endeavours. Then they are expected to exercise a 'socialist' moral conscience and use their wealth to find ways to universally enrich the masses:

> Wealth is most commendable, provided the entire population is wealthy. If, however, a few have inordinate riches while the rest are impoverished, and no fruit or benefit accrues from that wealth, then it is only a liability to its possessor. If, on the other hand, it is expended for the promotion of knowledge, the founding of elementary and other schools, the encouragement of art and industry, the training of orphans and the poor — in brief, if it is dedicated to the welfare of society — its possessor will stand out before God and man as the most excellent of all who live on earth and will be accounted as one of the people of paradise.[10]

Bahá'í beliefs about the creation and sharing of wealth are more than a tidy way to eliminate economic extremes. They are a way of building moral strengths in society.

This process of income generation and sharing of wealth has profound effects.[11] The system develops individuals by encouraging them to use their own capacities. By establishing service to humanity as the criterion for individual success, it fosters generosity, spirituality, and concern for others. The experience of giving away substantial wealth for a good cause adds depth and force to an individual's spiritual and material life. The Bahá'í entrepreneur can enjoy creating wealth, give a substantial part of it away, and then do what he or she does best, and make a lot of money again. The spiritual obligation of Ḥuqúqu'lláh ('the Right of God'), which asks (but does not force) each Bahá'í to offer a portion of their wealth[12] to the centre of the Faith,[13] is intended to foster spiritual strengths in the individual and in society, as well as provide the material basis for social progress.

A Bahá'í economic system also develops society. Bahá'í philanthropy is supposed to create structural changes which eliminate poverty; it is not a food-basket system that relieves the consciences of the rich while keeping the poor alive in a state of poverty. Contributions do not reinforce perceptions that the poor are inferior, because assistance for development is distributed through the network of Bahá'í administrative institutions. Local spiritual assemblies that receive funds have initiated, and bear responsibility for, their own development activities. People who have benefitted as recipients in this system become able to participate as donors. When people share their material assets because they want to and not because they are forced to, they become connected spiritually as well as economically. As the community becomes more prosperous, it also becomes more united.[14]

Spiritual reality is an immensely practical element of economic life: reliance on God inspires individual creativity, and love of God harnesses the ego for the benefit of society. Spiritual principles offer solutions to the social problems which are the product of every existing economic system. In order to move beyond the emptiness of consumer societies, the stagnation of socialist economies, the failure of the welfare State or the brittleness of inter-communal conflicts, people need to pry themselves out of the debilitating framework of materialistic thought. Each of these issues has a spiritual dimension. By understanding the whole reality of a problem, and recognizing the power of spiritual tools to resolve it, people can move themselves and their societies forward.

NOTES

1. 'This Wronged One testifieth that the purpose for which mortal men have, from utter nothingness, stepped into the realm of being, is that they may work for the betterment of the world and live together in concord and harmony.' Bahá'u'lláh, *Trustworthiness* comp. Research Department of the Universal House of Justice (London: Bahá'í Publishing Trust, 1987), p. 5.
2. The Universal House of Justice, *The Promise of World Peace: A Statement by the Universal House of Justice* (London: Bahá'í Publishing Trust, 1985), p. 3.
3. Norman Myers, gen. ed., *The Gaia Atlas of Planet Management*, (London: Pan Books, 1985), p. 218.
4. *World Development Forum*, vol. 5, no. 18 (15 October 1987); and vol. 4, no. 21 (30 November 1986).
5. '. . . man should know his own self and recognize that which leadeth unto loftiness or lowliness, glory or abasement, wealth or poverty. Having attained the stage of fulfilment and reached his maturity, man standeth in need of wealth, and such wealth as he acquireth through crafts and professions is commendable and praiseworthy...' Bahá'u'lláh, *Tablets of Bahá'u'lláh revealed after the Kitáb-i-Aqdas* comp. Research Department of the Universal House of Justice, trans. Habib Taherzadeh and others, rev. ed. (Haifa: Bahá'í World Centre, 1982), p. 35.
6. Loraine Granado, 'The Link of Classism', *Sojourners*, vol 16, no. 10 (November 1987).
7. '. . . it is impossible for a human being to turn aside from his own selfish advantages and sacrifice his own good for the good of the community except through religious faith. For self-love is kneaded into the very clay of man, and it is not possible that, without any hope of a substantial reward, he should neglect his own present material good. The individual, however, who puts his faith in God . . . will for the sake of God alone abandon his own peace and profit and will freely consecrate his own heart and soul to the common good.' 'Abdu'l-Bahá, *The Secret of Divine Civilization* trans. Marzieh Gail, 2nd ed. (Wilmette, IL: Bahá'í Publishing Trust, 1970), pp. 96-7.
8. 'Mine aim hath ever been, and still is, to suppress whatever is the cause of contention amidst the peoples of the earth, and of separation amongst the nations, so that all men may be sanctified from every earthly attachment, and be set free to occupy themselves with their own interests.' Bahá'u'lláh, *Epistle to the Son of the Wolf* trans. Shoghi Effendi (Wilmette, IL: Bahá'í Publishing Trust, 1969), p. 33.
9. 'Abdu'l-Bahá, *The Secret of Divine Civilization*, p. 24.
10. Ibid.
11. 'Man reacheth perfection through good deeds, voluntarily performed, not through good deeds the doing of which was forced upon him. . . . Voluntary sharing, the freely-chosen expending of one's substance, leadeth to society's comfort and peace. It lighteth up the

world; it bestoweth honour upon humankind.' 'Abdu'l-Bahá, *Selections from the Writings of 'Abdu'l-Bahá* comp. Research Department of the Universal House of Justice, trans. Marzieh Gail and others, rev. ed. (Haifa: Bahá'í World Centre, 1982), p. 115.

12. The amount paid is equivalent to 19 per cent of the excess of income over expenditure. 'It is clear and evident that the payment of the Right of God is conducive to prosperity, to blessing, and to honour and divine protection.' 'Ḥuqúqu'lláh is indeed a great law. It is incumbent upon all to make this offering, because it is the source of grace, abundance, and of all good. It is a bounty which shall remain with every soul in every world of the worlds of God, the All-Possessing, the All-Bountiful.' Bahá'u'lláh, *Ḥuqúqu'lláh: The Right of God* comp; Research Department of the Universal House of Justice, rev. ed. (London: Bahá'í Publishing Trust, 1989), p. 2.

13. That is, to the Universal House of Justice.

14. 'Co-operation, mutual aid and reciprocity are essential characteristics in the unified body of the world of being, inasmuch as all created things are closely related together and each is influenced by the other or deriveth benefit therefrom, either directly or indirectly. . . .

'This is the basic principle on which the institution of Huqúqu'lláh is established, inasmuch as its proceeds are dedicated to the furtherance of these ends.' 'Abdu'l-Bahá, *Ḥuqúqu'lláh*, pp. 20-1.

THE WORLD ORDER OF NATURE

Arthur Lyon Dahl

WE seem so small in relation to the natural world that it has always appeared unlimited. Yet the environmental problems currently making the headlines — toxic wastes, accumulating carbon dioxide, holes in the ozone layer, acid rain, nuclear reactor accidents — underline the fact that our technological development and growing population are now affecting natural systems at a world scale.

What is less evident, but perhaps more alarming in the long term, is the world crisis in the conservation of nature. The natural areas that once clothed the planet are steadily eroding under pressures from our rapidly expanding population. The rich and the poor both contribute to the problem: the rich through their headlong rush for economic development, and the masses of the poor through their desperate efforts to eke out a living from diminishing resources.

The biosphere, that thin layer of air, water and soil surrounding the earth that supports all life, is a single, complex, interrelated system. The conditions that keep our planet surface a suitable environment for living things were in part created, and are maintained by, life itself. We are far from understanding how these systems work, but as much as we would like to overlook the fact, it is increasingly evident that we depend on these natural systems of the biosphere for our very survival. It has also become alarmingly apparent that, at the present rate of destruction, much of the natural heritage of the earth may be irretrievably lost within a few decades.

The climates are changing, forests are being cleared, soils are washing away, deserts are expanding, fisheries are declining or collapsing, and pollution is spreading. As a result, the wild species that maintain the balance of natural systems and represent most

---

Revised from a paper, 'A Bahá'í perspective on nature and the environment,' prepared for the Bahá'í International Community. The views expressed in this paper are the author's own and do not necessarily represent those of the United Nations.

of the earth's genetic resources accumulated over millions of years are being driven to extinction in increasing numbers. As long as significant fragments of natural areas remain to harbour such species, there is always the hope that a wiser and more stable society could maintain and even restore the natural richness of the planet. It is those last fragments of natural ecosystems that are now threatened in many places. When they are gone, many species and potential resources will be lost forever, and it will prove more difficult to maintain or restore balanced natural systems.

These are the symptoms of a civilization that has gone out of control and is heading for self-destruction.

The Bahá'í teachings place this and the other grave problems facing the world today in a broader perspective which both accounts for their origin and suggests practical solutions. Technological progress has confronted the peoples and institutions of the nation-States with the reality of a physically united world, but their behaviour and values have yet to adapt to this fundamental change. Science and technology have greatly magnified our impacts on the environment to the extent that they affect the whole planet, yet each nation still insists on its sovereign right to exploit and destroy its natural resources and dispose of its wastes, regardless of the consequences for neighbouring countries or the rest of the world. For the Bahá'ís, therefore, the problem is basically spiritual: all people must come to accept the oneness of mankind, as 'the first fundamental prerequisite for the reorganization and administration of the world as one country.'[1] Without such a spiritual solution, other measures can only be temporary palliatives; solve the fundamental spiritual problem, and the difficulties of the world will resolve themselves naturally. The biosphere can only be managed within the context of a new world order built on universal values.

The Natural World System

The unity underlying natural systems has become one of the tenets of modern science. It is also fundamental to the view of the world expressed in the writings of Bahá'u'lláh and of his son 'Abdu'l-Bahá, which reflect the basic harmony of science and religion. The origins of the universe are described in the Bahá'í writings in terms that correspond well with present scientific theories, even though written before many of these theories and the physical and chemical terminologies used to describe them were developed. The endless universe is seen as having neither beginning nor end.[2]

> That which hath been in existence had existed before, but not in the form though seest today. The world of existence came into being through the heat generated from the interaction between the active force and that which is its recipient.[3]

This description is quite close to that of the functioning of stars through fusion reactions involving positive and negative forces as understood by modern physics. Individual celestial bodies may coalesce or disintegrate without upsetting the perpetual order of the universe.[4] A single original state of matter differentiated into the different chemical elements with stable forms and their own particular characteristics. These elements combined to form an infinite variety of molecules which, through their many combinations, form and disintegrate in complex reactions which have led to existence and life as we know it today.[5] The earth came into existence through these universal processes and evolved gradually to its present condition where it can support innumerable forms of life in a complex organized system.[6]

Nature is seen as following scientific laws that are themselves the expression of a divine reality. 'Nature is God's Will and is its expression in and through the contingent world.'[7] And further:

> This Nature is subjected to an absolute organization, to determined laws, to a complete order and to a finished design, from which it will never depart — to such a degree, indeed, that if you look carefully and with keen sight, from the smallest invisible atom up to such large bodies of the world of existence as the globe of the sun or the other great stars and luminous spheres, whether you regard their arrangement, their composition, their form or their movement, you will find that all are in the highest degree of organization and are under one law from which they will never depart.[8]

Nature is defined as those inherent properties and necessary relations underlying the realities of all things. All natural beings, though highly diverse, are intimately connected with each other.[9] Different levels of natural organization are distinguished. Minerals are composed of various combinations of elements; plants have in addition the capacity for growth; animals are further distinguished by sense perceptions; and humans are the highest specialized organism of the physical creation, with the qualities of the mineral, vegetable and animal plus an endowment totally lacking in the lower forms — the power of intellectual investigation into the mysteries of nature. The outcome of this intellectual process is science, the unique human characteristic, which reveals the nature and laws of the universe. The attainment of scientific knowledge is thus humankind's most noble and praiseworthy accomplishment.[10]

The Bahá'í writings accept the scientific evidence for evolution. However, they make the distinction between the potential for all types of beings, which is inherent in the substance and laws of the natural world and has thus always existed, and the process by which that potential is revealed.

> ... as man in the womb of the mother passes from form to form, from shape to shape, changes and develops, and is still the human species from the beginning of the embryonic period — in the same way man, from the beginning of his existence in the matrix of the world, is also a distinct species, that is, man — and has gradually evolved from one form to another.[11]

The gradual growth and development of all beings is a basic characteristic of natural systems.[12] As 'Abdu'l-Bahá explained further, 'All beings, whether large or small, were created perfect and complete from the first, but their perfections appear in them by degrees.'[13]

Thus, the evolution of existence is the expression of a single divine system of organization. The endless beings which inhabit the world, whether human, animal, vegetable, or mineral, are expressions of relative perfection composed of elements combined in appropriate ways and proportions through processes involving other beings. All beings are connected together like a chain. Reciprocal interactions and influences are among their essential properties, causing the existence, development and growth of created beings.[14] The natural world is therefore in its very essence a single interrelated system. The scientific discovery of the universality of the genetic code has demonstrated that all living things are related and have descended from the same origin.

THE WORLD ORDER OF NATURE

The concepts of essential ecological processes and life-support systems also appear in the Bahá'í writings.

> Consider for instance how one group of created things constituteth the vegetable kingdom, and another the animal kingdom. Each of these two maketh use of certain elements in the air on which its own life dependeth, while each increaseth the quantity of such elements as are essential for the life of the other. In other words, the growth and development of the vegetable world is impossible without the existence of the animal kingdom, and the maintenance of animal life is inconceivable without the co-operation of the vegetable kingdom. Of like kind are the relationships that exist among all created things. Hence it was stated that co-operation and reciprocity are essential properties which are inherent in the unified system of the world of existence, and without which the entire creation would be reduced to nothingness.[15]

> In the physical realm of creation, all things are eaters and eaten: the plant drinketh in the mineral, the animal doth crop and swallow down the plant, man doth feed upon the animal, and the mineral devoureth the body of man. Physical bodies are transferred past one barrier after another, from one life to another, and all things are subject to transformation and change, save only the essence of existence itself — since it is constant and immutable, and upon it is founded the life of every species and kind, of every contingent reality throughout the whole of creation.[16]

Human beings have a special place in the natural world. While the human body is, like the animal's, subject to natural laws, a human being's second reality, the rational or intellectual reality, predominates over nature,[17] and gives him or her the power to guide, control and overcome nature.[18] There is in addition a third reality in each person, the spiritual reality, which delivers us from the material world. Escaping from the world of nature, we find an illuminating reality, transcending the limited reality of humankind with our superstitions and imaginations, and leading to the infinitude of God.[19] Humankind should be freed from the world of nature, for as long as man is captive to nature he is a ferocious animal, as the struggle for existence is one of the exigencies of the world of nature.[20]

The Bahá'í view of the origins of the natural world and of our place in it accords fully with the evidence of modern science. The underlying theme of the interrelationships of all things demonstrates the importance of wise conservation and management of the biosphere. The fact that we can interfere with and control nature also gives us the responsibility to manage nature wisely. However conservation problems are not rooted in any lack of a scientific understanding of nature, they result largely from the social and structural problems of present day society. The Bahá'í Faith provides social perspectives which are equally important to the problem of the conservation of nature.

Threats to the World System

The scientific and technological revolution of the last 150 years have transformed the nature of civilization and the means at our disposal to meet our needs and desires. However, the major environmental problems now threatening the planet suggest that our material civilization in its present form may not be sustainable. While the basic social aim of humanity is to carry forward an ever-advancing civilization,[21] the form that such progress takes is open to question. Our present value systems have become highly materialistic. Development is measured in the economic terms of goods and services, with little attention paid to other aspects of the quality of life. The very institutions and structures of our society reflect this. Industrial enterprises and multinational corporations hold much of the power in western society; it is only with great difficulty that even the strongest governments succeed in limiting their impacts on the environment. The extreme poverty in which the masses of the developing countries are maintained drives them to destroy the very resources on which they depend for survival.

Bahá'u'lláh warned more than a hundred years ago about the hazards to the planet of too much material civilization.

> The civilization, so often vaunted by the learned exponents of arts and sciences, will, if allowed to overleap the bounds of moderation, bring great evil upon men . . . If carried to excess, civilization will prove as prolific a source of evil as it had been of goodness when kept within the restraints of moderation . . . The day is approaching when its flame will devour the cities . . .[22]

In a reference that could well apply to nuclear energy, but written long before its discovery, he wrote:

THE WORLD ORDER OF NATURE

> Strange and astonishing things exist in the earth but they are hidden from the minds and the understanding of men. These things are capable of changing the whole atmosphere of the earth and their contamination would prove lethal.[23]

The pollution and resource problems of today bear out these warnings. Obviously the civilization of the future must seek out a more moderate balance between material development and the requirements of the natural world.

The destruction of the natural resource base of the biosphere has two distinct origins: the over exploitation required to meet the high market demands in the wealthy countries, and the erosion of resources by the masses of the poor in their desperate bid to survive. Both are symptoms of the serious imbalances in the distribution of wealth on a world basis. The population problem itself is largely a result of an unstable intermediate state in which much of the world's population is maintained by the present world system. Sufficient modern medical knowledge has been shared to lower death rates, but not enough wealth has been shared to raise standards of living enough to lower birth rates. The roots of the world environmental crisis thus lie in the defects of the present world system.

Solving such problems will require changes in the basic values and structures of society. The injustices that maintain extremes of wealth and poverty and drive the poor to destroy their resources must be resolved through a combination of spiritual, moral and practical approaches.[24] Universal education would allow the masses of the people to understand and modify their behaviour. At the same time, the inordinate consumption of resources by the wealthy must be controlled.

World Approaches to Environmental Management

The environmental systems of the biosphere function on a global scale; they can only be managed on a global basis. The limitations of national sovereignty in this respect are particularly apparent. The present global environmental anarchy must be replaced by new structures and approaches at the scale of the problems.

The necessary changes will require fundamental alterations in the structure of human society. The Bahá'í teachings provide guidelines for the kind of transformation necessary to achieve a new world order.

> The unity of the human race, as envisaged by Bahá'u'lláh, implies the establishment of a world commonwealth in which all nations, races, creeds and classes are closely and permanently united, and in which the autonomy of its state members and the personal freedom and initiative of the individuals that compose them are definitely and completely safeguarded. This commonwealth must, as far as we can visualize it, consist of a world legislature, whose members will, as the trustees of the whole of mankind, ultimately control the entire resources of all the component nations, and will enact such laws as shall be required to regulate the life, satisfy the needs and adjust the relationships of all races and peoples. A world executive, backed by an international Force, will carry out the decisions arrived at, and apply the laws enacted by, this world legislature, and will safeguard the organic unity of the whole commonwealth. A world tribunal will adjudicate and deliver its compulsory and final verdict in all and any disputes that may arise between the various elements constituting this universal system. . . . The economic resources of the world will be organized, its sources of raw materials will be tapped and fully utilized, its markets will be coordinated and developed, and the distribution of its products will be equitably regulated . . .
>
> . . . economic barriers and restrictions will be completely abolished, and the inordinate distinction between classes will be obliterated. Destitution on the one hand, and gross accumulation of ownership on the other, will disappear. The enormous energy dissipated and wasted on war, whether economic or political, will be consecrated to such ends as will extend the range of human inventions and technical development, to increase the productivity of mankind, to the extermination of disease, to the extension of scientific research, to the raising of the standard of physical health, to the sharpening and refinement of the human brain, to the exploitation of the unused and unsuspected resources of the planet, to the prolongation of human life, and to the furtherance of any other agency that can stimulate the intellectual, the moral, and spiritual life of the entire human race.[25]

Note that such a world federal system would control the entire resources of all the nations, would tap and fully utilize the sources of raw materials and regulate the distribution of products, and would aim to exploit the unused and unsuspected resources and all available sources of energy on the surface of the planet. With the abolition of economic barriers and restrictions, the world economy would finally become a globally balanced and effective system, in which each component part would produce what it can most efficiently, given its situation and resources. Only such a

THE WORLD ORDER OF NATURE

system would be able to manage the life support systems of the biosphere and to implement a world strategy for the conservation of nature.

Sustainable development would be fundamental to such a civilization. Unlike today's almost exclusive reliance on short-term planning, the Bahá'ís are laying the foundations for the first thousand years of a cycle which should last five hundred thousand years. The economy of such a society would have to work on a fully-sustainable basis, using renewable or recyclable resources and highly efficient resource utilization.

The Bahá'í Attitude towards Nature

Humanity will only be willing to move towards a new world order with nature if it prizes the values that nature represents. The importance of the natural world must become rooted in the fundamental moral and spiritual values of society. The Bahá'í Faith proposes a value system that integrates the scientific and spiritual views of the world, and gives an important place to nature and to respect for ecological principles.

For Bahá'ís, while nature is not an end in itself to be worshipped and adored,[26] the creation does reflect the qualities and attributes of God.

> When . . . thou dost contemplate the innermost essence of all things, and the individuality of each, thou wilt behold the signs of thy Lord's mercy in every created thing, and see the spreading rays of His Names and Attributes throughout all the realm of being . . . Then wilt thou observe that the universe is a scroll that discloseth His hidden secrets, which are preserved in the well-guarded Tablet. And not an atom of all the atoms in existence, not a creature from amongst the creatures but speaketh His praise and telleth of His attributes and names, revealeth the glory of His might and guideth to His oneness and His mercy . . .
> And whensoever thou dost gaze upon creation all entire, and dost observe the very atoms thereof, thou wilt note that the rays of the Sun of Truth are shed upon all things and shining within them, and telling of that Day-Star's splendours, Its mysteries, and the spreading of Its lights. Look thou upon the trees, upon the blossoms and fruits, even upon the stones. Here too wilt thou behold the Sun's rays shed upon them, clearly visible within them, and manifested by them.[27]

The contemplation of nature thus has a spiritual significance for Bahá'ís. Indeed the spiritual, social and physical environments are all interrelated.

> We cannot segregate the human heart from the environment outside us and say that once one of these is reformed everything will be improved. Man is organic with the world. His inner life moulds the environment and is itself also deeply affected by it. The one acts upon the other and every abiding change in the life of man is the result of these mutual reactions.[28]

The genetic diversity that underlies the richness of living things is thus a reflection of the qualities of God. Bahá'ís are encouraged to appreciate such diversity, whether in humanity or in the natural world.

> Consider the world of created beings, how varied and diverse they are in species, yet with one sole origin. All the differences that appear are those of outward form and colour. This diversity of type is apparent throughout the whole of nature ...
> Let us look ... at the beauty in diversity, the beauty of harmony, and learn a lesson from the vegetable creation. If you behold a garden in which all the plants were the same as to form, colour and perfume, it would not seem beautiful to you at all, but, rather monotonous and dull. The garden which is pleasing to the eye and which makes the heart glad, is the garden in which are growing side by side flowers of every hue, form and perfume, and the joyous contrast of colour is what makes for charm and beauty. So is it with trees. An orchard full of fruit trees is a delight; so is a plantation planted with many species of shrubs. It is just the diversity and variety that constitutes its charm; each flower, each tree, each fruit, beside being beautiful in itself, brings out by contrast the qualities of the others, and shows to advantage the special loveliness of each and all.[29]

This same principle of diversity is fundamental to the efficiency and stability of most natural ecosystems. Respect for the material world and moderation in the use of its resources are also reflected in the Bahá'í prohibition of cruelty to animals.

> Briefly, it is not only their fellow human beings that the beloved of God must treat with mercy and compassion, rather must they show forth the utmost loving-kindness to every living creature ... The feelings are one and the same, whether ye inflict pain on man or on beast. Train

THE WORLD ORDER OF NATURE

your children from their earliest days to be infinitely tender and loving to animals. If an animal be sick, let the children try to heal it, if it be hungry, let them feed it, if thirsty, let them quench its thirst, if weary, let them see that it rests.[30]

Similarly, we are counselled

> Unless ye must
> Bruise not the serpent in the dust
> How much less wound a man.
> And if ye can
> No ant should ye alarm
> Much less a brother harm.[31]

'Abdu'l-Bahá said of his father during his imprisonment, 'Bahá'u'lláh loved the beauty and verdure of the country. One day He passed the remark: "I have not gazed on verdure for nine years. The country is the world of the soul, the city is the world of bodies."'[32] Once Bahá'u'lláh was free to leave the prison, he often used to pitch his tent among the trees on the side of Mount Carmel.

In many religions, including the Bahá'í Faith, the founders or leaders have retired to the wilderness for meditation and contemplation prior to taking on the burdens of their message, or for spiritual renewal. Bahá'u'lláh spent two years in the mountains, where 'the birds of the air were my companions and the beasts of the field My associates...'[33] and Shoghi Effendi, the late Guardian of the Bahá'í Faith, found for himself a partial healing from the weight of his responsibilities high in the Swiss Alps.[34]

Bahá'ís thus approach nature with an awareness of the interrelatedness of themselves and the natural world, with an indication of the importance of all the world's resources for the civilization they are building, and with the example of their leaders showing the ecological, spiritual and aesthetic values of wilderness, the countryside, and the diversity of natural life.

Building a World Order in Support of Nature

The goals for the protection of the world's vital interests in nature have been spelled out in the World Conservation Strategy.[35] They are: to maintain essential ecological processes and life-support systems, to preserve genetic diversity, and to ensure the sustainable utilization of species and ecosystems. The report of the UN World Commission on Environment and Development[36] has also highlighted the importance of sustainable development for the future of the planet. But as with many global undertakings in today's fragmented world, these prescriptions suffer from the lack of world-scale institutions capable of implementing them. Action at the national level will never be more than a partial solution to world problems. The establishment of the world commonwealth anticipated in the Bahá'í writings will finally make world management and conservation of the resources of the biosphere possible.

There is thus no special solution to today's problems of nature and the environment, any more than the problems of peace or international economic instability can be solved in isolation. The human race must first recognize its oneness on a world scale and then build the new institutions needed to reflect that oneness in world organization. Change in both basic values and structures are necessary. As such changes are implemented, it will be possible to begin the long and complex process of learning how to correct the imbalances in the systems of the biosphere and to manage them for our long-term survival.

At the same time, new approaches to sustainable development in harmony with natural resources will need to be evolved at the local and national levels. This essentially means rebuilding the very foundations of civilization along patterns that are ecologically sound and more in harmony with both humanity and nature. Guiding principles such as those set out in the Bahá'í Faith can set the direction, but an enormous scientific effort will be necessary to identify the means, and new institutional structures will be required to put them into practice. Again the material and spiritual aspects must be in balance; science can provide the practical solutions, but only spiritual principles can provide sufficient motivation to implement them.

The existing Bahá'í communities around the world are a pilot-scale experiment of the kind of transformation required. They demonstrate that such new approaches to world order can go beyond utopian idealism, and have the capacity to become a practical reality. The natural world order of the biosphere can thus find its parallel in a new world order of humanity.

NOTES

1. The Universal House of Justice, *The Promise of World Peace: A Statement by the Universal House of Justice* (London: Bahá'í Publishing Trust, 1985), p. 17.
2. 'Abdu'l-Bahá, *Some Answered Questions* comp. and trans. Laura Clifford Barney, 5th ed. (Wilmette, IL: Bahá'í Publishing Trust, 1981), p. 180.
3. Bahá'u'lláh, *Tablets of Bahá'u'lláh revealed after the Kitáb-i-Aqdas* comp. Research Department of the Universal House of Justice, trans. Habib Taherzadeh and others, re. ed. (Haifa: Bahá'í World Centre, 1982), p. 140.
4. 'Abdu'l-Bahá, *Some Answered Questions*, pp. 180-1.
5. Ibid., pp. 181-2.
6. Ibid., pp. 182-3.
7. Bahá'u'lláh, *Tablets*, p. 142.
8. 'Abdu'l-Bahá, *Some Answered Questions*, p. 3.
9. See 'Abdu'l-Bahá's 'Tablet to Dr. August Henri Forel', in *The Bahá'í World*, vol. XV (1968-73) (Haifa: Bahá'í World Centre, 1976), pp. 37-43.
10. 'Abdu'l-Bahá, *Bahá'í World Faith* (Wilmette, IL: Bahá'í Publishing Trust, 1956), p. 242.
11. 'Abdu'l-Bahá, *Some Answered Questions*, pp. 193-4.
12. Ibid., pp. 198-9.
13. Ibid., p. 199.
14. Ibid., pp. 178-9.
15. 'Abdu'l-Bahá, in *Conservation of the Earth's Resources* comp. Research Department of the Universal House of Justice (London: Bahá'í Publishing Trust, 1989), p. 4.
16. 'Abdu'l-Bahá *Selections from the Writings of 'Abdu'l-Bahá*, comp. Research Department of the Universal House of Justice, trans.Marzieh Gail and others, rev. ed. (Haifa: Bahá'í World Centre, 1982), p. 157.
17. 'Abdu'l-Bahá, *Foundations of World Unity: Compiled from Addresses and Tablets of 'Abdu'l-Bahá* (Wilmette, IL: Bahá'í Publishing Trust, 1968), p. 51.
18. 'Abdu'l-Bahá, *Paris Talks: Addresses Given By 'Abdu'l-Bahá in Paris in 1911-1912*, 11th ed. (London, Bahá'í Publishing Trust, 1971), p. 122.
19. 'Abdu'l-Bahá, *Foundations of World Unity*, p. 51.
20. 'Abdu'l-Bahá, *Selections*, p. 302.
21. Bahá'u'lláh, *Gleanings from the Writings of Bahá'u'lláh* trans. Shoghi Effendi, 2nd rev. ed. (Wilmette, IL: Bahá'í Publishing Trust, 1976), p. 215.
22. Bahá'u'lláh, *Bahá'í World Faith*, pp. 138-9.
23. Bahá'u'lláh, *Tablets*, p. 69.
24. The Universal House of Justice, *The Promise of World Peace*, p. 13.
25. Shoghi Effendi, *The World Order of Bahá'u'lláh: Selected Letters*, 2nd rev. ed. (Wilmette, IL: Bahá'í Publishing Trust, 1974), pp. 203-4.
26. 'Abdu'l-Bahá, *Paris Talks*, p. 123.
27. 'Abdu'l-Bahá, *Selections*, pp. 41-2.
28. Letter written on behalf of Shoghi Effendi, in *Conservation of the Earth's Resources*, p. 15.

29. 'Abdu'l-Bahá, *Paris Talks*, pp. 51-3.
30. 'Abdu'l-Bahá, *Selections*, pp. 158-9.
31. Ibid., p. 256.
32. 'Abdu'l-Bahá, in J. E. Esslemont, *Bahá'u'lláh and the New Era* (Wilmette, IL: Bahá'í Publishing Trust, 1970), p. 35.
33. Bahá'u'lláh, in Shoghi Effendi, *God Passes By* (Wilmette, IL: Bahá'í Publishing Trust, 1970), p. 120.
34. Rúḥíyyih Rabbaní, *The Priceless Pearl* (London: Bahá'í Publishing Trust, 1969), p. 120.
35. IUCN/WWF/UNEP, *World Conservation Strategy* (Gland, Switzerland: International Union for Conservation of Nature, 1980).
36. World Commission on Environment and Development, *Our Common Future* (Oxford: Oxford University Press, 1987).

INDEX

'Abdu'l-Bahá, 2, 4, 14, 19, 20, 22, 23, 25, 30, 41, 42, 72, 76, 77, 90, 91, 117, 134, 138, 140, 142, 162
  quotes from, 3, 19, 22, 23, 24, 34, 40, 42, 73, 77, 92, 95, 117, 118, 133-4, 157, 163, 164, 165, 169, 171
aggression, 78, 101, 102, 109,.112-16, 120, 125
agriculture, 82, 147
anarchy, 83, 88, 103, 167
animals, 165, 170-1
animus dominandi, 110-11, 122
arbitration, 25, 92
Ardrey, Robert, 113
arms, 5, 26, 88, 90, 91, 92, 121, 122, 132, 141
Aron, Raymond, 12
art, 7, 157
Augustine, Saint, 102-3, 105, 106, 108, 110

Báb, 4, 14, 16, 117
Bahá'í Faith, 34, 119, 132, 169, 172
  administrative order, 35, 37-41, 43, 45, 158
  growth, 17, 21
  teachings, 4, 7, 17, 38, 43, 72, 86, 89, 91, 162
  view of origins of universe, 162-4, 165-6
  writings, 1, 19, 20, 21, 22, 24, 26, 29, 30, 31, 41, 42, 43, 45, 49-50, 72-3, 87, 88, 89, 117, 126, 150, 155, 162, 164, 172
Bahá'í International Community, 14, 78, 96
Bahá'ís, 20, 29, 35, 43, 121, 131, 136, 169
  development activities, 149-51, 152
  teaching activities, 17, 131
Bahá'u'lláh, 1, 4, 14, 16, 18-19, 21, 22, 24, 26, 27, 28, 29, 30-1, 35, 37, 38, 72, 76, 90, 117, 125-6, 131, 134, 136, 138, 150, 151, 162, 168, 171
  quotes from, 2, 4, 5, 14-15, 16, 17, 19, 20, 21, 23, 26-7, 27, 29, 40, 73, 76, 86-7, 90, 95, 117, 118-19, 132-3, 134, 135, 137, 163, 166, 167, 171

bellicism, 106
Bernhardi, Gen. F. von, 106
borders (national boundaries), 24, 25, 26, 71, 91, 136
Bull, Hedley, 1, 12, 46

calamity ('catastrophe'), 27, 30-2, 87
capitalism, 123, 125, 145-6, 147-8, 149, 150, 151, 153
centralization, 34, 89, 93
Christ, 103
Christianity, 8, 16, 21, 102, 106, 138
civilization, 18, 28-9, 32, 114, 118, 152, 162, 166, 171, 172
  ever-advancing, 126, 149
  material, 133, 166-7
  spiritual (true), 3, 35, 36, 37, 38, 43, 133
classes, 10, 35, 44, 85, 94, 122, 168
  conflict, struggle, 8, 124, 148, 149, 154
Claude, Inis, 75
Coffin, William, 10
Cold War, 121
collective security, 5, 22, 23, 71, 76-7, 90-3, 95, 132-3
colonialism, 6
commerce, 6, 41, 80, 94, 157
communications, 36, 73, 94, 147
communism, 8
Concert System, 75
conflict, 3, 23, 73, 81, 92, 104-5, 107, 109, 112, 114
conflict resolution, 4
conscience, 42, 82, 157, 158
consultation, 41, 44, 45, 150
co-operation, 10, 15, 34, 78-9, 80, 88, 93, 95, 104, 146, 156
  between East and West, 74
  international, 123, 141
creeds, 34, 35, 44, 168
culture, 6, 23, 44, 74, 86, 136
currency, 94

Dahl, Gregory, 5
Danesh, Hossain, 4
decentralization, 93
decolonization, 78
democracy, 10, 74, 124, 135
detachment, 42, 118

175

deterrence, 132
development, 23
  cultural, 123
  economic, 23, 79, 90, 96, 123, 146-60, 161, 166
  political, 123
  social, 23, 96, 146-60
  sustainable, 169, 172
dictatorship, 89
dignity, 10, 12
diplomacy, 133
disarmament, 5, 22-5, 75, 92, 96, 123, 124-5
Dolman, Antony, 47
drug abuse, 79

East, 8, 37, 74, 95, 123, 125, 134
economic barriers, 26, 94
  collapse, 87
  development, 79
  gain, 122
  interdependence, 72
  needs, 44
  relationships, 6
  resources, 36
  rights, 136
  systems, 122, 156
  structures, 16
  theories, 109
  welfare, 10
  woes, 32
economy, global, 83, 87, 141, 168, 172
education, 5, 11, 23, 24, 74, 82, 147, 148, 151
  in principle of human unity, 86-7, 91
  of girls and women, 80, 150
  universal, 4, 16, 90, 125, 167
entrepreneurs, 147, 158
environment, 6, 9, 10, 30, 87, 122, 153, 161-72
equality of men and women, 4, 15, 16, 90, 125, 149
eschatology, 26-7, 33, 136
Europe, 16, 71, 116, 123, 147
  Eastern, 74, 124, 125
European Community, 71, 72
evolution, 164
extremes of wealth and poverty, 6, 36, 90, 94, 125, 151, 152, 157, 167, 168

Falk, Richard, 9-10, 11, 112, 122
family, 7, 38, 41
fascism, 108, 116

federalism, global, 25, 35, 36, 72, 89, 96, 121-2, 134, 139, 140, 168
Finland, 77
First World, 5, 6, 10, 44
Food and Agriculture Organization (FAO), 82
foreign policy, 124, 131, 136, 139, 141
freedom (liberty), 5, 10
  of expression, 42
  personal, 35, 89
  unity in, 19
free will, 3
Freud, Sigmund, 112, 113, 128
Fromm, Erich, 114

Galtung, Johan, 12
General Agreement on Tariffs and Trade (GATT), 80, 83
genocide, 99
God, 2, 3, 4, 17, 19, 20, 21, 23, 29, 30, 32, 33, 42, 95, 109, 119, 137, 146, 149, 154, 155, 157, 165, 170
  and nature, 169
  Kingdom, 4, 33, 103, 134
  knowledge of, 2
  love of, 2, 155-6, 158
  manifestation (messenger), 15, 138, 150
  plans, 16, 18
  will, 132-4, 135, 136, 139, 150, 163
government, 45, 93
  international (world), 9, 12, 16, 37, 45, 85, 89, 109-10, 121-2
  national, 5, 6, 8, 20, 22, 24, 25, 34, 36, 79, 88, 91, 122, 124, 141, 150, 153, 166
  new forms, 13
Gulf War, 32, 90

Hague Conference, 75, 97
Hainsworth, Philip, 20, 30
harmony of science and religion, 4, 36, 162-3, 169, 172
health care, 4, 5, 36, 80, 94, 147, 148, 151, 167, 168
Hegel, 106
history, 18, 101, 123, 134, 136
Hitler, 77
Hobbes, Thomas, 104
Hoffmann, Stanley, 12, 47
housing, 5, 147
Huddleston, John, 20
human nature, 101-26, 146, 153
  Bahá'í concept, 2, 3, 117, 120-1, 149, 165

176

negative image, 11-12, 102-116, 117, 120, 121-6
positive image, 102, 120-1, 154
human potential, 4, 10, 123, 126, 146, 150
human race, coming of age, 73
purpose of creation, 2, 4, 101, 146
service to, 2
unification of, 7, 18, 33-4, 73
unity (oneness, wholeness), 8, 14, 16, 19, 27, 34, 35, 44, 79-80, 81, 85, 86-7, 88, 91, 94, 95, 97, 101, 162, 168, 172
human rights, 4, 5, 6, 10, 71, 79, 89, 92, 96, 141
third generation, 136
Universal Declaration, 79, 81-2, 98-9
Huqúqu'lláh, 158, 160
Huxley, Aldous, 139, 140

ideologies, 7, 8, 13, 120, 122, 125, 145-6
capitalist, 145-8, 152-3, 154, 155-6
socialist, 145-6, 148-9, 152-4, 155, 156
imperialism, 6
independence, 78
individual, 45, 117, 145, 157
agent of social change, 38, 147-9, 150, 155, 156
creativity, 10, 146
freedom, 35, 42, 145, 168
initiative, 35, 146, 168
privacy, 136
rights, 145
industrialization, 123, 147
industry, 74, 157, 166
injustice, 9, 37, 148, 149, 152
institutions, 5, 11, 12, 13, 25, 108, 136
economic, 29
global, 73, 85, 109, 121
new, 10, 14, 93, 172
political, 22, 29, 140
religious, 120
social, 14, 29, 140, 166
interdependence, 74, 75, 76, 80, 94, 95
cultural, 86
economic, 72, 86
global, 9, 79, 83, 93
political, 72, 86
social, 72, 86, 154
inter-governmental organizations, 71, 72, 75, 168

International Court of Justice, 76, 93
International Executive, 25, 36, 88, 91, 92
International Labour Organization, 76
International Monetary Fund, 79, 83, 141
international organizations, 71-100, 122
international police force, 24
international relations, 12, 44, 81, 107, 108, 110, 123, 140
International Teaching Centre, 31, 32, 40
International Year of Peace, 81, 131
Iran, Bahá'ís in, 119, 151
Isaiah, 33
Islam, 8, 16

Jaspers, Karl, 140
Johansen, Robert, 10, 12
justice, 4, 5, 10, 16, 19, 44, 45, 76, 125, 134, 145, 153

Kant, Immanuel, 123-4, 138
Khan, Janet, 15
Khan, Peter, 31
Kitáb-i-Aqdas, 16, 21
Klineberg, Otto, 115
Kothari, Rajni, 10, 12

Laborit, Henri, 115
language, unity of, 19, 35
universal auxiliary, 22, 36, 90, 94, 125
law, international, 74, 121, 123, 168
laws, 5, 13, 35, 43
League of Nations, 75-7, 78, 79-80, 81, 84, 88, 91, 97, 107-8
legislature, 35-6
Lesser Peace, 18-22, 24, 25, 32, 35, 37, 95
speculative definitions, 20
liberalism, 104, 108
literacy, 80, 147, 149, 150-1, 152
Lorenz, Konrad, 112, 113-4
love, 42, 87, 103, 106, 117, 150
of country, 111, 137

MacGregor, Douglas, 140, 142
Machiavelli, Niccolo, 104-5, 106
Marxism, 123-4, 138
materialism, 7, 8, 13, 120, 158
Mayan, Alfred Thayer, 106

177

media, 36, 140
Mendlovitz, Saul, 11
Middle East, 32, 84
military force, 25, 78, 92, 108
morality, 13, 16, 23, 29, 37, 82, 94, 108, 110, 114, 122, 150, 152, 157, 169
Morgenthau, Hans, 110
Most Great Covenant, 24
Most Great Peace, 19, 29, 33, 35, 37, 95
Muhammad, 138
multinational corporations, 136, 141, 166
music, 7

nationalism, 8, 26, 34, 77, 84, 85, 95
nations (nation-States), 6, 7, 10, 12, 19, 23, 35, 44, 39, 43, 72, 73, 78, 79, 82, 88, 90, 104, 107, 109, 111, 115, 132, 139, 162, 168
  autonomy, 10
  security, 124
  sovereignty, 121, 134, 137, 141, 162, 167
nature, 163
  and God, 169
  conservation of, 161, 166, 169
  contemplation of, 170
  unity underlying, 162, 164, 166, 170, 171
new diplomacy, 107
Niebuhr, Reinhold, 108-10
Nietsche, 106
Nineteen Day Feast, 38-9, 43, 45
nineteenth century, 1, 15-16, 74, 108, 119
non-governmental organizations (NGOs), 14, 71, 72, 78, 79
nuclear energy, 166-7

Old Testament, 118, 136
oppression, 3, 43, 148, 149
original sin, 103, 109

pacifism, 106
Paris Peace Conference, 107
patriotism, 111
peace, 3, 4, 10, 13, 19, 21, 22, 25, 71, 72, 73, 74, 75, 76, 77, 80-1, 85-6, 88, 90-1, 95, 96, 97, 101, 106, 116, 120, 121, 123, 124, 131, 132-3, 136, 139, 150, 172
peoples, 36, 72, 73, 126, 132, 139, 162

philanthropy, 157, 158, 160
political consciousness, 9-10
  dignity, 12
  energy, 11, 94, 168
  interdependence, 72
  institutions, 35
  issues, 3, 79, 83, 114
  realism, 4, 12, 102, 108, 109, 111, 122
  relationships, 6
  science, 112
  structures, 16, 44
  systems, 1, 7, 122, 139
  theories, 13, 109
  unity, 18, 19, 20
politicians, 8, 138, 140
pollution, 167
population growth, 6, 122, 161
poverty, 5, 9, 23, 36, 110-11, 141, 158, 166
power, 122, 136, 137, 148
  national, 109
  political, 108, 132
prayer, 42, 155
prejudices, 4, 5, 14, 16, 36, 84, 85, 121, 125
prestige, 109, 137
  national, 122,
pride, 109
Promise of World Peace, 44, 101
  quotes from, 2, 8, 9, 13, 26, 44, 72, 73, 74, 80, 80-1, 82, 86, 87, 88, 91, 96, 101, 102, 120, 121, 125, 126, 146, 162
Promised Day is Come, 7, 33
prosperity, global, 5
Protestant work ethic, 157
provincialism, 34
psychology, 112

races, 19, 35, 36, 168
racism, 8, 26, 36, 84, 90, 150
Radano, John, 47
reason, 103-4, 105, 106
religion, 7, 13, 16, 29, 40, 71, 85, 86-7, 112, 118, 119, 138, 156
  discrimination, intolerance, fanaticism, prejudice, strife, 7, 8, 26, 36, 84, 90
  unity, 19, 87
repression, 6
resources, 6, 35, 44, 94, 122, 123, 134, 150, 161, 162, 166, 168, 169, 170, 171, 172

economic, 36
Richardson, Lewis F., 116
Rome (ancient), 137
rulers, 18, 19, 20, 22, 33-4, 76, 90, 134, 135
    convocation, 22, 25, 95, 125, 132, 133
Russia, 75
    revolution, 123

San Francisco Conference on International Organization, 77
science, 6, 74, 86, 94, 112, 162, 164, 166, 168, 172
self-determination, 45, 107, 137
self-interest, 11, 102, 109, 148, 153
selfishness, 101, 102, 110-11, 120, 126, 156
self-sacrifice, 83, 150, 151, 154, 156
Shoghi Effendi, 2, 4, 7, 14, 16, 20, 21, 27, 31, 35, 41, 44, 72, 117, 120, 132, 171
    quotes from, 7, 13, 17, 18, 19, 25-6, 27, 28, 28-9, 32-3, 33, 33-4, 35-6, 37, 45, 76, 77, 87, 88, 89, 91, 92, 93, 94, 119-20, 131-2, 134, 140, 168, 170
social Darwinism, 106-7
socialism, 123, 125, 145-6, 148-9, 152, 155, 158
society, evolution, 2, 13, 18, 28, 35, 43, 126
    transformation, 11, 14-15, 148, 150, 156, 167
Sorokin, P. J., 120
South Pacific Commission, 14
sovereignty, varieties of, 134-6
Spinoza, Benedict de, 103-4, 105, 106, 109
spiritual assemblies, 41, 43
    local, 39, 40, 150, 158
    national, 39-40
spirituality, 2, 3, 5, 13, 14, 37, 42, 94, 132, 140, 156, 157, 158, 165, 169
State system, 5-7, 8, 104, 121, 123, 134, 136, 138, 140, 141, 152
    autonomy, 35, 89
    sovereignty, 84-5, 88
statecraft, 102, 111
structures, 124, 137, 172
    economic, 16, 44
    political, 16, 44
    social, 7, 10, 44, 167
suffering, 87

Supreme Tribunal (world court), 25, 26, 36, 88, 91, 92-3, 168

taxation, 22, 25, 40, 88, 141
technology, 4, 6, 36, 71, 74, 94, 147, 152, 161, 162, 166, 168
terrorism, 5, 7, 83
Third World, 5, 6, 10, 44, 45, 78, 82, 83, 147
    debt crisis, 83, 152
torture, 6
trade, 35, 36, 71, 80, 108
treaties, 91
Trietschke, 106, 107
twentieth century, 1, 20, 25, 32, 34, 72, 73, 95, 108, 121
Tyson, Jay, 30

unemployment, 5, 148, 154
UNEP, 14
UNESCO, 14, 80, 115
UNICEF, 14, 82
uniformity, 10, 34, 89
United Nations, 71, 77-80, 81-5, 88, 89-90, 91, 92, 93-4, 96, 97, 121-2, 131, 141
    Development Programme, 83
    Secretary-General, 78, 81
    Security Council, 78, 84
    World Commission on Environment and Development, 172
United States, 28, 77, 78, 108, 115, 123, 138-9, 140, 145, 153
unity in diversity, 4, 34, 89
Universal House of Justice, 2, 3, 8, 9, 13, 14, 16, 18, 20, 21, 26, 34, 40, 41, 43, 44, 72, 90, 101, 102, 116, 117, 121, 125, 126, 170, 171
    quotes from, 4, 16, 16-17, 17, 17-18, 21, 29-30, 31, 32, 32-3, 33, 35, 38-9, 39, 90, 95 (see also *Promise of World Peace*)
urbanization, 122
USSR, 77, 123, 124, 125
utopianism, 43, 101, 110, 172

values, 4, 119, 167, 172
    materialist, 166
    global (universal), 11, 162
    moral, 2
    new, 7, 10, 13-14, 169
    spiritual, 2, 157, 171
violence, 5, 6, 9, 10, 11, 12, 112-16, 126

virtues, 17, 150

war, 5, 23, 24, 25, 27, 30, 36, 37, 73, 74, 77-8, 81, 83, 84, 87, 88, 90, 94, 102, 107, 121, 131, 134, 135, 141, 168
  nuclear, 27, 30, 73
wastes, 161, 162
wealth, 118-19, 137, 157, 158, 167
weapons, 23, 73, 75, 95, 122, 123
welfare State, 154, 158
West, 8, 37, 74, 95, 123, 124, 125, 134, 166
  Bahá'ís in, 27, 30
Will and Testament of 'Abdu'l-Bahá, 2, 40
will to power, 109, 111-12
Wilson, President Woodrow, 76, 107, 108
women, 79, 96
work, 6, 147, 150, 153, 154, 156, 157
World Bank, 79, 83, 147
world commonwealth, 21, 35, 37, 38, 87-9, 91, 92, 93, 95, 96, 132-3, 168, 172
World Conservation Strategy, 171-2
World Health Organization, 14, 79
World Legislature, 91, 168
world order, 1, 43, 72, 126, 162, 169
  models, 10, 33, 44
    Bahá'í, 1, 3, 4-5, 12, 13, 17, 29, 33, 38, 40, 45, 86, 131, 135, 167-8, 172
  transition to, 3, 9, 10, 11, 12, 15-16, 18, 21, 32, 33, 131-2
    disintegration process, 16-17, 26-7, 32, 73
    integration process, 16, 17, 32
World Order Models Project (WOMP), 10, 11, 12, 49
world parliament, 25, 88, 89, 92, 93
world super-state, 25-6, 88, 136, 138, 140, 141
World War I, 31, 74, 75-6, 107
World War II, 31, 72, 77, 84, 108, 110, 121, 123